GROUP DYNAMICS

CONNECTING THROUGH COMMUNICATION

NICOLE BLAU

Kendall Hunt
publishing company

Cover image © Shutterstock, Inc.

www.kendallhunt.com
Send all inquiries to:
4050 Westmark Drive
Dubuque, IA 52004-1840

DEDICATION

For Chris and Lane…the other two members of my favorite group.

BRIEF CONTENTS

TABLE OF CONTENTS

PREFACE

Like so many other things in life, the study of group communication continues to evolve. At some point in our lives, we will all partake in group communication. As groups and teams continue to be a significant part of our personal and professional lives, it is exciting to learn what makes groups effective and how we can embrace group situations.

Because students often have quite a bit of experience working in groups, teaching group communication courses are some of my favorites to teach. In this book, the goal is to equip students with the tools necessary to enhance their own group communication skills. Particularly, some distinctive features of this text include the following:

- Each chapter includes a *Learning by Action* section in which hands-on activities that may be used in- or out-of-class are provided. This enables students to apply the group communication concepts covered in the chapter and engage in higher-level learning.
- Video clips from popular culture television shows and movies are included for each chapter. When concepts from each chapter are illustrated in video clips that students enjoy, it should lead to meaningful conversations and analyses about group communication.
- At the end of each chapter there is a section on *Contemporary Communication* in which timely communication channels are presented. Various websites and apps that are very commonplace today are shared to help increase the effectiveness of group communication.
- Every chapter in the text concludes with an original case study related to group communication. The case studies are aimed at providing experiences that students can relate to in order to further analyze the group communication concepts covered in the chapters.

Chapters in this text are organized in way that will help students begin with the foundations of group communication theory and build on this knowledge as they work through the entire text.

Chapter 1 introduces the concept of group communication and provides theoretical foundations. It is important to set a solid foundation for students to work from as they learn about effective group communication strategies throughout the remainder of the textbook.

In *Chapter 2* students will learn about various types of groups as well as group member roles. Moreover, students will learn about the well-known phases of group development and challenges that often arise when groups are created.

Chapter 3 introduces the ideas of diversity and culture as they relate to group communication. The importance of diversity and culture in group settings cannot be understated. In order to become an effective group communicator, it is important that students understand how culture and diversity impact our communication with others.

In *Chapter 4* problem-solving and decision-making in groups are addressed. Nearly every group is faced with either solving a problem or decision-making, so the chapter is quite important in terms of providing students the skills they need to successfully work in groups.

Chapter 5 discusses the role of power in group contexts. It is highly unlikely that students will find themselves in a group setting in which power struggles do not exist. The goal of the chapter is to provide students the knowledge needed to understand the role of power within groups and mange it effectively.

Chapter 6 logically follows the information surrounding power in groups. The focus of the chapter is conflict within group situations. The information further fills the student toolbox with tips on how to successfully manage conflict in groups.

Chapter 7 examines the importance of leadership within a group. As our students strive to become leaders in their own personal and professional groups, the chapter should provide theory and application strategies to help them thrive.

In *Chapter 8* students will learn the difference between groups and teams. Specifically, the information provided in the chapter will help students identify effective communication behaviors necessary for positive teamwork.

Chapter 9 focuses on group communication within specific contexts. After studying the chapter students will be able to identify group communication theory and strategies in health settings, workplace contexts, as well and social groups.

Finally, in *Chapter 10* virtual group communication is examined. In the current times, so many group discussions occur online that it is imperative we learn how to effectively communicate in this virtual world.

The overall goal of this text is to provide not only theoretical guidance with regard to group communication, but also to provide students real life application-based tools they can use in their own personal and professional groups. It is unlikely to imagine a world in which we do not consistently find ourselves working in groups. Therefore, it is the hope that the information provided in this text will provide students a tool kit that they can use to enhance future group communication experiences.

Nicole Blau
Ohio University

ABOUT THE AUTHOR

© N. Blau

Nicole Blau (Ph.D., University of Kentucky) is an Associate Professor of Communication Studies at Ohio University, Lancaster. Dr. Blau's research may be found in *Communication Quarterly, Journal of Health Communication, Ohio Communication Journal* and *the Florida Communication Journal*. She is also a co-author of *Family Communication: Relationship Foundations*. Dr. Blau enjoys teaching group communication and working on research that examines the interpersonal nature of groups.

CHAPTER ONE

What is Group Communication? Foundations and Theory

LEARNING OBJECTIVES

After studying chapter 1, you should be able to:

- Explain the importance of effective group communication.
- Define the need for affiliation and explain how that need can be satisfied in groups.
- Define communication, group, and small group communication.
- Explain communication principles as they relate to groups.
- Define theory.
- Explain and apply various theories of group communication.

DID YOU KNOW...

- The largest group hug in history included 10, 554 people.
- The best-selling music group (in terms of sales) is the Beatles.
- The longest group hug lasted 30 hours and one minute.
- The largest group of carol singers included 25, 272 people in Nigeria.
  (Guinness Book of World Records, 2019)

Though you have likely never been included in a group setting as large as the groups who have made it into the *Guinness Book of World Records*, you have probably been a part of at least a couple of groups during your lifetime. Further, you will undoubtedly be involved in group situations in the future. The world records above show us how groups can take on all forms, sizes, and missions. As we begin our journey to study group communication, think of the groups that you are a part of and your role in those groups. In this chapter, we will take a look at some core group communication concepts, as well as theory that help explain how and why groups communicate.

THE IMPORTANCE OF GROUP COMMUNICATION

Groups are a large part of our everyday lives. This includes both our personal and professional lives. Think about your personal life—what groups are you a part of? Most of us are part of multiple groups simultaneously. For instance, I am part of my family, my group of friends, work groups, and a small group at my church. In addition, you may be part of a sports group, a group centered on a hobby (such as a sewing group or book club), or even a support group.

Now that you are beginning to think of all the groups you belong to, can you imagine how lonely life would feel without being a part of those groups? Though we all need "alone time" on occasion, these groups help us handle tough times as well as celebrate good times. Groups in general, but especially social groups, such as friends and family, are important for our needs for affiliation. As humans, we have **affiliation needs** meaning we need to be connected to others. Connection with others can help us handle situations mentally, emotionally, and even impact our health. We know that people who live in isolation from others tend to have more mental and physiological issues. If you recall the movie *Castaway (2000)* starring Tom Hanks, the main character's plane crashed, and he was isolated on a deserted island. The lack of affiliation caused him severe physical, mental, and emotional challenges. This movie illustrates an extreme case where one's affiliation needs are not met, but nevertheless, it shows how our needs for affiliation impacts every part of our life.

Affiliation Need

a human need to be connected to others

© OlegRi/Shutterstock.com

Although we all have affiliation needs, we do so to differing degrees. While some people need constant connection with others, you may be someone who thrives on being alone and only feels the need to connect with others from time to time. To quote the movie *The Hangover (2009)*, some people are "lone wolves." Not only do our needs for affiliation vary, but these needs also may change during different parts of our lives. The amount of human connection you crave now may not be the same five years from now. Regardless, we all have needs for affiliation, and group membership (social or professional) can often help satisfy the need for connectedness.

It is pretty clear how social groups, such as our family and friends, impact our lives, but what about other types of groups? You may have a job currently for which you have to work in groups. If not, you likely will in the future. Groups in the workplace are important. In fact, teams and groups are very common in corporate America. For this reason, at some point in your career, you will likely have to work in a group setting. There are many benefits to group work in the workplace including increased productivity, better decision-making and problem-solving, and better idea creation.

Think about a group project you have worked on in the past. Perhaps, as a group, you had many tasks you were required to complete. Finishing several tasks may go more quickly and be more likely to be finished if more than one person can work toward the goal. As a group, you can "divide and conquer" which results in more productivity. Not only will groups be more productive when tasks can be delegated, but the job also may be done more efficiently.

Groups can also promote better decision-making and problem-solving than working individually. Have you ever heard the saying, "two heads think better than one"? When people work together to make a decision or solve a problem, more ideas can be generated. Often, more ideas can lead to more thoughtful processes when decision-making and/or problem-solving. Instead of coming up with only one idea individually, if all members have ideas, the group can then pick which one is best and/or combine ideas to make the best decision. We will look more closely at group decision-making and problem-solving in chapter 4.

Thirdly, groupwork can lead to more innovative ideas. From my own experience, I have had many ideas that I thought were amazing *until* I began to talk through my ideas with others. When talking with others, I was able to generate even greater, more innovative ideas. Often when working together, groups can talk through ideas to generate a superior idea than one can create individually. Imagine a huge corporation such as Walt Disney. If Disney theme parks were based on the ideas of only one person, it would not likely be near as complex and innovative as it is today. Special engineers called "Imagineers" work together in teams to create new rides, ensure safety, and develop all components of the experience. A huge enterprise such as Disney could never be developed by one or two good ideas; it takes many ideas and many people to make the dream a reality.

In addition to the social and professional functions of groups, there is a support function of groups. In other words, we look to others for physical, emotional, mental, and sometimes financial support. You have probably heard of multiple types of support groups for things such as grief, dealing with illnesses, and even substance abuse support groups. For instance, Alcoholics Anonymous (AA) is a support group for people who have had issues with alcohol. Related to AA, is a group called Al-Anon which provides support for family and friends of persons with drinking problems. The amount of support groups is ever-growing and can be found in many outlets such as social media, websites, chat rooms, and face-to-face meeting locations. Support groups can be formal, such as Alcoholics Anonymous, or informal, such as your own circle of friends. Neither type is more or less important, and both can meet people's needs. We all need support at some point in our lives, and it is really nice to have options when we need help.

Groups are even important in terms of our physical health. According to an article in *Healthline* (2017), people who work out in group settings are more likely to "stick with it" and gain more health benefits. Health-related groups, such as Weight Watchers, actively provide support to help people reach health goals. Weight Watchers offers weekly meetings for members to talk through issues and share ideas of how to stay on track to achieve a healthier lifestyle. For those who cannot attend face-to-face meetings, the company also offers online support where you can connect with other members and weight loss coaches. Research shows that when people are trying to

SUPPORT GROUP CONTEXT	BENEFIT	EXAMPLE
Personal	Connection with others	Suzy has suffered from depression that resulted after a traumatic event in her life. Suzy's family persuaded her to join a support group that meets weekly to help her cope with her depression. In that group, Suzy met a couple of women who quickly became close friends and truly could understand her situation. Suzy found the connection she needed through this group to help her manage her depression and learn to enjoy life again.
Professional	Shared resources	Chris works for an organization that audits financial institutions. For each audit, teams are placed in an organization to analyze various elements such as finances, technology issues, federal regulation compliance and other important areas. Each team member specializes in one of the areas of the audit and, as a group, they share resources to complete the task. Without sharing resources, they would not be able to thoroughly audit all parts of an institution.
Health	Support to attain a healthy lifestyle	Bobbi recently received a poor report from her doctor and needs to lose weight to avoid serious health issues. In order to motivate herself to lose weight, Bobbi asks friends and family members if they would like to form a weight loss group where they hold one another accountable. Specifically, they must weigh in weekly and report their weight loss/gains to the group. At the end of eight weeks, whomever lost the most weight wins a prize. While Bobbie did not win the prize for the most weight lost, she did lose a significant amount of weight in no small part to the support and motivation from her weight loss group.

lose weight, working with others increases accountability and helps them achieve goals. Often, weight loss group members connect with one another and when such groups increase cohesion, they are more likely to attend meetings and achieve weight loss goals (Taylor, et al., 2019). In our digital world, support groups can be accessed 24-hours per day, seven days per week.

All of these group benefits are a result of quality communication. In order for groups to be successful, it is essential the communication be effective. Thus, let's define *communication* and investigate important principles that may ultimately impact our communication in groups.

WHAT IS COMMUNICATION?

We are repeatedly told that communication is important. In fact, most of us believe that effective communication is an important part of our daily lives. Because communication is crucial in groups, it is important that we know how to define it. In this book, **communication** is defined as sharing meaning with others through verbal and nonverbal codes. While neither verbal nor nonverbal communication is more important than the other, we do use both forms and should be able to differentiate between the types. **Verbal communication** includes using words to send a message between sender and receiver. We can communicate through the use of language because every word represents a symbol for some meaning. On the other hand, **nonverbal communication** occurs when we send a message to a receiver using non-speech symbols (such as gestures, body movements, and non-speech vocalics). Regularly, verbal and nonverbal behaviors are used simultaneously.

It would be impossible to work in a group without communication. Sometimes people have trouble verbally communicating and this can be difficult in group situations. In fact, we often perceive no verbal communication as the person just refusing to communicate or not sending any message at all. This begs the question, is it possible to not communicate *at all*?

Many communication scholars argue that we are always communicating. There is a well-known communication principle that "one cannot not communicate" (Watzlawick, Beavin, & Jackson, 1967). According to this principle, even when we are not intentionally communicating, or even realize we are sending a message, we are still communicating. For instance, imagine you are not feeling well and decide to skip class one day. No one in the class knows where you are or why you are not in class—you did not contact anyone. Are you sending a message to your classmates? A better question may be, are your classmates receiving a message from you? Perhaps some of your classmates notice you are

Communication
sharing meaning with others through verbal and nonverbal codes

Verbal Communication
using words to send a message between sender and receiver

Nonverbal Communication
sending a message to a receiver using non-speech symbols (such as gestures, body movements, and non-speech vocalics)

absent and assume you are running late, sick, or just needed a "mental health day." Even in your absence, you have communicated a message. In this situation, you cannot *NOT* communicate. In addition to one's inability to communicate, there are several other communication principles that are central to our study of group interactions.

PRINCIPLES OF COMMUNICATION

When studying any type of communication, it is important to review some common beliefs and principles. This is certainly not an exhaustive list of communication principles, but each of the following is important to the study of group communication.

Communication is a process. Communication does not occur in a vacuum. Communication involves several moving parts such as a sender, a receiver, the message (verbal or nonverbal), the channel of communication, and the context in which the interaction takes place. All of these parts work together as a process. Each part is interdependent meaning they depend on one another. Put differently, a change in one component of the process will create change in the other components.

Groups may be formed in multiple ways, but each will follow its own process as the group develops and moves toward a goal. Sometimes this process goes smoothly, sometimes it does not. Often, the ease in this process depends on the competence level of the group members.

Some people are more competent communicators than others. Competent communicators are able to effectively send and receive verbal and nonverbal messages. They are able to speak in a way that others can understand and receive messages with accurate understanding. Competent communicators often use a variety of communication behaviors such as listening, paraphrasing, concrete language use, and the like when interacting with others. Competent communication is a skill that can be learned and should be practiced on a regular basis. It is important to remember that no one is born a competent communicator. Much like any sport or hobby, the ability to communicate competently is something that is honed over time.

Communication is dynamic. Because communication is transactional and we are consistently reacting to the behavior of others, communicative behaviors are always changing. Even if you send the same message to the same person, other pieces of the communication situation have changed (i.e. time of day, location, etc.) which changes the overall message in some way.

Communication is irreversible. Have you ever said something that you wished you could take back or perhaps say differently? Communication, like so many other things in life, is something that cannot be taken back once it is put out there. In other words, it is not reversible.

Interdependence

a change in one component of the process will create change in the other components

Competent Communication

effectively sending and receiving verbal and nonverbal messages; a person's ability to speak in a way that others can understand and receive messages with accurate understanding

When working in a group, certain messages can be very damaging to group relationships and, because communication is irreversible, may create a difficult situation to overcome.

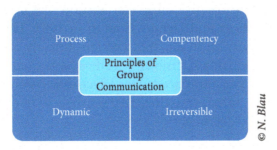

© N. Blau

WHAT IS GROUP COMMUNICATION?

Before we can examine group communication, we must be able to define group. When you think of "groups," what are you imagining? Do two people make up a group—or is that a pair? Three people… or more than three? If there are five people standing around not interacting while they wait on a bus to arrive, is that a true group or a conglomerate of people? In this textbook, we will define group as three or more people brought together by a common goal who depend on one another to achieve their goals.

Group communication may be defined as "an interaction among a small group of people who share a common purpose or goal, who feel a sense of belonging to the group, and who exert influence on one another" (Beebe & Masterson, 1997, p. 6). Over the years, there have been several theories of group communication advanced that help explain how and why we communicate in groups. In this section, we will briefly review some common group communication theories that will help guide our studies. First, let's make sure we know what we mean by "theory."

A theory may be thought of as ideas that are logically linked together that can be used to explain, predict, and

© Rawpixel.com/Shutterstock.com

understand human phenomena. Theories help us describe behavior and explain *why* people behave a certain way. For instance, why do some people naturally take on the leadership role in a group while others prefer to blend into the background? Why do some people question everything while others tend to agree with whatever others in the group prefer? Theories of group communication help us to understand the dynamics of groups a bit better. This can ultimately lead to more effective group communication.

GROUP COMMUNICATION THEORIES

Functional Perspective on Group Decision Making

The functional perspective on group decision making was developed by Randy Hirokawa and Dennis Gouran in 1983. They believed the interaction that occurs in group discussions directly impacts a group's ability to make quality decisions. Specifically, they argued that there are four specific functions needed for effective decision-making. These are **requisite** (required) **functions** that must occur in order for a group to make a quality decision.

Frist, groups must analyze the problem. In this step, a group must work to determine the extent of the situation they are facing. When trying to make a decision or solve a problem, the group needs to spend time figuring out the nature of the problem, the cause(s) of the problem, who is affected, and what is impacting the issue. When groups assume they know the nature of the problem without fully looking at all angles, they may risk missing something that will help them make a quality decision. For this reason, group members should not rush through this step. Knowing the entire situation is necessary when working to solve a problem and make a quality decision.

The second requisite function is goal setting. It is fair to say that when engaged in decision-making, we hope to accomplish some goal. For instance, when you decided to take a college class, perhaps it was with the goal of earning a college degree or getting a certain job. When groups engage in decision-making, it is crucial to set goals to be used to evaluate potential solutions.

According to this theory when groups set goals, they create criteria to evaluate decisions/solutions. Put differently, group members decide in advance what needs to happen in order for the decision to be a good one. If criteria are not advanced early in the decision-making processes, it is possible a group will come to a decision that seems good but does not accomplish everything needed by the group.

For instance, imagine you are making a large purchase, such as a new car. You could go car shopping and find many cars you like, but will they all be the best decision for you? Perhaps some will be too expensive, have too much mileage, or not be practical for what you need. If you set goals for your car-buying experience *before* you begin looking for cars (such as price range, age of the vehicle, etc.), you are more likely to focus your shopping and end up with a car that meets all of your needs.

The third function is the identification of alternatives steps. This function includes group members identifying as many possible options as possible. The more alternatives a group can think of, the more likely the "right" or best one will be found. How many times have you had a decision to make and you just go with the first idea that pops into your

Requisite Functions

functions necessary for a group to perform in order to make a quality decision

head, only to find out later it was not the best possible decision? By taking the time to pinpoint as many options as possible, it increases the likelihood that the most effective decision will be made.

The final function includes the evaluation of positive/negative characteristics for each alternative identified. In this step, group members must take every alternative they came up with and evaluate each based on the criteria set forth in the goal-setting phase. When group members examine each alternative in detail and analyze the pros and cons for each against the goals created for the situation, the group can narrow down the best options. Once this has been done, the group can make a decision on how to proceed.

Hirokawa and Gouran argue that if groups spend the time and energy needed to communicate about each of these requisite functions, they will be more likely to make a quality decision. Many groups fail to tend to the four requisite functions. Though acceptable group decisions have been made without completing all four functions, this theory help explains how effective group interactions can only increase the quality of decisions made by groups.

Group Decision-Making Functions

© N. Blau

Group Think

Picture this: You are part of a group of five students in your Group Communication course. As a group, you must create a video highlighting the positive aspects of your campus. You have only one week to create and edit this video. This project is worth a lot of points and can significantly impact your grade in the course. While planning, someone in the group suggests filming the gym locker rooms as a comedy portion of the video. You think this is a bad idea, but no one seems to say anything. After very little discussion, everyone seems to be "on board" with the idea and the plan is set. After the project is completed and turned in, you find out that two other group members also thought it was a bad idea but chose not to say anything. All three of you went along with the group feeling pressured to do so. It is possible, this group was in a state of groupthink.

First developed by social psychologist Irving Janis in 1972, **groupthink** occurs when a less than optimal decision is made by the group in

Groupthink

extreme pressure felt by group members to agree with the behavior(s) of the group; a less than optimal decision is made by the group in order to come to an agreement

order to come to an agreement. In other words, people in a group form a consensus just to come to an agreement on the issue at hand. When a group has entered a state of groupthink, members (especially in smaller groups) feel pressured to "go along with the group." This behavior typically does not result in a good decision being made.

Think of large groups you have been part of versus smaller-sized groups. When there is a large amount of people, there is likely to be differing opinions. When more than one person shares an opinion, they may speak up. On the converse, the smaller the group, the less likely there are for differing opinions, and the more likely for groupthink to occur. In addition to group size, Janis (1972) described eight symptoms of groupthink:

- *Illusion of invulnerability*: Group members feel they are unstoppable; this often leads to greater risk-taking.
- **Collective rationalization**: Group members work together to create justifications/rationalizations for the decisions made and/or actions taken.
- **Belief in inherent morality of the group**: Group members believe they are behaving ethically and are moral in their actions so this belief can lead to unethical decisions/actions being taken.
- **Stereotyped view of outgroups**: Members view outsiders as stupid, dumb, bad/evil; they are often underestimated.
- **Direct pressure on dissenters**: Peer pressure is placed on anyone who does not agree with the group.
- **Self-censorship**: Group members typically do not disagree or openly communicate ideas that go against the groups (watch what they say) so as not to be criticized by the rest of the group.
- **Illusion of unanimity**: Members believe that everyone agrees; silence is perceived as consent.
- **Self-appointed mindguards**: These are members who "guard" the rest of the group from outside information/pressures that could be perceived as criticizing the group.

Though we tend to think that our own groups will never enter a state of groupthink, we need to be careful. When engaged in group settings, be mindful of the communication that takes place among group members. Keep an eye out for the eight symptoms of groupthink, especially in smaller-sized groups. Groupthink is a phenomenon that is generally not intended, but once entered can lead to poor group decision-making and problem-solving.

SYMPTOM OF GROUPTHINK	MESSAGE EXAMPLE
1. Illusion of Invulnerability	*"There is no way we are making the wrong decision; we are a really good group and we know how to do things correctly. We never make mistakes!"*
2. Collective Rationalization	*"Every group has 'hiccups.' Just because we failed that group project does not mean we did bad work. It was just because we are a new group and need time to gel."*
3. Belief in Inherent Morality	*"No matter what anyone says, we know that we have strong values and morals. We are not doing anything bad or wrong."*
4. Stereotyped View of Outgroups	*"Our group rocks! We are clearly the best group on this campus. The other student group is full of dummies."*
5. Direct Pressure on Dissenters	*"Wait... are you suggesting we are making a mistake? We are NOT making a mistake and if you are a GOOD group member, you will be supportive instead of being critical. Do you want to be a part of this group or not?"*
6. Self-censorship	*(Thinking to self) "Gee, I don't know that this is going to work, but if I say anything, they will all be so mad at me. I better just keep my ideas to myself."*
7. Illusion of Unanimity	*"Well no one spoke up after I suggested we move the meeting to Friday afternoon, so we must all be in agreement."*
8. Self-appointed Mindguards	*"Eh, don't worry about what he was saying. He was making comments, but they don't relate to us. Now, back to what we were talking about..."*

Communication Accommodation Theory

If you have ever changed your speech pattern to blend in with a group of people, your behavior can be explained by the communication accommodation theory. Originally called the speech accommodation theory, in 1987, Howard Giles renamed it the communication accommodation theory. According to this theory, when we perceive differences between ourselves and others, we sometimes adapt (or accommodate) our communication behavior to more effectively interact with others.

There are two ways in which we accommodate our communication: convergence and divergence. Convergence occurs when a person changes his/her communication to better match others. For example, my husband is from a very small town in Texas. His family and friends use some words differently than we do in the Midwest, and their accents are very different in Texas. Every time we go visit his family in Texas, I notice that his speech patterns change to match that of his family and friends. He speaks (and sounds) very different than he does when at home. In essence, he converges to fit in with his Texas family.

Convergence

changing your communication to better match others

Conversely, **divergence** happens when you modify your communication to set yourself apart and stress the differences between yourself and others. When I was a graduate student teaching lower-level communication courses, I was very close in age to my students. In fact, until I told people my role, many just thought I was a student in the class. In an attempt to stand out as the instructor of the course, I diverged in my speech patterns. I intentionally spoke differently than my students in order to stress the difference in my position within the class.

Group members' decisions to adapt speech patterns can undoubtedly impact communication. This impact can be positive or negative depending on the circumstances. Can you think of a time that you engaged in either convergence or divergence within a group situation? Why did you do so? What was the outcome?

Although we sometimes engage in convergence and/or divergence unknowingly, when we do so purposefully the intent behind our action is important. Often, the intent behind opting to converge or diverge impacts the outcome. If the intent is good, often the outcome will be positive; if the intent is bad, then the consequence may also not be favorable. Keep this in mind while working in groups. Be mindful when trying to converge of "fit in" or diverge and recognize why you are doing so.

Convergence

- Bryce has recently been elected to the Student Senate on his campus. He is getting ready to attend his first meeting and is unsure how to communicate in this new role. In an effort to fit in, Bryce aims to use similar language and nonverbals as the students in the group.

Divergence

- After having served on the Student Senate for two years, Bryce would like to run for president of the student senate. In order to stand out and distinguish himself as a good candidate for president, he begins to speak differently than other students in the group. He feels using more formal language and speaking about unique topics will help him stand out and successfully be seen as a leader in the group.

Systems Theory

Think of any group. Groups are made up of people (members) and each individual brings something to the group. Collectively, however, the group may take on its own identity that is unique—unlike the identity of any one group member. When viewing groups this way, we are essentially seeing the group as a system—with various working parts.

The last theory we will cover in this chapter was advanced in 1969 by Ludwig von Bertalanffy and is called the General Systems Theory. Because multiple groups such as family units, work groups, and social groups can be thought of as systems, this theory has been applied in many different contexts. Bertalanffy defined as system as "a set of elements standing in interrelation among themselves with the environment" (von Bertalanffy, 1975, p. 159). In other words, the components of a system (group members) relate with one another in such a way they create a new phenomenon (the group).

If we view groups as systems, von Bertalanffy would argue that we can no longer view the group in terms individual members, but as a larger entity. This is what is referred to as wholeness. If you have ever been a part of a group project in a class and received a "group grade" instead of an "individual grade," the instructor was likely viewing the group as a system. The instructor knew that each person contributed different amounts of work and accomplished different tasks, but the grade was based on the whole group product—not individual outputs.

Sports teams are great examples of systems. We can easily apply the general systems theory to sport teams because each player on the team has a specific role, but they must play together as a system to be successful. For instance, a football team is made up of several positions such as the offensive linemen, the defense, the running back, the wide receivers, kicker, and quarterback (to name a few). Each part of the football team system is important. They cannot play without each role being filled. However, they cannot win games and succeed if only the kicker performs well. They need a sense of wholeness to win games.

System

"a set of elements standing in interrelation among themselves with the environment" (von Bertalanffy, 1975, p. 159)

Wholeness

viewing a system as a larger, whole entity instead of as a summation of individual parts

© aceshot1/Shutterstock.com

There are many other theories that help us explain communication in groups not covered in this chapter. Further, there are broader models of group development that will be covered in later chapters. The theories discussed in this chapter will be a useful foundation as we dive deeper in the communication common in group contexts. Moreover, these theories will be useful as we work through explanations of how and why groups communicate. Keep this foundation in mind as you participate in your own personal and professional groups as the ability to understand group behavior will help you to become a more effective communicator yourself.

SUMMARY

Love 'em or hate 'em, groups are a part of our lives. At work, school, and in social settings, groups are common. Because we cannot live our lives in isolation, it is important to learn how to effectively communicate in group situations. In this first chapter, we have set the groundwork for the remainder of the text. Now that we have defined important terms such as communication, group, and small group communication, we can continue learning strategies to successfully communicate with others. In addition, the group communication theories covered in this chapter will help us evaluate small group interactions and explain human behavior.

Not all groups are the same. Some groups are larger than others, some are more diverse, and group goals differ. In fact, groups change over time and the way groups look today may very well appear differently next year or even next week. In part, changes in groups may be due to group development. In the next chapter, we will take a look at different types of groups, group roles, and how groups grow and change over time.

REFLECTION QUESTIONS

1. Why is effective group communication important? How does it impact our lives?
2. What are needs for affiliation?
3. What does it mean to refer to communication as a "process"?
4. Why is competent communication important in group situations?
5. What is a theory? What are theories used for?
6. What are the requisite functions of group communication?
7. What is groupthink? How do we know when a group is in groupthink?
8. In what situations should we converge and/or diverge with group members?
9. How are groups "systems"? What does this mean to refer to a group as a system?

LEARNING BY ACTION

In groups (four-five students per group), students should go out and experience an activity that no one in the group has ever done before. Some examples may be canoeing, playing a sport, line dancing, or pitching a tent. Group should spend a significant amount of time sharing the activity (three to five hours) and the activity should be challenging to some degree. Groups will subsequently report their experience with classmates. There should be a discussion of how the experience ties in with course content being covered in class. This is a good introductory learning project to help students become acquainted and start learning about small group communication.

VIDEO CLIP

"Dead to Me" (2019)—Starring Christina Applegate—Episode 1 (Pilot), Season 1. Jennifer (Applegate) attends a grief support group following the death of her husband. Jennifer meets Judy when getting coffee before the start of the meeting and they quickly form a friendship. During the season, we see both ladies attend support meetings on a regular basis.

CONTEMPORARY COMMUNICATION

Chances are you have text messaged someone from your smartphone. Have you ever texted more than one person at one time? If so, you were involved in a group text. Texting has become such a large part of our lives; apps have been developed to create chat rooms for groups via text messaging. One of the most popular group text messaging apps is call GroupMe. Members in the group chat can opt out or leave the group at any time. This is a perfect app to use when keeping in touch with working groups that are temporary!

CASES IN COMMUNICATION

You just transferred from to a new university. It is your first semester at your new school, and you don't know many people. You recently found out that there is a golf club on campus. You really enjoy playing golf and decide to join the club so that you can play golf regularly as well as meet new people. Shortly after you join the golf club, you begin to notice that there are certain members of the club that openly speak their mind and voice their opinions quite aggressively. Even though everyone does not always agree with those members, no one seems to step up and say anything. After your first outing with the golf club, you notice that there are a lot of side conversations wherein some group members disagree with the louder members of the group but are afraid to speak up and say anything to them. Therefore, people just kind of go along with whatever those particular group members suggest.

On your second weekend trip with the golf club, Nick and Jerry, the louder group members, decide that after the team is checked in for the night, everyone should sneak out of their hotel rooms and attend a party at a local fraternity house. Nick knows someone in the fraternity and tells the entire golf club they are welcome to go to the party. You know that if you sneak out past curfew and attend this party, you all will be in big trouble and the golf club could possibly be disbanded. You talk with some other members of the group and they are a bit hesitant to sneak out also. When the time comes, however, everyone in the group sneaks out just as Nick and Jerry instructed them to do so because they don't want to be the ones to say no.

1. What symptoms of groupthink are illustrated in this case?
2. Do you think the group is in a state of groupthink? Why or why not?
3. What communication can be helpful in this situation?

REFERENCES

Beebe, S.A., & Masterson, J.T. (1997). *Communicating in small groups* (5th ed). New York, NY: Addison-Wesley Longman.

Gouran, D. S. , & Hirokawa, R. Y. (1983). The role of communication in decision-making groups: A functional perspective. In M. S. Mander (Ed.), Communications in transition (pp. 168–185). New York: Praeger.

Guinness Book of World Records. (2019). Retrieved from www.guinnessworldrecords.com

Janis, I.L. (1972). Victims of groupthink: A psychological study of foreign policy decisions and fiascoes. Boston: Houghton Mifflin Company.

Poole, M. S., & DeSanctis, G. (1990). Understanding the use of group decision support systems: The theory of adaptive structuration. In J. Fulk & C. Steinfeld (Eds). Organizations and Communication Technology. Newbury Park, Ca: Sage.

Radcliffe, S. (2017, November). *People who exercise in groups get more health benefits.* Retrieved from: https://www.healthline.com/health-news/exercise-in-groups-get-more-health-benefits#1

Taylor, S.S., Olsen, M.K., McVay, M.A, Grubber, J., Gierisch, J.M., Yancy, W. S., & Voils, C.I. (2019). The role of group cohesion in a group-based behavioral weight loss intervention. *Journal of Behavioral Medicine, 42,* 162-168. doi:10.1007/s10865-018-9953-4.

von Bertalanffy, L. (1968). General systems theory. New York: George Braziller.

von Bertalanffy, L. (1975). Perspectives on general systems theory: Scientific-philosophical studies. New York: George Braziller

Watzlawick, P., Beavin, J., & Jackson, D.D. (1967). *Pragmatics of human communication.* New York, NY: Norton.

CHAPTER TWO

What Kind of Group is This, Anyhow? Group Types and Roles

LEARNING OBJECTIVES

After studying chapter 2, you should be able to:

- Explain the importance of group roles.
- Explain task and social dimensions of groups.
- Describe and apply the five stages of group development.
- Explain the types of group roles.
- Understand the process of group socialization.

Have you ever heard of the legendary band named, The Beatles? Chances are, you have. Many consider The Beatles to be the most influential band of all times. Originally created by Paul McCartney and John Lennon, the group started off playing small gigs at local clubs and began their first large tour in 1960 after adopting the group name "The Beatles." For decades to follow, the group influenced millions of people all over the world in various ways. This group of four men would go down in history as the "Fab Four" – John Lennon, Paul McCartney, George Harrison, and Ringo Starr. Though viewed as one "group," this infamous group is made up of individuals who all took on different roles in the group:

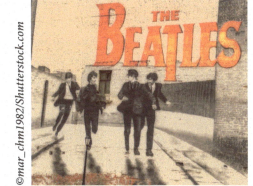

©mar_chm1982/Shutterstock.com

- John Lennon – *Rhythm guitar, vocals*
- Paul McCartney – *Bass guitar, some piano, vocals*
- George Harrison – *Lead guitar, backup vocals*
- Ringo Starr – *Drummer*

Without any of these group roles being fulfilled, The Beatles may not have been nearly as successful. Because each member excelled at his role within the group, the world was able to experience great songs such as "*Hey Jude*" and "*The Abbey Road*."

Group roles are important to the overall structure of the group. Whether the roles are explicit (well-defined) or implicit and grow organically from the group interaction, each participant should "bring something to the table." In this chapter, we will examine the importance and function of group roles. In addition, because not all groups are the same, we will take a look at different types of groups and the importance of each.

THE IMPORTANCE OF GROUP ROLES

Have you ever been a part of a group where you knew the group goal, but had no idea what your specific task or role was? Or have you ever worked on a group project for a class and everyone assumed others were completing certain jobs, so the task never actually got accomplished? If so, you have experienced the importance of group roles first-hand.

Thinking back to what we learned about systems theory in chapter 1, in order for the group to function as a complete system, it is important that each part of the system does its job. This is a great way to think of roles within a group. Each person must effectively enact his or her role in the group so that, as a whole, the group can function as a system and achieve goals.

Role Clarity

when group members to know exactly what they are responsible for and how their contribution will help achieve the group goal

One important component of group roles is clarity. Role clarity allows group members to know exactly what they are responsible for and how their contribution will help achieve the group goal. Imagine you are working on a group project for a class and you do not know what you are responsible to complete. Odds are that you won't be motivated to complete the work if you are unsure of what you are supposed to do. If you know, however, that you are responsible for writing a specific part of the group paper, this clarity will allow you to focus on your task and contribute to the project. Thus, group roles not only help group members know what they should focus on, roles can *motivate* members to contribute to the overall goal in a meaningful way.

Motivation

one's drive to accomplish a goal or behave in a certain way

Motivation may be defined as one's drive to accomplish a goal or behave in a certain way. When group roles are made clear, each individual is more likely to be motivated to fulfill his or her assigned role. In turn, when each member effectively carries out his or her role, it is more likely that the group will achieve his or her goal. Group goals may be very task-oriented or more social in nature, depending on the group. No matter the type of group, however, it is important to understand that in all groups there are two dimensions: task and social dimensions.

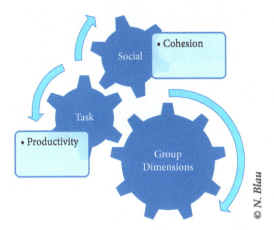

© N. Blau

Task Dimension

the functions and work achieved by the group; productivity is the output of this dimension

Social Dimension

the relationships formed among group members as a result of their interaction; the output of this dimension is cohesiveness.

The **task dimension** includes the functions and work achieved by the group. Productivity is the output of this dimension. In other words, when groups perform tasks, they produce a result. This output may be a decision made, a problem solved, or a goal accomplished. The **social dimension** refers to the relationships formed among group members as a result of their interaction. The result from the social dimension is cohesiveness.

The Jury Trial

Selena received a summons in the mail to report to jury duty in her county. Dreading the obligation to serve on a jury and disrupt her daily schedule, Selena reported as requested. On day one of jury duty, she, along with several strangers also summoned, were sent to a courtroom where a trial was beginning. As part of the trial process, Selena and her peers were questioned extensively by the attorneys (a process called *voir dire*) and eventually the jurors were selected. The jury consisted of twelve members with one alternate juror. Over the course of the next two weeks, the 13 strangers developed into a cohesive group who exemplified both task and social dimensions. The jury was tasked with listening to witness and expert testimonies, analyzing legal arguments made by attorneys, and learning the law as it related to the case. In addition, they were asked to make a decision on the guilt or innocence of the defendant. Over the two weeks, not only did they focus on their tasks, they began to form relationships. Over lunch breaks and talks about family, work, and other interests, friendships were formed. This speaks to the social dimension of the group. By the conclusion of the trial, Selena was thankful for the opportunity to serve on jury duty and was proud of the work they completed (productivity) as well as the connections formed with new friends (cohesion).

The two dimensions are closely tied to one another. Consider a group where relationships are maintained, and members feel a sense of cohesion. In a group such as this, with a strong social dimension, they are more likely to be focused on their task and be productive.

If group members, through individual roles, positively contribute to the group goal, it is possible that they will feel dependent on one another

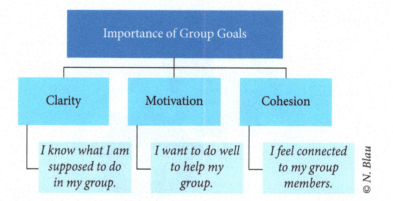

and are united in achieving success. This feeling of connectedness is group cohesion and can have positive effects on the group overall. As long as groups do not get *too* cohesive and enter a state of groupthink, there are many benefits to group cohesiveness. Some benefits include:

- **Increased productivity**: The more connected a group is, the more they can work together and work to achieve goals (see Weinberg, 1979); When each member fulfills his or her role, collectively he or she is better able to accomplish goals.
- **Satisfaction:** The more a person feels united (cohesion) with group members, the more he/she will feel satisfied within the group. Frey (1997) said that the more cohesive the group, the more one will be attracted to it, which is directly related to satisfaction.
- **Efficiency:** The more cohesive a group is, the more they will work together (as opposed to fighting with one another) to reach goals. Ultimately, this should lead to efficiency in achieving tasks and attaining goals.
- **Motivation:** According to Mudrack (1989), the more cohesion experienced in a group, the more committed one will be to the group goals. The more connected we feel with others, the less we want to let them down. As a result, we are driven to do well and contribute positively to the group.
- **Quality communication:** We are more likely to communicate openly and honestly with those with whom we feel connected. Conversely, we are less likely to engage in poor communication practices (such as not listening, aggressive communication, etc.) when the group is unified. The group atmosphere is typically more open in cohesive groups, allowing members to feel free to ask more questions and engage in open dialogue (Bormann, 1990).

The United States Women's National soccer team (USWNT) is a great example of what groups can achieve when they are cohesive. The group of ladies worked together to achieve their goals and not only did they win the World Cup in July 2019, but they also became the first women's national soccer team to win four Women's World Cup titles. That is a remarkable accomplishment that could have never been attained had the players been disconnected from one other. This group of ladies did not experience such strong cohesion overnight, and just because they were all on the same team does not mean the group developed automatically. Next, we will take a look at how groups develop.

© Mikolaj Barbanell/Shutterstock.com

EXAMPLE OF GROUP COHESION	
Increased Productivity	Brad's fraternity is a cohesive group who enjoy spending time together. Because they are such a close group, they don't mind working together on the Homecoming float for their fraternity. Almost every guy in the fraternity shows up to help and they are able to build an amazing float together. As a group they are much more productive than had only one or two members worked on the project.
Satisfaction	Judy was assigned to a group at work in which they were trying to create a new policy manual for the organization. The group, however, was not very cohesive and no one felt "connected." As a result, Judy and many of her peers were unhappy working in this group. When switched to a different group that was more cohesive, Judy was able to experience satisfaction in her group as they worked toward their goals.
Efficiency	Lyndsey had to complete two projects in her Communication course this semester. Though the work for the projects were similar, she noticed that the one she did individually took much longer than the one she completed with a group. When working with the group, members were able to take on different tasks and work more efficiently than she could when she had to complete all of the tasks on her own.
Motivation	Kellan recently received news from the doctor that he must lose weight in order to lower his cholesterol and be healthier. He could not seem to stay motivated to work out until he joined an exercise group at the local YMCA. Once he joined the group and experienced the group unity, he was much more motivated to show up, workout, and support others in the group. As a result, he did lose weight and increased his health.
Quality Communication	Kurt is a Human Resources Manager at XYZ Company. Kurt created small groups of employees to formulate ideas on how to create a better work environment. Kurt noticed that in the groups where members did not appear to be cohesive, they had a hard time communicating with one another and sharing ideas. In more cohesive groups, however, the discussions were open, and everyone felt free to honestly express their opinions. Overall, the quality of communication was better in the groups that were cohesive.

GROUP DEVELOPMENT

Forming Phase

when group members
are placed together
in a group by either
assignment or choice

Storming Phase

communication is
increased, and group
members are getting
to know one another
and trying to figure
out group roles; con-
flict often occurs in
this phase

Norming Phase

power struggles and
other issues begin
to get resolved and
group members begin
to understand what is
normal for the group

Norms

rules and guidelines for
the group

Explicit Norms

guidelines for the
group that are clearly
stated so there is little
to no uncertainty

Implicit Norms

guidelines that are
understood by group
members, though not
necessarily expressed
outright

Many times, the level of cohesiveness within a group depends on how the group was developed. Though you may have been placed in a group and view the group as having been developed instantly, this is really not the case. The assignment is only one phase of group development.

The most well-known group development research by Tuckman in 1965 advanced four phases of group development: forming, storming, norming, and performing. The first phase is called the forming phase of group development. This phase occurs when group members are placed together in a group (by assignment or choice). Often, group members do not know each other very well at this point and communication may be tentative. Only those who are very assertive will voice strong opinions/ideas during this phase.

Eventually, group members become more comfortable interacting with one another, and the novelty of the group begins to wear off. This is characteristic of the storming phase where communication is increased, and subgroups may be formed. It is in this phase that conflict and disagreements arise. Group members are getting to know one another and trying to figure out group roles, which frequently results in confrontation. Thus, the label "storming." A metaphorical storm arises in groups in this phase.

Third is the norming phase. In this phase, power struggles and other issues begin to get resolved and group members begin to understand what is normal for the group. Norms, or rules and guidelines, for the group are established and roles become clear at this point. Some norms are explicit, and some are implicit.

Explicit norms are guidelines for the group that are clearly stated so there is little to no uncertainty. Guidelines about meetings, due dates, and assigned tasks are frequently made explicit so that everyone is aware of the expectations. Implicit norms are guidelines that are understood by group members, though not necessarily expressed outright. For example, group members may take turns bring snacks to each meeting. Bringing a snack is not an official rule or obligation, but a group norm that is understood by all. Once group members begin to understand roles, they are better able to work on tasks and stabilize group relationships. With task and social group dimensions aligned, group members often begin to feel satisfaction within the group.

The fourth phase put forth by Tuckman is the performing phase. At this point, the group has evolved, and communication is better defined. While there still may be disagreements among members, it is better understood how to communicate differing ideas and opinions while staying focused on the group goal. Group roles are solidified by the performing phase and this is often considered the final stage in group development. Many groups never make it to this phase due to time constraints or groups separating before getting to this phase.

More than a decade after Tuckman published the four phases of group development, a fifth phase was added – the adjourning phase (Tuckman & Jensen, 1977). The **adjourning phase** can be considered a "wrap-up" phase where groups are no longer focused on task achievement but wrapping up any loose ends and concluding the group. For permanent groups, this is the last phase of the group development in which the group is disbanded. For work groups that have a specific task to accomplish, once the job is complete, the group work is officially over, and the group can be dismissed.

Although these phases appear linear in nature, group development is not as straightforward as it seems. There is no set amount of time a group may spend in each phase. Some groups will spend a lot of time in the forming phase and very little time in storming, for instance. Other groups may differ. Some groups may start in the forming stage, quickly enter storming, and decide to alter the group structure and start over again in the forming phase. Each and every group is unique and, as a result, group development will vary based on group attributes such as its size, membership, and goals.

You have probably heard of the late Michael Jackson. Many referred to Jackson as the "King of Pop" with hits such *Thriller* and *Beat It*. Jackson's career started off in a group setting. Together with his brothers, Jackie, Tito, Jermain, and Marlon, a group was formed by their father called, The Jackson Five. Their father, Joe Jackson, recognized his sons had great musical talent, created the music group, and the forming phase of the group was completed.

Being brothers, they knew each other very well (unlike many other groups when initially formed), but nevertheless they experienced a storming phase. Early on, the brothers faced conflict about group roles and conflict with their father and manager who pushed them nonstop. Unlike other kids their age, the Jackson brothers were forced to spend many, many hours rehearsing and performing in talent competitions. Learning to live such a life at young ages led to conflict and stormy times within the group.

After a short period, the Jackson brothers recorded their first hit and were subsequently picked up by a famous recording label. By this point, the boys knew what they had to do, how to perform and what was expected of them. They grew popular and released many big musical hits that led them to fame. By this point, the

Performing Phase

communication is better defined within the group and group members better understand how to communicate differing ideas and opinions while staying focused on the group goal; group roles are solidified

Adjourning Phase

the "wrap-up" phase where groups are no longer focused on task achievement but wrapping up any loose ends and concluding the group

©ZUMA Press, Inc./Alamy Stock Photo

CHALLENGES OF GROUP DEVELOPMENT BY PHASE	
PHASE	*CHALLENGE(S)*
Forming	• Expectations may be unknown or unclear. • Members are not sure what is acceptable behavior/norms. • Communication may be uncomfortable.
Storming	• Power struggles in this stage may lead to conflict. • Cliques/subgroups may form, and tension may increase among subgroups. • There may be competition to have voices be heard.
Norming	• Group members may become too comfortable. • Socializing may increase causing the group to get off task.
Performing	• Once group members feel united, it is easier to fall into a state of groupthink. • Expectations may be escalated making tasks more difficult to achieve.
Adjourning	• Group members may be saddened when groups end. • It may be confusing knowing what to do when the group is over. • Emotions may run high leading to tension/conflict.

Working Through Group Development Challenges

- Be open-minded to all group members.
- Avoid judgment (especially when initial ideas/opinions are presented).
- Engage in active listening.
- Work to build strong relationships with group members.
- Avoid social loafing and messing around during work time.
- Stay focused on the group task.
- Remember tough phases will pass.
- Enjoy the experience as best you can.

group had surpassed the norming phase and was into the performing phase. The Jackson Five had solidified and was incredibly productive and talented.

Eventually, however, Michael Jackson began to record solo hits and The Jackson Five (aka, "The Jacksons") separated and Michael Jackson continued his musical career on his own. This marked the adjourning phase for The Jackson Five. As with other groups, each member of The Jackson Five had a role within the group. By taking on various roles, it helped the group attain goals and gain success. Group roles are important for the structure of the group.

TYPES OF GROUP ROLES

From your own experience working in groups, you undoubtedly learned quickly that often people take on various roles within the group. Sometimes roles in the group are formally recognized. Formal roles may be assigned by a group leader or voted on by group members. For example, the president of a student organization on campus is often voted on by members of the group and is considered a formal role. Formal roles are needed to make sure specific tasks are fulfilled and are typically found in larger groups. Formal roles can also be found in small groups, but the larger the group, the more likely the opportunity for persons to take on formal roles.

Informal roles in groups are positions that transpire from group interactions and are not formally assigned. Less formal roles are common in smaller groups where there isn't a need to assigned formal roles, but people still "step up to the plate" to perform a certain group function. In my neighborhood, for example, we frequently have block parties and other social events. More often than not, there is one person who adopts the leadership role without being asked to do so. Because we don't have a neighborhood group or committee to plan the events, there is no formal structure; thus, no formal roles. When everyone in the group recognizes a person as leader, however, an informal role has emerged.

Whether a group role is formal or informal, we can classify roles into various types. Task roles help the group function in ways to achieve a specific assignment or goal, solve a problem, or make a decision. Just as there are several possible tasks a group may face, there are various types of task roles such as gathering information for the group, keeping the group organized, and facilitating group discussions.

Maintenance roles are centered on creating and sustaining relationships within the group. Typically, maintenance roles are focused on sustaining the social factors of the group. These roles may be more prevalent in groups that are more social than formal, such as a fraternity/sorority versus executive board of a large company.

Finally, disruptive roles are performed by group members who are more focused on themselves than the group and work to disturb the group. The disruptive role occurs frequently in groups and is generally not considered good or positive. There are several ways disrupters can cause chaos in a group such as hogging attention, messing around, and inciting conflict.

Task and maintenance roles are classically considered "good" or "positive" roles, while disruptive roles are often thought of negatively. As you review specific types of task, maintenance, and disruptive roles in the charts below, think of your participation in groups. What roles have you had? Which roles would you like to have in a group setting?

Formal Roles

positions assigned by a group leader or voted on by group members; official roles in the group

Informal Roles

positions that transpire from group interactions and are not formally assigned

Task Roles

roles that help the group function in ways to achieve a specific task or goal, solve a problem, or make a decision

Maintenance Roles

roles that are focused on creating and sustaining relationships within the group

Disruptive Roles

roles enacted by group members who are more focused on themselves than the group and work to disturb the group

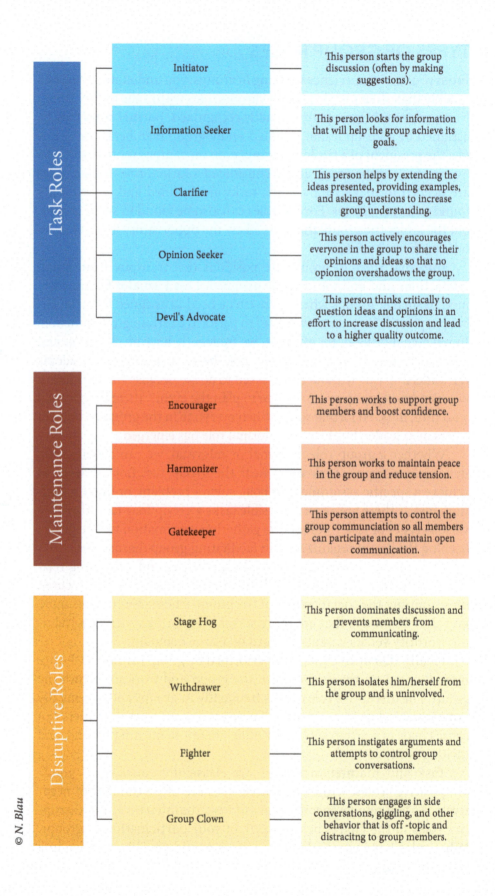

Task Roles

- **Initiator** — This person starts the group discussion (often by making suggestions).
- **Information Seeker** — This person looks for information that will help the group achieve its goals.
- **Clarifier** — This person helps by extending the ideas presented, providing examples, and asking questions to increase group understanding.
- **Opinion Seeker** — This person actively encourages everyone in the group to share their opinions and ideas so that no opionion overshadows the group.
- **Devil's Advocate** — This person thinks critically to question ideas and opinions in an effort to increase discussion and lead to a higher quality outcome.

Maintenance Roles

- **Encourager** — This person works to support group members and boost confidence.
- **Harmonizer** — This person works to maintain peace in the group and reduce tension.
- **Gatekeeper** — This person attempts to control the group communciation so all members can participate and maintain open communication.

Disruptive Roles

- **Stage Hog** — This person dominates discussion and prevents members from communicating.
- **Withdrawer** — This person isolates him/herself from the group and is uninvolved.
- **Fighter** — This person instigates arguments and attempts to control group conversations.
- **Group Clown** — This person engages in side conversations, giggling, and other behavior that is off-topic and distracitng to group members.

© N. Blau

ROLE CONFLICT AND ROLE AMBIGUITY – WHAT ROLE SHOULD I PLAY?

Considering the various parts of our lives, it is possible that we embody different roles simultaneously. For instance, as a mom and wife, in my personal life I may take on the role of "provider" or "nurturer" for my family. Professionally, however, I may be in a leadership role where I must manage other people. Thus, at work, I take on more of a "boss" or "manager" role. When our roles contradict each other, we experience role conflict.

Role conflict can certainly be stressful and lead to emotional tension. For example, a study done by Magdalena Obermaier and Thomas Koch in 2015 investigated the role conflict of persons employed dually as journalists as well as public relations professionals. In their role as journalists, they felt an obligation to report honest and straightforward information to the public. At the same time, however, their work as a public relations professional included the need to communicate information in a way that protects the organization they represent. This does not always include sharing all information available. The study found that the tension resulting from such role conflict led to a decrease in job satisfaction.

Within group settings, we may be asked to take on different roles and those roles could contradict one another. A similar problem we may experience in group settings, especially in the forming phase, is role ambiguity. Role ambiguity has been defined as a lack of understanding about how to fulfill one's role (Kahn, Wolfe, Quinn, Snoek, & Rosenthal, 1964).

Role ambiguity occurs when you are unsure of what to do in the role assigned. For example, you may be assigned the role of treasurer in your student organization. You may not know what tasks are involved in this role or how to fulfill your duties. This role may not conflict with other roles you have, but the uncertainty is evidence of role ambiguity.

Just like with role conflict, role ambiguity can lead to anxiety and possibly make you feel dissatisfied in the group. Thus, it is important to take measures to reduce the role ambiguity before it becomes problematic. Effective communication with others (both in and out of the group) should help reduce the uncertainty experienced. First, you must figure out what is causing the ambiguity. Put differently, what are you unsure about? What information do you need to help clarify your role?

Role Conflict

when our roles contradict each other

Role Ambiguity

a lack of understanding about how to fulfill one's role

Once you have this figured out, you can work with others or take necessary steps to figure out how to fulfill your role. Creating relationships with other group members, asking questions, and being open to advice are all ways you can work to reduce role ambiguity. Learning your role and developing relationship with group members will help the socialization process and potentially lead to a satisfying group experience.

GROUP SOCIALIZATION – FINDING YOUR WAY

Group socialization

the process group members use to influence one another and communicate in order to create agreed-upon norms for the group

Group socialization refers to the process group members use to influence one another and communicate in order to create agreed-upon norms for the group (Anderson, Riddle, & Martin, 1999). Similar to the phases of group development, socialization into groups often occurs in stages. One cannot enter a group and expect to be fully integrated into the group immediately. It takes time.

In the 2018 comedy *Game Night*, there was a group of friends who met each week for game night. When one of the group member's brother came to town and joined the group, he became the newcomer in the group and tried to find ways to fit in. The socialization process did not go well for the newcomer because instead of easing his way into the group of friends, he behaves a bit over-the-top.

Newcomers to a group must take on the newcomer role. In other words, they must play the part of the new person in the group so as not to upset the group dynamic. Newcomers should focus on learning the group norms, embracing the group culture, and learning about the group as part of the socialization process.

SMALL GROUP SOCIALIZATION SCALE

Directions: Complete each item in regard to your experience thus far in your small group. Rate each item in relation to the following scale by filling in the blanks with what you consider an appropriate answer.

If you strongly agree with the statement, write 5 in the blank.
If you agree with the statement, write 4 in the blank.
If you neither agree nor disagree with the statement, write 3 in the blank.
If you disagree with the statement, write 2 in the blank.
If you strongly disagree with the statement, write 1 in the blank.

_____ 1. I understood what was appropriate dress for group meetings.
_____ 2. I understood the authority the group had for doing its work.
_____ 3. I did not see myself as an effective group member.*
_____ 4. I understood the "group talk" the group used to do its work.
_____ 5. I found someone in the group who could provide me with emotional support.
_____ 6. It was clear what was expected of me in this group.
_____ 7. I found someone in the group with whom I could talk about career plans.
_____ 8. It was not at all clear what was expected of me in this group.*
_____ 9. I depended on other group members for support in the group.
_____ 10. I found someone in the group who could help me adjust to the group.
_____ 11. I found someone in the group on whom I could depend for support.
_____ 12. I had no clear idea of what this group was to accomplish.*
_____ 13. I found someone in the group with whom I could discuss personal matters.
_____ 14. There was no one in the group on whom I could depend for support.*

Scoring: Reverse score all items marked with an asterisk. (If you put a 5 for item 3, change this score to 1; if 4, change this score to 2; if 2, change this score to 4; if 1, change this score to 5.) Sum all items to create a general socialization outcome score. The higher the score, the more positive the socialization experience.

Source: Bruce L. Riddle, Carolyn M. Anderson, Matthew M. Martin, _Small Group Research_, Vol. 31, No. 5, pp. 554-572, copyright © 2000 by SAGE Publications. Reprinted by Permission of SAGE Publications, Inc.

SUMMARY

After studying chapter 2, you should now understand the nature and importance of roles within groups. The larger the group, the more roles become defined and, also, important. Knowing what your role within the group system will help make the group more productive and likely increase your own satisfaction.

Though many groups are created quite quickly, the development process can take time. Not all groups will reach every phase in the process, but it is essential to understand the development stages as you enter into groups in your personal and professional lives. Finally, understanding the group socialization process is necessary – especially if you are the newcomer to the group.

In our lives, we will partake in many group situations. Some will go more smoothly than others, and our roles within those groups will differ. Nevertheless, understanding your role and importance of group roles will help make us more productive and, likely, more cohesive. This can only benefit our experience in groups.

REFLECTION QUESTIONS

1. Why are group roles important?
2. How do group roles contribute to the overall group structure?
3. What are the task and social dimensions of groups? Why is each important?
4. Why is cohesion important in groups?
5. What can groups do to increase levels of cohesion?
6. What are the phases of group development? What goes on in each phase?
7. What is the difference between implicit and explicit group norms?
8. What are examples of task, maintenance, and disruptive roles in groups?
9. What is the difference between role conflict and role ambiguity?
10. What is group socialization and why is it important?

LEARNING BY ACTION

In groups (four-five students per group), students should decide on a problem facing the department or campus. This may include issues with class scheduling, parking problems, or any issue specific to your academic studies. Once a problem has been identified, in order to research the problem and come up with a reasonable solution, each group member should be assigned a specific role. Possible roles include leader, researcher, interviewer (to interview persons on campus), reporter (to report back to the class when complete), and group organizer (to organize resources and keep track of meetings, important information, etc.).

Each person must focus on his/her own role and write a two-three page reflection paper on how his/her role impacted the group system. In addition, each member must reflect on how other groups roles impacted his/her role. Finally, together the group should report (to the class) on their experience in group development (addressing each of the five phases).

VIDEO CLIP

"Ocean's Eight" (2018) – Starring Sandra Bullock, Cate Blanchett, and Anne Hathaway - is an action comedy spin-off of the box-office hit *Ocean's Eleven* (2001). In this film, Debbie Ocean (Bullock) reconnects with her former crime partner, Lou (Blanchett) and shares her plan to rob the Museum of Art at the upcoming Met Gala. Together, Debbie and Lou contact other friends, and the ladies form Ocean's Eight. This movie illustrates the phases of group development as well as different group roles played by each lady in the group.

CONTEMPORARY COMMUNICATION

So, you have a group you are a part of and scheduling face-to-face meetings is becoming a nightmare! For most people, between school, work, and other obligations, fitting time in to meet with a group is difficult. There are several online meeting formats that you can access for free to help alleviate scheduling issues. One format is Google Hangouts. Google has created an easily accessible, and user-friendly way for groups not only to meet and video chat, but to collaborate and share documents and other resources.

CASES IN COMMUNICATION

You work as a customer service manager at the Caring company which employees approximately 500 employees. Company policy strictly prohibits supervisors from dating their employees. While the policy is clear that superiors and subordinates must not be romantically involved, it is unclear on the consequences of such a relationship. One of your coworkers, Jerod (who is the manager of the marketing department) has recently started dating one of his newest employees. The new employee, Tara, has only worked for the Caring company for about five months. Jerod and Tara went on their first date approximately three months ago, and the relationship has continued to develop over the couple of months. About one month ago, Jerod disclosed to his boss that he is romantically involved with Tara and when asked, he was honest and that they had been dating for the past few months. An ethics committee has been called to review Jerod and Tara's case and to determine what action, if any, should be taken. Considering all members of the committee are the same rank in the organization, it is unclear who should lead the committee and what role each person has in this work.

1. What can the group do to increase role clarity?
2. During interactions group members tend to disagree on how to handle this case. What can be done to help the group through the storming phase?
3. What norms might help the group successfully accomplish their goals?

REFERENCES

Anderson, C. M., Riddle, B. L., & Martin, M. M. (1999). Socialization processes in groups. In L. R. Frey (Ed.), D. S. Gouran, & M. S. Poole (Assoc. Eds.), *The handbook of group communication theory & research* (pp. 139–163). Thousand Oaks, CA: Sage.

Bormann, E. G. (1990). *Small group communication: Theory and practice (3rd ed.).* New York: Harper & Row.

Fox, J. (Producer), & Daley, J.F. & Goldstein, J. (Directors). (2018). *Game night* [Motion Picture]. United States: Warner Brothers Pictures.

Frey, L. R. (1997). Individuals in groups. In L. R. Frey & J. K. Barge (Eds.), *Managing group life: Communicating in decision-making groups* (pp. 52-79). Boston: Houghton Mifflin Company.

Kahn, R.L., Wolfe, D.M., Quinn, R.P, Snoek, J.D., & Rosenthal, R.A. (1964). *Organizational stress: Studies in role conflict and ambiguity.* New York, NY: John Wiley & Sons.

Mudrack, P. E. (1989). Defining group cohesiveness: A legacy of confusion? *Small Group Behavior, 20,* 37-49.

Obermaier, M., & Koch, T. (2015). Mind the gap: Consequences of inter-role conflicts of freelance journalists with secondary employment in the field of public relations. *Journalism, 16(5),* 615–629. https://doi-org.proxy.library.ohio.edu/10.1177/1464884914528142

Riddle, B. L., Anderson, C. M., & Martin, M. M. (2000). Small group socialization scale: Development and validity. *Small Group Research, 31,* 554–572. Thousand Oaks, CA: Sage.

Tuckman, B. (1965). Developmental sequences in small groups. *Psychological Bulletin, 63,* 384-399.

Tuckman, B. & Jensen, M. (1977) Stages of small group development. *Group and Organizational Studies, 2,* 419-427.

Weinberg, S. B. (1979). Measurement of communication aspects of group cohesion. *Journal of Applied Communication Research, 8,* 55-60.

CHAPTER THREE

Embracing Difference: Diversity and Culture in Groups

LEARNING OBJECTIVES

After studying chapter 3, you should be able to:

- Define and explain diversity.
- Define and explain culture.
- Differentiate between race and ethnicity.
- Understand various cultural orientations.
- Discuss and provide examples of challenges faced by diverse groups.
- Discuss and provide examples of benefits faced by diverse groups.

When we think about the idea of the United States as a "melting pot," we can easily picture our country as a place where people who differ culturally and ethnically can come together as one. Though we have evolved in terms of acceptance and tolerance for diversity as a country, we often still face challenges when communicating with other cultures. As you think about your future professionally and personally, it is imperative you think about the impact of diversity will have in your life. Consider the following "fast facts" about diversity in the United States:

- According to the Pew Research Center, by the year 2065, there will be no racial/ethnic majority in the United States.
- According to a research study published in the *American Sociological Review*, organizations that report the highest levels of racial diversity report 15 times more sales revenue than less diverse organizations.
- According to the Pew Research Center, the majority of Americans perceive the country's increasing diversity positively.

In chapter 3, we will examine the impact of diversity on our group communication. As you know, group communication is an important part of our social and professional lives. Therefore, you will likely find yourself in a diverse group at some point. When faced with diversity, do you know what communication challenges you may face? Do you know how to effectively communicate with someone from a different culture than your own? Before we look at communication strategies for working in diverse groups, we need to first understand what diversity is and how it impacts our lives.

WHAT IS DIVERSITY?

Diversity

the state of being distinctive, or unlike others

When you hear the word *diversity*, what comes to mind? For many, the image of different cultures, races, or ethnicities is common. For others, diversity signifies uniqueness. As with the term *communication*, there are many, many definitions of diversity. In this textbook, **diversity** is defined as the state of being distinctive, or unlike others.

Think about the student body on your campus. In all likelihood, there are students of various races, ethnicities, socioeconomic statuses, religions, and so forth. These differences create a diverse study body. Next, consider your own interests and hobbies. For example, you may enjoy multiple types of music including rock, pop, and country. One could say your musical interests are diverse.

The term *diversity* is not limited to cultural or racial diversity, as we often think of it. The term refers to distinction and uniqueness and can be applied to any phenomenon. This can include distinct genders, religions, education levels and many, many more. This being said, it is common for us to first think of diversity as it relates to culture.

Culture

the values, beliefs, attitudes, opinions, behaviors and practices of a group of people

WHAT IS CULTURE?

Culture may be defined as the values, beliefs, attitudes, opinions, behaviors, and practices of a group of people. Simplistically, some refer to culture as a "way of life" for a group of people. Often, cultural practices are passed down from generation to generation. If you have ever

© aceshot1/Shutterstock.com

watched the hit television show *This is Us*, you have seen this phenomenon. In the show, you see the life of a family played out in more than one time of life. You see a family of five when the children are young and then you see the same children (perhaps even in the next scene) when they are grown with their own families. In this show, we can often see cultural norms passed down from one generation to the next. In addition, you see a family that is diverse in terms of race.

Race refers to a group of people who share common biological traits. This is different from ethnicity which is a group of people who share common cultural characteristics. The differences may become apparent. Though each unique race and ethnicity can share values and beliefs and be considered their own culture, the term culture is not restricted to race and ethnicity. Culture can include *any group* of people who share meaning and behaviors. For instance, different colleges and universities often display their own unique culture. You may have certain songs, mottos, mascots, and ways of doing things on your campus that may be different than those things at another school.

No matter if diversity presents as differences in race, ethnicity, or other cultural characteristics, it can significantly impact our communication in groups. Cultural differences can impact many things in life, including communication patterns. When communicating with others from differing cultures, understanding cultural norms can be challenging.

For example, my mother was born and raised in Puerto Rico—a culture that greatly differs from the Midwest United States. In Puerto Rico, the common communication patterns, both verbal and nonverbal, contrast from the culture in which I was raised. In Puerto Rico, speech rate is usually must faster than it is in the United States, which can easily confuse midwesterners. In a group situation, different speech patterns can create a challenge for some group members.

Because group members often come from varied cultural backgrounds, like my mother, when groups are developed, we can readily find ourselves working with people who communicate very differently than we do. For this reason, it is important to understand cultural differences so that we can accept, acknowledge and communicate effectively when diversity exists.

The culture that we identify with not only impacts our own communication patterns, but also our expectations for how interactions should take place. These expectations are often referred to as our cultural orientation.

CULTURAL ORIENTATION

Think about the culture in which you were raised. Were you taught to prioritize the needs of your family (or any group that you are a part of) ahead of your personal needs? How is power viewed in your culture? How are norms and rules communicated in your culture? Is there more of an emphasis on competition or cooperation?

All of these characteristics indicate your cultural orientation, or your perspective on phenomena based on your cultural beliefs and practices. In 2004, Hofstede and Hofstede introduced several cultural

Race

a group of people who share common biological traits

Ethnicity

a group of people who share common cultural characteristics

Cultural Orientation

one's perspective on phenomena based on your cultural beliefs and practices

orientations that may help us better understand communication patterns within groups. As you read about each cultural orientation, refer to Table 3.1 to see a sampling of countries who exhibit each orientation, as well as common communication patterns.

Table 3.1: Cultural Orientations

ORIENTATION	SAMPLE OF COUNTRIES	COMMUNICATION PATTERNS
Individualism vs. Collectivism	**Individualism:** United States, Australia, Ireland, Germany, Austria, Spain, South Africa **Collectivism:** China, India, Argentina, Singapore, Greece, Japan, Portugal	**Individualism:** "Me-oriented;" Focus on the needs of the individual over the group **Collectivism:** "We-oriented;" Focus on the needs of the group over individual
Masculinity v. Femininity	**Masculinity:** United States, Japan, Ireland, Italy **Femininity:** Netherlands, Spain, Korea, Portugal, Thailand	**Masculinity:** Success / achievement is priority **Femininity:** Relationships are priority
High v. Low Power Distance	**High Power Distance:** Mexico, India, Brazil, Nigeria **Low Power Distance:** United States, Germany, Ireland	**High Power Distance:** Hierarchy is present; most do not hold power **Low Power Distance:** Equality is prioritized; power is more evenly shared
High v. Low Uncertainty Avoidance	**High Uncertainty Avoidance:** Greece, Portugal, Japan, Spain, Israel **Low Uncertainty Avoidance:** United States, Singapore, Ireland, China	**High Uncertainty Avoidance:** Uncertainty is uncomfortable, and attempts are made to evade it **Low Uncertainty Avoidance:** Uncertainty is okay and can lead to positive communication
Indulgence v. Restraint	**Indulgence:** Mexico, Nigeria, Columbia, Sweden **Restraint:** Pakistan, Egypt, Iraq, Ukraine	**Indulgence:** Having fun and enjoying life is a priority **Restraint:** Instant gratification should be delayed; following rules and social norms is a priority
High-Context v. Low-Context	**High-Context:** Japan, China, France, Spain, Brazil **Low-Context:** United States, Canada, Germany, Netherlands	**High-Context:** Communication is direct **Low-Context:** Communication is more implied; more emphasis on context and nonverbal cues

Individualism vs. Collectivism

An **individualistic culture** is one in which the focus is on personal needs as opposed to that of the larger group. Individualistic cultures often emphasize independence and autonomy. In other words, there is not a strong reliance on others or groups, but rather a tendency toward self-reliance. Imagine a team at work who are put together to work on a specific product. There may be one person who is concerned with doing what he/she needs to do to be noticed by upper management without regard to the needs of the group. A person with an individualistic mindset will work to set him or herself apart to earn accolades.

Sometimes, we see team members who do not care as much about individual needs as the overall success of the group as a whole. These people tend to be more collectively oriented. A **collective culture** is one that prioritizes the needs of the group over personal needs. Collectivist cultures emphasize community over independence. The stress is selflessness and nurturing others. Think of groups you are a part of and how you would classify the orientation of the group. Are they more individualistic or collectivist?

Individualistic Culture

a culture in which the focus is on personal needs as opposed to that of the broader group

Collective Culture

a culture that emphasizes community over independence

Masculinity vs. Femininity

Many times, people associate the terms *masculinity* and *femininity* with biological sex (i.e., males/females). While there may be some relationship, masculine and feminine cultural orientations are not directly related to biological sex. A **masculine culture** focuses on achievements and being successful. In order to "win" or "succeed," masculine cultural members are often describe as assertive and dominant. The attitude is one of competition.

In contrast, **feminine cultures** stress more conventional gender role characteristics such as accommodation and nurturing behaviors. As opposed to being focused on success, members of feminine cultures are more relationship oriented. Creating and sustaining strong bonds among group members is important to feminine cultures.

As most of us know, professional sports teams frequently focus on winning games and/or championships. As a group, competition is key and there is little to no interest on making everyone in a league content. For instance, the Kansas City Chiefs want to win the Super Bowl without regard to other NFL teams. When facing an opponent on a Sunday afternoon in the fall, the Chiefs are focused on dominating their opponent without worrying about relationships and such. Sports teams are great examples of masculine cultures.

Masculine Culture

a culture that focuses on achievements and being successful

Feminine Culture

a culture that stresses more conventional gender role characteristics as accommodation and nurturing behaviors

© dotshock/Shutterstock.com

High vs. Low Power Distance

In addition to attributes of individualism/collectivism and femininity/masculinity, cultures vary in how the power is distributed among members. In some cultures, the majority of the power is concentrated in the hands of a few people. In others, power is more evenly distributed among cultural members. When a minority of people have most of the power within a group, the group is said to have a high-power distance orientation.

Consider a business that employs 500 employees, but all company decisions are made by a committee of two people—the CEO (Chief Executive Officer), and CFO (Chief Financial Officer). If the additional 498 people in the company have no impact on decision-making in the organization, there is a large distance between those who have power (i.e., the CEO and CFO) and those who do not (all others in the company).

Now, imagine that same 500-personal business had no formal leadership roles and all decisions were made democratically. In other words, any time a business decision was made, there was a vote and all members got a vote in the decision. In this instance, power would be much more evenly distributed making the distance between those who have power (and those who do not) much smaller. This type of group would be characterized as having a low-power distance orientation.

In groups where power is more evenly circulated, members often feel as if they are being treated more equally than those in high-power distance groups. This can lead to greater group cohesiveness and satisfaction among members. This being said, in groups where efficiency in problem-solving or decision-making is needed, a high-power distance orientation can be helpful. If time is of the essence, it is frequently faster to work with only a few people (or individually) to make a decision rather than listening to many opinions and ideas.

High vs. Low Uncertainty Avoidance

How do you feel when you experience feelings of uncertainty? Maybe you are uncertain about a relationship in your life, or how to complete a project for class. Uncertainty is defined as a state of not knowing or inability to predict phenomena. For some, uncertainty is not bothersome at all; for others, the feeling of "not knowing" is frustrating, scary, and creates anxiety.

In cultures that are characterized as high uncertainty avoidant, uncertainty is dodged at all costs. Communication in high uncertainty avoidance cultures is very direct and explicit, leaving little room for interpretation. When groups are high in uncertainty avoidance, group members regularly create explicit rules so that everyone understands how things should be done within the group. The clearer the communication and more rigid the policies, the less room for uncertainty among group members.

Low uncertainty avoidance cultures, by contrast, do not shy away from uncertainty. In fact, in such cultures, spontaneity and flexibility

---

High-power Distance Orientation

when a minority of people have most of the power within a group

Low-power Distance Orientation

when power in a group is more evenly distributed making the distance between those who have power (and those who) do not much smaller

Uncertainty

a state of not knowing or inability to predict phenomena

High Uncertainty Avoidant Culture

cultures that avoid uncertainty as much as possible

Low Uncertainty Avoidance Cultures

cultures that do not shy away from uncertainty

are valued. Members embrace uncertainty knowing that being open to change can be positive. The group that leaves rules and policies open to interpretation allows for change and new ideas to present as needed.

Intolerance of Uncertainty Scale—Short Form

Please circle the number that best corresponds to how much you agree with each statement. Add up scores for each item. The lower your score, the more likely you are to be okay with uncertainty.

	Not at all characteristic of me	A little characteristic of me	Somewhat characteristic of me	Very characteristic of me	Entirely characteristic of me
1. Unforeseen events upset me greatly.	1	2	3	4	5
2. It frustrates me not having all the information I need.	1	2	3	4	5
3. Uncertainty keeps me from living a full life.	1	2	3	4	5
4. One should always look ahead so as to avoid surprises.	1	2	3	4	5
5. A small unforeseen event can spoil everything, even with the best of planning.	1	2	3	4	5
6. When it's time to act, uncertainty paralyses me.	1	2	3	4	5
7. When I am uncertain, I can't function very well.	1	2	3	4	5
8. I always want to know what the future has in store for me.	1	2	3	4	5
9. I can't stand being taken by surprise.	1	2	3	4	5
10. The smallest doubt can stop me from acting.	1	2	3	4	5
11. I should be able to organize everything in advance.	1	2	3	4	5
12. I must get away from all uncertain situations.	1	2	3	4	5

Score: _____

Source: Reprinted from *Journal of Anxiety Disorders*, Vol 21, issue 1, R. Nicholas Carleton,M.A. Peter J. Norton,Gordon J.G. Asmundson, Fearing the unknown: A short version of the Intolerance of Uncertainty Scale, pp. 105–117, © 2007, with permission from Elsevier.

cultures that focus on doing whatever will provide instant gratification; the goal is enjoyment with little regard to social rules and norms

Restraint-Based Cultures

cultures that do not worry about instant gratification and are more focused on following norms set forth

High-Context Culture

a culture that places great emphasis on the context to interpret messages

Low-Context Culture

cultures that do not relay on the context in order to understand communication

Static

unchanging

Indulgence vs. Restraint

We have all felt as if we are being pulled in two opposite directions at some time. On one hand, we have a strong desire for enjoyment and fun, while on the other hand we feel a need to restrain our own desires to meet social norms and expectations.

Indulgent cultures place a focus on doing whatever will provide instant gratification. Put differently, the goal is enjoyment with little regard to social rules and norms. Restraint-based cultures, however, worry less about instant gratification and more about following norms set forth.

A class group that is indulgent may be less motivated by a grade on a project or securing the approval of the teacher, and more in tune with enjoying group interactions and having fun with one another. A group working on a class project that is more restrained would be exceedingly motivated to earn a good grade; thus, less focused on the "fun" aspect of group work and more task oriented.

High-Context vs. Low-Context

In addition to the cultural orientations introduced by Hofstede and Hofstede, Hall (1997) examined the extent to which cultures rely on context to infer the meaning of message. Cultures considered high-context place great emphasis on the context to interpret messages. In other words, nonverbal messages, and other aspects such as time and location of communication, are key to assigning meaning to a message. The context aids understating of the communication.

Low-context cultures, however, do not relay on the context in order to understand communication. The focus is on direct and explicit communication so that little is left to the imagination. Because there is less ambiguity in low-context cultures, there is also less room for interpretation and/or confusion.

It is important to remember a couple of things about these cultural orientations. First, no orientation is necessarily better or worse than another. For instance, groups that are uncertainty avoidant than others are not better (or inferior). There are positives and negatives to both orientations.

Next, these cultural orientations may be thought of as falling on a continuum. While some cultures may be strongly influenced by one orientation or another, many fall somewhere in the middle. Just as cultures differ, groups differ in orientations.

Finally, while most countries favor one orientation over another, and the tendencies are fairly static (or unchanging), groups *can* change over time. A group you are part of at the start of the semester that is individualistic in nature may be more collectivistic by the end of the semester.

HOW IS DIVERSITY IN GROUPS HELPFUL?

Considering so many business and organizations turning to team-based work and groups, a large amount of time has been spent studying work groups. The research shows us that diversity in the organization can have several benefits.

For instance, Knouse and Dansby (1999) found that diversity in groups enhances quality decision-making. This is due to a greater variety of solutions being posed by group members and more evaluation of possible solutions. A research study conducted in the early 1990's investigated workplace diversity among 72 manufacturing teams. The researchers found that increased work group diversity positively impacted group performance (Magjuka & Baldwin, 1991).

Diversity is not only beneficial in work groups but can be helpful in any type of group. Specifically, group diversity can positively impact group decision-making, creativity, problem-solving. There are numerous theoretical perspectives to explain the impact of diversity in groups.

According to the information / decision making perspective of group diversity, ethnic diversity within the group can increase individual's creativity and learning by exposure to multiple perspectives (see Antonio et al., 2004). Think of a group where all group members are similar, perhaps even think alike. Although similarity can bring people together and even help develop group cohesion, brainstorming creative and unique ideas may be difficult.

Researchers from MIT, Union College, and Carnegie Mellon University (2010) did a study in which they studied more than 700 people working in small groups. Each group was problem-solving—some small tasks, some more complicated. They found that groups that were more diverse in terms of intelligence level and gender performed better than less diverse groups. Groups that included more women tended to perform best as women are typically more sensitive to reading others' social cues and considering other viewpoints.

Source: *Forbes*, 2019

I find that when I try to make decisions or solve problems with others that are different than me, I get fresh perspectives and begin to think of ideas that I never would have thought of with someone too similar to myself. Thus, diversity can be helpful when it comes to creativity in groups. Group diversity, though beneficial, can also pose challenges that must be overcome in order for a group be to effective.

**Social Categoriza-
tion Perspective
of Diverse Group
Decision-Making**

on an individual level,
group members who
differ ethnically are
often less cohesive,
which can lead to
lower individual per-
formance; at the group
level, the social cat-
egorization perspective
states that ethnically
diverse groups often
experience increased
conflict and decreased
group cohesion

Ethnocentrism

the belief that our own
culture is superior to
other cultures

Perception

how we sense and
attribute meaning to a
phenomenon

CHALLENGES TO DIVERSE GROUPS

Especially within cultures such as the United States that value indi-
vidualism, diversity in groups can pose challenges. For instance, the
social categorization perspective of diverse group decision-making, states that on an individual level, group members who differ
ethnically are often less cohesive, which can lead to lower individual
performance (see Chatman & Flynn, 2001). At the group level, the
social categorization perspective states that ethnically diverse groups
often experience increased conflict and decreased group cohesion.
This can often lead to a decrease in group productivity (Jehn, Northcraft, & Neale, 1999).

As we have seen, there is research to support diversity in groups,
as well as research indicating diversity can pose challenges for groups.
Nevertheless, at some point, we will find ourselves in a diverse group.
In such case, we need to know how to communicate effectively in order
to achieve goals.

First, we must look at what makes the group diverse. More often
than not, considering our inclusive definition of culture addressed
earlier in this chapter, we may differ from others in terms of cultural
backgrounds. As a result, cultural sensitivity is an important part
of diverse groups. Cultural sensitivity includes recognition of cultural differences without judgment. In other words, when working
in diverse groups, it is important to make ourselves aware of our cultural differences and be understanding of others so as not be offensive or disrespectful.

Next, we must avoid ethnocentrism—or the belief that our own
culture is superior to other cultures. If we subscribe to an ethnocentric attitude, this is likely to shine through in our communication with
others, verbally and nonverbally, and result in a negative interaction.

Ethnocentric communication can also make others feel uncomfortable in a group setting and unwilling to speak up. If group members
do not share their own perspectives, ideas, and opinions, there will be
less information available when it comes time to make a decision. This,
of course, can be problematic. Culturally *insensitive* behavior will only
alienate group members and possibly create conflict within the group.

Not only is cultural sensitivity important to consider in group
interactions, it is a topic that should be discussed openly within the
group. One way to manage diversity challenges in a group could be to
develop group rules or guidelines regarding cultural sensitivity.

For example, think back to a group meeting you had for a class
project where one member was late to the meeting. Perhaps this person is always late to meetings. Perhaps this person is you! Keeping that
situation in mind, recall that perceptions of time differ from culture
to culture. Perception is how we sense and attribute meaning to a

phenomenon. Thus, for the person who was late to the group meeting, getting there by a certain point in the meeting was perceived by him/her as being on time. Moreover, it is possible that the group member that is consistently late to meetings was raised in a family where everyone is always late and that is considered acceptable.

In a situation such as this, how do you react as a group? One way to handle this issue may be to establish group rules that everyone agrees upon. This is especially important when it comes to matters of culture and diversity in groups. Working together to create group rules or guidelines centered on effective communication will not only help everyone work better together but will address culturally sensitive issues and help identify ways to manage challenges that may arise.

Finally, as diversity in groups—especially in the workplace—continues to grow, it is impossible to ignore the impact of diversity on communication practices. Sometimes the impact is positive, other times it is negative (Shaw & Barrett-Power, 1998).

Most of the time, diversity increases uncertainty in the group dynamic. Always be willing to not only be open to different viewpoints but to also encourage others to share their thoughts. Sometimes when people find themselves in diverse groups, they may communicate less due to uncertainty of how others may react to comments. In a study of multicultural decision-making groups, researchers found that in mixed groups of Americans and East Asians, Americans tended to increase group participation, and East Asians tended to withdraw (Aritz & Walker, 2009).

Because diversity can sometimes stifle participation, we must learn to manage uncertainty created by diverse workgroups. Charles Bantz (1993) presented sound advice on how to manage diversity in groups:

1. Gather information and learn about group member differences.
2. Adapt to a variety of situations, issues and needs of group members.
3. Focus on group cohesion, on both social and task dimensions.
4. Make sure to identify clear goals.

Examples of Communication Guidelines for Groups

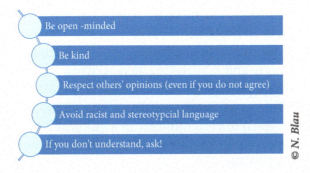

Be open -minded

Be kind

Respect others' opinions (even if you do not agree)

Avoid racist and stereotypcial language

If you don't understand, ask!

© N. Blau

Keep in mind that "diverse groups" are not only groups that include multiple races or cultures. Jackson, May, and Whitney (1995) argued that some forms of diversity are "readily detectable" (easily seen and identifiable), and some are "underlying attributes" (not indefinable just by looking at someone). For instance, groups may be diverse in terms of age, gender, sexual orientation, socioeconomic status, and other important factors.

READILY DETECTABLE DIVERSITY ATTRIBUTES (Examples)	UNDERLYING ATTRIBUTES (Examples)
Age	Cultural beliefs
Biological sex	Religious beliefs
Ethnicity	Personality characteristics
	Intelligence level

Perhaps you have brothers and sisters. Now think of a family with only one child. Does it seem likely that the family (group) culture is different in a family with only one child versus multiple children? This is just one more example of diverse cultural experiences we bring to groups contexts. No matter what form of diversity present in a group, cultural sensitivity and a willingness to remain open-minded is important to the success of the group.

SUMMARY

Diversity is something we will encounter in many forms of interaction, including group communication. When we find ourselves in a group where members represent various races, cultures, genders, religious beliefs and other differences, it is important to know how to effectively communicate.

Always keep in mind that when diverse groups (or any group) interact, there is potential for disagreement among group members. We have reviewed several communication strategies in chapter 3 that you may use when engaging in diverse group interactions, but the first step is learning to tolerate differences. The more we can recognize that "different" isn't "bad," the more we will be motivated to accept diversity, and learn to embrace it.

Although we may face challenges, such as language barriers, cultural uncertainty, and contrasting perspectives, we can also benefit from diverse groups. Groups that are diverse are often more creative and more effective at problem-solving and decision-making. It is imperative we learn to communicate in a culturally sensitive manner. When we learn to communicate in groups effectively, we will most certainly reap the benefits.

TOLERANCE FOR DISAGREEMENT SCALE (TFD)

Instructions: This questionnaire involves people›s feelings and orientations. Hence, there are no right or wrong answers. We just want you to indicate your reaction to each item. All responses are to reflect the degree to which you believe the item applies to you. Please use the following system to indicate the degree to which you agree that the item describes you:

5 = Strongly Agree, 4 = Agree, 3 = Undecided, 2 = Disagree, 1 = Strongly Disagree

_____ **1.** It is more fun to be involved in a discussion where there is a lot of disagreement.

_____ **2.** I enjoy talking to people with points of view different than mine.

_____ **3.** I don't like to be in situations where people are in disagreement.

_____ **4.** I prefer being in groups where everyone's beliefs are the same as mine.

_____ **5.** Disagreements are generally helpful.

_____ **6.** I prefer to change the topic of discussion when disagreement occurs.

_____ **7.** I tend to create disagreements in conversations because it serves a useful purpose.

_____ **8.** I enjoy arguing with other people about things on which we disagree.

_____ **9.** I would prefer to work independently rather than to work with other people and have disagreements.

_____ **10.** I would prefer joining a group where no disagreements occur.

_____ **11.** I don't like to disagree with other people.

_____ **12.** Given a choice, I would leave a conversation rather than continue a disagreement.

_____ **13.** I avoid talking with people who I think will disagree with me.

_____ **14.** I enjoy disagreeing with others.

_____ **15.** Disagreement stimulates a conversation and causes me to communicate more.

Scoring:

Step 1. Add the scores for the following items: 1, 2, 5, 7, 8, 14, 15.

Step 2. Add the scores for the following items: 3, 4, 6, 9, 10, 11, 12, 13.

Step 3. Complete the following formula: TFD = 48 + total of Step 1 - total of Step 2.

Scores > 46 indicate High TFD; Scores < 32 indicate Low TFD. Scores between

32 and 46 indicate moderate TFD.

Source: Measurement of tolerance for disagreement, Jason J. Teven, James C. McCroskey, et al, *Communication Research Reports*, 5/1/1998, Taylor & Francis, reprinted by permission of the publisher Taylor & Francis Ltd, http://www.tandfonline.com.

REFLECTION QUESTIONS

1. What is diversity? Provide an example.
2. What is culture? What cultures are represented in your own life?
3. How does culture impact communication in groups?
4. What are some characteristics of an individualistic culture? Collectivist culture?
5. What are some indicators that a culture is masculine? Feminine?
6. What is high-power and low-power distance in terms of cultural orientation? Describe and provide examples for each.
7. What role does uncertainty avoidance play in cultures?
8. What are some challenges diverse groups may face? What are some ways to "tackle" those challenges?
9. What are benefits of diverse groups?

LEARNING BY ACTION

Break the class into small groups (three-four students per group) and ask them the following questions:

1. What communication behaviors will make group interactions productive?
2. What communication behaviors will make group interactions unproductive?
3. How can group members communicate in a culturally sensitive manner?

After each group has had sufficient time to discuss each question and craft thoughtful responses, have each group share their thoughts with the class. Next, as a larger group (i.e., the class) compile a list of "class guidelines" to be used to guide interactions the remainder of the term. These guidelines should be applied to whole class and small group interactions. Make sure to post the class guidelines in a place that is readily accessible.

VIDEO CLIP

Big Brother (2000—present) is a reality television show where several strangers are chosen to live together in a house where their actions are monitored 24 hours per day. Typically, 16 houseguests are chosen to play "Big Brother" and move into the house for an entire summer. Throughout the summer, houseguests compete for various benefits (such as immunity and prizes) and fight for power. Each week, at least one houseguest is voted off the show. In the 2019 season of

Big Brother, the group that entered the Big Brother house on the first night was diverse in many ways. Cultural differences included age (ages ranged from 22 to 53), sexual orientation, race (at least seven different races were included), and regional differences (southerners, northerners, east and west coast) to name a few. Cultural diversity is exemplified in the first three episodes of the season when the houseguests are getting to know one another. After viewing one of the first few episodes (available at cbs.com/bigbrother), identify various cultural orientations of each houseguest and how their cultural backgrounds impacted their communication. Also, as small groups (aka: alliances) formed by episode two in the show, examine the cultural diversity in the groups and how their communication practices impacted the group goals. What challenges did they face? How did they overcome those challenges (if at all)?

CONTEMPORARY COMMUNICATION

Imagine you find yourself in a group with members from other cultures. You want to be culturally sensitive but know very little about other cultures. What do you do? One place to start is the Internet. Another, even more convenient, option is to download a free app—*Memrise*—to your smartphone or tablet. *Memrise* is an app that not only helps with language barriers but provides lessons about various cultures. There is information included about cultural history, geography, pop culture and other interesting topics.

CASES IN COMMUNICATION

For the past ten years you have worked for a small marketing firm in rural Ohio. In your firm, you were part of a group of five people all of whom are the same race and similar ethnicities. Moreover, you were all raised in rural Ohio and shared similar backgrounds, experiences, and values with regard to work. You have recently accepted a new position at a large marketing firm in downtown Chicago. You will be in charge of the marketing department at this new firm and there are 56 people in your department. You call the very first meeting in your department to introduce yourself and begin brainstorming ideas for a marketing strategy for the local college (your newest client), and you quickly notice a few things.

Out of the 56 people in the department, 17 different races are represented. In addition, English is not everyone's first language. As the group begins brainstorming ideas for a new marketing strategy for your client, you quickly realize that some people are much more aggressive than others, and communication styles greatly differ within the group. It becomes quite apparent that this group does not share the same cultural values, beliefs, and opinions as did your small marketing firm did in Ohio.

1. What are some differences in terms of cultural orientations that might be evident in this new marketing firm?
2. What communication barriers might such a diverse group when working toward this marketing strategy for the client?
3. What communication strategies will help you be successful in leading this group to successfully complete the project?

REFERENCES

American Sociological Association. (2009, April 3). Diversity linked to increased sales revenue and profits, more Customers. *Science-Daily*. Retrieved from www.sciencedaily.com/releases/2009/03/090331091252.htm

Antonio, A. L., Chang, M. J., Hakuta, K., Kenny, D. A., Levin, S., & Milem, J. F. (2004). Effects of racial diversity on complex thinking in college students. *Psychological Science, 15,* 507-510.

Aritz, J., & Walker, R. C. (2009). Group composition and communication styles: An analysis of multicultural teams in decision-making meetings. *Journal of Intercultural Communication Research, 38*(2), 99–114. https://doi-org.proxy.library.ohio.edu/10.1080/17475751003787346

Bantz, C. R. (1993). Cultural diversity and group cross-cultural team research. *Journal of Applied Communication Research, 21*(1), 1. https://doi-org.proxy.library.ohio.edu/10.1080/00909889309365352

Beilock, S. (2019, April 4). How diverse teams produce better outcomes. *Forbes*. Retrieved from https://www.forbes.com/sites/sianbeilock/2019/04/04/how-diversity-leads-to-better-outcomes/amp/

Carleton, R. N., Norton, M. A., & Asmundson, G. J. G. (2007). Fearing the unknown: A short version of the intolerance of uncertainty scale. *Journal of Anxiety Disorders, 21,* 105-117. doi: S0887-6185(06)00051-X [pii]10.1016/j.janxdis.2006.03.014

Chatman, J. A., & Flynn, F. J. (2001). The influence of demographic heterogeneity on the emergence and consequences of cooperative norms in work teams. *Academy of Management Journal, 44,* 956-974.

Hall, E.T. (1997). *Beyond culture*. Garden City, NY: Anchor Publishing.

Hofstede, G., & Hofstede, G. (2004). *Cultures and organizations: Software of the mind*. New York, NY: McGraw-Hill.

Hobman, E. V., Bordia, P., & Gallois, C. (2004). Perceived dissimilarity and work group involvement: The moderating effects of group openness to diversity. *Group & Organization Management, 29*(5), 560–587. Retrieved from EBSCOHost.

Jackson, S.E., May, K.E., & Whitney, K. (1005). Understanding the dynamics of diversity in decision-making teams. In R. Guzzo, E. Salas, and Associates (Eds.), *Team effectiveness and decision-making in organizations*. San Francisco, CA: Jossey-Bass.

Jehn, K. A., Northcraft, G. B., & Neale, M. A. (1999). Why differences make a difference: A field study of diversity, conflict, and performance in workgroups. *Administrative Science Quarterly, 44,* 741-763.

Knouse, S.B., & Dansby, M.R.1999. Percentage of work-group diversity and work-group effectiveness. *The Journal of Psychology, 133, 486–494.*

Magjuka, R.J., & Baldwin, T.T. (1991). Team-based employee involvement programs: Effects of design and administration. *Personnel Psychology, 44,* 793-812.

Pew Research Center. (2015). Retrieved from https://www.pewresearch.org/fact-tank/2015/10/05/future-immigration-will-change-the-face-of-america-by-2065/

Pew Research Center (2018). Retrieved from https://www.pewresearch.org/fact-tank/2018/06/14/most-americans-express-positive-views-of-countrys-growing-racial-and-ethnic-diversity/

Shaw, J. B., & Barrett-Power, E. (1998). The effects of diversity on small work group processes and performance. *Human Relations, 51*(10), 1307–1325. Retrieved from EBSCOHost.

Teven, J. J., Richmond, V. P., & McCroskey, J. C. (1998). Measuring tolerance for disagreement. *Communication Research Reports, 15,* 209-217.

CHAPTER FOUR

Decisions, Decisions! Problem-Solving and Decision-Making in Groups

LEARNING OBJECTIVES

After studying chapter 4, you should be able to:

- Define stage model and provide an example.
- Explain Fisher's model of group decision-making.
- Explain Tubb's model of group decision-making.
- Describe and apply the Standard Agenda.
- Identify questions of fact, policy, and value.
- Describe and provide examples of barriers to effective decision-making.
- Identify communication practices used for effective decision-making.

Have you ever gone to an escape room? Escape rooms have become very popular outings for groups in the past several years. When you go to an escape room, you must be in a group (at least three people) and you are given clues to solve puzzles, complete tasks, and make decisions in an effort to get out of the room. You have a specific amount of time to figure out how, as a group, to escape the room. The escape room is a fun outing for groups that requires effective decision-making and problem-solving in order to be successful. According to an article in *USA TODAY,* there are more than 2,000 escape rooms in the United States, so if you have not tried out the experience yet, you will have plenty of opportunities to do so in the future. Once you learn about effective means of problem-solving, your odds of escaping can only increase!

In chapter 4, we will examine how decisions are made and problems are solved in groups. Even if a group is not formed for the sole purpose of solving a problem, it is likely that the group will be faced with a decision to make or problem to solve at some point. Recall from chapter 3 the discussion of the importance of groups in the workplace and think about your future (or present) career. What is the likelihood that you will be working in groups in your organization? One of our country's top employers, Google, strongly encourages all

© Sundry Photography/Shutterstock.com

employees to not only work together in groups but to also create groups to increase innovation and creativity in their product. Employees are rewarded for leading groups that serve as "think tanks."

No matter the type of group, it is important to learn effective strategies for group decision-making and problem-solving. The functional perspective on group decision-making we learned in the first chapter of this text is one effective strategy. In this chapter, we will review several additional models of decision-making, as well as barriers groups may face and ways to overcome challenges when engaged in group decision-making and problem-solving.

FISHER'S MODEL OF GROUP DECISION-MAKING

In 1970, B. Aubrey Fisher, a professor at Utah University, developed a model of group communication may be considered a stage model or theory. A **stage model** is one that explains behaviors as it moves through various phases in a particular order. Stage models show communication processes as occurring in a specific order. The interactions must be ordered and systematic in order for the group to be effective. Moreover, no phase can be skipped or ignored when working toward a goal.

One of the most frequently cited stage models of group decision-making is Fisher's model consisting of four phases: orientation, conflict, emergence, and reinforcement. The first stage, the **orientation stage**, is where group members get to know one another and share information about themselves. It is common at this point for group members to experience uncertainty, anxiety, and interpersonal tension. Especially when we join a new group, we may feel nervous and a bit uneasy. It is in this first stage that Fisher argued group members get familiarized with one another and relive some of this tension.

The second stage is called the **conflict stage**. In this phase, group members share their own perspectives and offer possible solutions. This may or may not lead to interpersonal conflict, but at this point, no decisions are made nor problems solved. In this stage, group members may individually brainstorm as many suggestions as possible and subsequently share their ideas with the larger group. When ideas are shared and the group begins to discuss ideas, negotiation may occur.

The third stage, **emergence**, is notable for being the stage in which a decision is made by the group. By this point, the goal of the group is clear, and the functions of the group are understood by members. Individual members should not be adding new ideas to the discussion, but instead focus on achieving unanimous agreement among the group. Achieving a **consensus** can be difficult. Thus, the emergence stage is often the longest stage.

Stage Model

a process model that explains behaviors as it moves through various phases in a particular order

Orientation Stage

the phase where group members get to know another and share information about themselves

Conflict Stage (Fisher)

the phase in which group members share perspectives and offer solutions; this may or may not lead to interpersonal conflict

Emergence Stage

the phase where a decision is made by the group

Consensus

when group members unanimously agree on the decision

The fourth, and final, stage of Fisher's model is the **reinforcement stage**. In this stage, a decision has been made and individual group members attempt to understand the decision through their own perspective. Often, when group members can see how the group decision aligns with their own viewpoint, it creates increased satisfaction. For this reason, groups must follow through all stages of the model and not just stop after a decision has been made.

Reinforcement Stage

the phase in which a decision has been made and individual group members attempt to understand the decision through their own perspective

Fisher's Model of Group Decision-Making Example

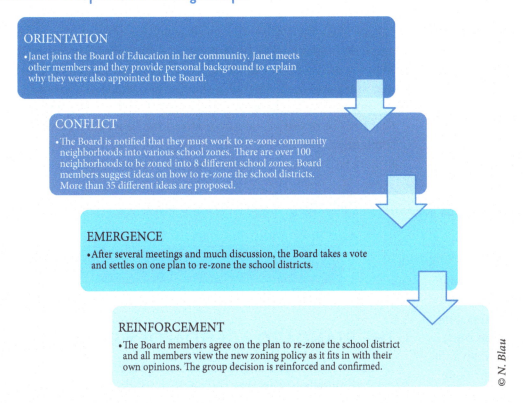

ORIENTATION
• Janet joins the Board of Education in her community. Janet meets other members and they provide personal background to explain why they were also appointed to the Board.

CONFLICT
• The Board is notified that they must work to re-zone community neighborhoods into various school zones. There are over 100 neighborhoods to be zoned into 8 different school zones. Board members suggest ideas on how to re-zone the school districts. More than 35 different ideas are proposed.

EMERGENCE
• After several meetings and much discussion, the Board takes a vote and settles on one plan to re-zone the school districts.

REINFORCEMENT
• The Board members agree on the plan to re-zone the school district and all members view the new zoning policy as it fits in with their own opinions. The group decision is reinforced and confirmed.

© N. Blau

ADDITIONAL MODELS OF GROUP DECISION-MAKING

Stewart Tubbs developed a model of group communication in 1983 very similar to Fisher's model. Tubbs' model also includes four stages: orientation, conflict, consensus, and closure. The first phase in group communication is the **orientation stage**. In this stage, just as the first stage in Fisher's model, group members get acquainted with one another.

During this initial stage, group members may share all kinds of information with each other including basic information (i.e., names, age, occupation) as well as more in-depth information that may be pertinent to the goal of the group. For example, if you join a group where the goal is to raise money for an organization, you might share your own personal experience in fundraising or expertise you can share with the group.

Orientation Stage

the phase where group members get to know another and share information about themselves

Conflict Stage (Fisher)

the phase in which the problem to be solved or decision to be made identified by group members

Consensus Stage

the phase that the group settles on one of the solutions posted in the previous stage of the model

Closure Stage

the phase where the group communicates any decisions made to whomever necessary and confirm that is the decision made as a group

Reflective Thinking

a process rooted in the scientific method that indicates a set of logical steps must be followed when a decision is to be made

Standard Agenda

a multi-step model of decision-making centered on analysis and reflection in order to identify the best solution possible which includes six steps: problem identification, problem analysis, solution criteria, alternative generation, solution evaluation and selection, and implementation

The second stage in this model is the conflict stage. In the conflict stage, the problem to be solved or decision to be made is identified by group members. As with Fisher's model in the second phase of this model, group members offer solutions and opinions. Using our earlier example, this would be the stage in which everyone suggests ideas on how to raise money for the organization presenting arguments as to why one idea is better than another.

Thirdly, groups enter the consensus stage. It is in this phase that the group settles on one of the solutions suggested in the previous stage of the model. As we mentioned earlier, reaching a consensus in a group can be difficult. Often, the more solutions offered, the harder it is to agree on only one. The final stage in Tubb's model is the closure stage. When a group comes to closure, they communicate decisions made as necessary and confirm that is the decision made as a group.

For example, the group may report to the organization's leaders that they have settled on one method for fundraising that they plan to implement. Depending on the group (long-term or short-term), many groups will disassemble following the closure stage.

Tubb's (1983) Stage Model of Group Communication

THE STANDARD AGENDA: DEWEY'S MODEL

Similar to the stage models advanced by Fisher and Tubbs, others have created models to describe the decision-making process that occurs in groups. Most of these models, at least in part, took into consideration the most well-documented small group communication decision-making model created - Dewey's (1910) model of reflective thinking.

The notion of reflective thinking is rooted in the scientific method and indicates a set of logical steps that must be followed during the decision-making process. Moreover, groups must systematically and strategically identify the problem, analyze, and then solve the problem. Put differently, Dewey argued that in order for effective problem-solving to take place, group members must *reflect and analyze* thoroughly so the best outcome may be achieved.

Based on Dewey's reflective thinking process, the Standard Agenda emerged. The Standard Agenda is a multi-step model of decision-making centered on analysis and reflection in order to identify the best solution possible. Specifically, the Standard Agenda includes six steps:

problem identification, problem analysis, solution criteria, alternative generation, solution evaluation and selection, and implementation.

In the first step, problem identification, group members must clearly identify the problem. Although this is seemingly straightforward, sometimes pinpointing the problem can be challenging. For instance, consider a family in which members are not speaking to one another and the group, as a whole, is riddled with conflict. When asked why the group is in such a negative state, different family members may provide different answers. What *is* the problem that is causing such turmoil? It is possible that the root of the problem has not been identified.

It is not uncommon for groups to experience problems without knowing, or fully understanding, the cause of the problem. Therefore, this first step is incredibly important so that all group members get "on the same page" before working through the remainder of the process. When identifying problems, a good practice is to also ascertain what *type* of problem the group is facing.

Problems are usually centered on questions of fact, questions of policy, or questions of value. Questions of fact inquire whether something is true or false. Questions of policy ask about the need for guidelines or rules that may be needed to enact change. Questions of value probe the worth of a phenomenon.

Problem Identification

step in which group members must clearly identify the problem

Questions of Fact

questions that inquire whether something is true or false

Questions of Policy

questions that ask about the need for guidelines or rules that may be needed to enact change

Questions of Value

questions that probe the worth of a phenomenon

Questions of Fact	Questions of Policy	Questions of Value
• Does our group have enough money to attend the upcoming National Convention?	• Should our group allow members from other organizations join?	• Is it more important for our group to win an award or form strong relationships?

© N. Blau

Once the group has successfully identified the problem, the next step is to analyze the problem. In the problem analysis step, group members must take care to strategically pinpoint the scope and cause of the issue. This step is much easier said than done!

Too often, groups rush through this step assuming they know the extent of problems without fully investigating the cause and impact. Effective communication is crucial in this second step. A good way to view problem analysis is to consider the "who," "what," "when," "where," "why," and "how" behind the problem.

In order for groups to find the best solution, it is necessary to understand the problem, who it impacts, how much of an impact it causes, and what the cause may be. Therefore, being open-minded to the viewpoints of all group members is important so that all parts of the issue

Problem Analysis

the step where group members must take care to strategically figure out the scope and cause of the issue can be discussed. It is more likely that the group will be able to thoroughly analyze the problem when multiple opinions are shared. When only one or two people analyze the problem, they may miss something because they are only looking at it from one viewpoint. In this instance, more is better.

This being said, as a group, you do not want to spend *too* much time analyzing the problem to the point where a decision never gets made. When this happens in groups, it is called **analysis paralysis**. Groups must find balance between under-analyzing and over-analyzing.

Step three is where **solution criteria** are set forth. This step is often skipped in group decision-making. In order to effectively solve a problem or make a decision, it is not enough to identify and analyze a problem and then advance a solution. In the solution criteria step, group members develop criteria (or standards) that will ultimately be used to evaluate possible solutions. Later in the process, then, group members will have benchmarks to use when deciding to keep or discard proposed solutions.

This step is essential to ensure groups are not simply making decisions based on what sounds good, but rather on established criteria deemed to be necessary. By creating solution criteria, groups can thoroughly discuss the "pros" and "cons" of each solution proposed. The most important thing to remember is that these criteria must be created *before* solutions are presented -not after.

Analysis Paralysis

when groups spend too much time analyzing the problem to the point where a decision never gets made

Solution Criteria

the step in which group members develop criteria that will ultimately be used to evaluate possible solutions

In a 2009 study focused on group decision-making, researchers investigated the use of the Standard Agenda in 17 seven-person corporate groups. Each group's decision was evaluated by experts on the process. Results showed that effective decision-making groups communicated more when establishing solution criteria and also more positively evaluated possible solutions. Groups deemed ineffective established and utilized solution criteria less.

Source: Graham, E. E., Papa, M. J., & McPherson, M. B. (1997). An applied test of the functional communication perspective of small group decision-making. *Southern Communication Journal, 62*(4), 269. https://doi-org.proxy.library.ohio.edu/10.1080/10417949709373064

Step four of the Standard Agenda is the phase groups tend to jump to right away – generating alternatives. When groups *generate alternatives,* they propose solutions for the problem. Essentially, this is the brainstorming stage in the process. At this point, group members should suggest as many possible solutions as they can. The more the better! In this step, the focus is not on determining which solutions are good or bad, but simply putting ideas on the table.

Each solution will be evaluated in the next step – solution evaluation and selection. In this stage, the group uses the criteria created in step three to assess each proposed solution. Think of the criteria as a check list to determine the worth and feasibility of each solution suggested. During this process, some solutions may be discarded completely. Others may be considered better or worse comparatively. Also, in this fifth step, one solution is selected.

Depending on the group and/or the problem itself, solution selection may be easy or difficult. Nevertheless, in this stage, group members must settle on a decision. Decisions may be made in several ways. One way a solution may be selected is via consensus. This occurs when group members unanimously agree on the decision. In jury trials, jurors must come to a unanimous decision regarding the guilt or innocence of the defendant. This often takes a long time (much deliberation) and sometimes results in a hung jury where all jurors cannot agree on a verdict.

Sometimes groups allow a small number of people (or even one leader) to make the ultimate decision. This is called minority rule. Often, minority rule is used when time is an issue and efficiency is needed. Finally, some groups choose to make decisions based on majority rule where group members may vote on the solutions and whichever has support from the largest group is the final decision. While there are positives and negatives for each type of decision-making, the issue at hand, group members, and other situational factors will impact which strategy will work best.

Once the solution has been selected, the final step is solution implementation. In this final step, the solution is employed and later evaluated. Once the decision has been made and applied for a specified amount of time, the group can assess whether or not the best solution was chosen. If the solution has proven to be effective, the decision-making process may be considered complete. If not, group members may go back to any stage in the process to re-analyze, set forth different criteria (if need be), and/or select a different solution.

The Standard Agenda is not always a quick process, nor an easy process. It is, however, a systematic method to thoroughly for groups to approach problem-solving. While some decisions can be made quickly, many problems experienced by groups are multifaceted and require a significant amount of communication to determine a viable solution. When groups must make important decisions or solve critical problems, the Standard Agenda is an excellent tool to use.

Solution Evaluation and Selection

the step where group uses the criteria set forth in step three to assess each proposed solution

Minority Rule

allowing a small number of people (or even one leader) to make a decision

Majority Rule

group members vote on the solutions and whichever has support from the largest group is the final decision

Solution Implementation

the final step in the Standard Agenda in which the solution is employed (and later evaluated)

The Standard Agenda

1. Problem Identification	You are on an advisory board for the local YMCA. The financial outlook is poor and YMCA leadership would like a solution to this problem. Following research and discussion, your group identifies the problem as a decrease in membership over the past few years.
2. Problem Analysis	In this step, the group assesses why membership has decreased, how much it has decreased, how marketing strategies have changed as well as class offerings and membership perks. The group notes that monthly/annual fees have increased and are now 43 percent higher than other fitness organizations within five miles. Membership has decreased approximately 18 percent resulting in a significant financial loss for the YMCA. In addition, it was noted that programs available for an additional fee (above membership costs) are not being populated as they have in past years; thus, resulting in less revenue for the organization.
3. Solution Criteria	Criteria identified to evaluate potential solutions include: • Must align with the organizational mission of the YMCA. • Must not cost more than $5,000 in marketing costs. • Must not necessitate hiring additional staff. • Must not decrease the number of classes/programs currently available to members. • Must have comparable benefits to similar organizations in the vicinity.
4. Generate Alternatives	Possible solutions generated by the advisory group include: • Raising monthly/annual membership fees. • Decreasing monthly/annual membership fees. • Waiving joining fee for a period of three months to recruit new members. • Raising fees for additional programs. • Reducing staff. • Increasing advertising via television ads. • Increasing advertising via social media. • Adding reduced rate memberships for those age 60+.
5. Solution Evaluation and Selection	Based on the criteria created in step 3, the advisory group automatically eliminated increased advertising via television ads (too expensive) and raising membership fees (to remain comparable to other organizations). Then, based on the criteria set forth, the group discusses the positives and negatives of other solutions presented. The group settles on a combination of solutions including waiving joining fee for a period of three months to recruit new members, increasing advertising via social media, and adding reduced rate memberships for those age 60+.
6. Solution Implementation	The three agreed upon solutions are implemented into the organization for a period of five months. At that time, the YMCA leadership, in consultation with the advisory board, will assess the financial situation.

BARRIERS TO EFFECTIVE DECISION-MAKING

As you most likely have experienced, when making decisions in groups, we often face challenges. There are several barriers to effective decision-making including issues related to group members, situational factors, or even outside influences. One barrier is groupthink.

Groupthink

Think back to chapter 1 where we learned about the groupthink phenomenon. Groups can enter a state of groupthink when members feel pressured to achieve a consensus. Ultimately, this frequently results in a low-quality group decision. The state of groupthink itself, as well as group think symptoms such as collective rationalization, direct pressure on dissenters, and the illusion of unanimity, can create barriers to effective decision-making. When group members resist ideas and opinions from those outside of the group, as well as inhibit group members ideas, important information needed to make a quality decision may never be shared.

Group Polarization

Similar to groupthink, group polarization occurs when individual group members are influenced by the remainder of the group to view things from a specific perspective. Often, entire attitudes of the group become polarized and are often extreme in one direction or another.

Group Polarization

individual group members are influenced by the remainder of the group to view things from a specific perspective

For example, imagine a group of high school seniors planning activities for prom weekend. When one or two friends mention activities that can be risky (i.e., could get the group in trouble), you may not think the plans are a good idea. This being said, when it seems everyone in the group are going along with the plans, you agree to participate as well. Now that everyone is "on board" with the prom weekend plans, the plans continue to get more involved and include more activities that could cause trouble.

Regularly, when groups become polarized, they are more easily susceptible to the risky shift phenomenon (Stoner, 1961). The risky shift phenomenon occurs when groups are more likely to engage in risky behaviors than members would have done individually. Thinking back to the prom weekend example, suppose the group decides to throw a party in a place they know they are not welcome. If you agree to help throw the party and engage in riskier behavior than you would had you not been part of the group, you have experienced the risky shift phenomenon.

Risky Shift Phenomenon

when groups are more likely to engage in risky behaviors than members would have done individually

When groups become polarized, and especially if they experience the risky shift phenomenon, pertinent information may not be shared, and good decisions may not be made. Once our viewpoints become extreme, it is much more difficult to accept information that does not support our position. This can result in poor problem-solving.

Close-mindedness

As addressed in chapter 3, being open-minded is important when working with others in groups. Being closed-minded, or unwilling to see other perspectives, can definitely be a barrier to effective decision-making. When we are closed-minded, we are typically not willing to learn new things and/or view things from other perspectives. It is important to remember that, individually, we do not know everything! No matter how much you do know about a topic, there is always room to learn.

One crucial part of decision-making is making an effort to seek out as much information as possible. When we are close-minded, it makes it difficult to think outside the box and discover ideas we may have never imagined. In addition to missing out on other perspectives and information, being close-minded occurs when we are unwilling to ask for help when needed. Decision-making can be difficult no matter if you are working in a group or alone. A willingness to reach out for help can make the process easier. I can think of several times that I have struggled to complete a task and when I finally allowed myself to ask others for help, all of a sudden, the burden was lifted. Had I just reached out earlier, I may have saved myself some time and aggravation.

Failure to Analyze the Problem Effectively

Early in this chapter, we defined analysis paralysis and indicated this can occur when groups spend *too much* time analyzing the problem. Conversely, if a group spends *too little* time in the analysis and criteria stages, and rushes to make a decision, this can also be problematic. When groups hurry to solve a problem, and skip key communication processes, it is likely they will not gather all of the information needed to effectively make a decision.

Not Speaking Up

Finally, when group members are unwilling to speak up and share opinions, this can present a challenge for the group. Group members may not share ideas for many reasons, but no matter the reason, a lack of sharing can be detrimental to the group. For example, I am part of our neighborhood homeowner's association group. Last year when the group was deciding on which landscaping company

© funnybear36/Shutterstock.com

to contract, several ideas were shared. Eventually, one landscaping company was chosen. When the company's contract began in spring, homeowners were very displeased with the quality of work. We later found out that one group member knew the company had a poor track record yet chose not to share that information with the group during the decision-making process. If the group had that information earlier, perhaps a different landscaping company would have been chosen and a better result achieved.

Therefore, it is important that groups acknowledge challenges and barriers in group decision-making so that they can be avoided. Knowledge can effectively motivate the group to proactively work to communicate in a manner that is inclusive and open to all ideas. Such communication should lead to more effective problem solving.

EFFECTIVE DECISION-MAKING

Now that we have reviewed group decision-making processes, as well as barriers to effective communication in groups, we can highlight strategies that may enhance group interactions. First, as a group, work to model other groups that make good decisions.

When I was asked to start a new student organization on my campus several years ago, I had no idea what to do! In fact, I had no idea what a "good" student organization looked like, nor what I would need to do once my group was established. Thus, I turned to other student organizations on campus that had been successful in terms of longevity and were actively involved on campus. I went to the faculty advisors of each group and sought their input on how to develop a strong group climate, encourage student leaders, and communicate the mission of the group. For several years, my student group modeled other groups on campus, and we learned a lot from other groups. I can proudly say we are now a very successful group which accomplishes many goals each year and hope to serve as a model for new groups developed in the future.

© Yuliia1996/Shutterstock.com

Next, always encourage creativity within the group. This is especially necessary when brainstorming alternatives. Remember to think outside the box! Sometimes we fear others' perceptions if we suggest ideas that are too different from the norm. Those ideas, however, can often be the best ideas. Even if a truly unique idea does not end up being the final solution, the fact that it was suggested may influence others to also offer distinctive ideas. As Einstein said, "Creativity is intelligence having fun!"

Finally, encourage others to speak up. An article in *Forbes* magazine in 2017 highlighted three best practices for high performance decision-making in groups. Frist, fill group roles. In other words, don't leave any roles vacant. Moreover, fill each role with the right person for the job. Do not fill the marketing position with someone who has no experience in marketing. Cover all your bases, and cover them well.

Second, collect group members' ideas individually and then share ideas with the group. This is an example of a nominal group technique (NGT), or a form of structured brainstorming where group members write down individual ideas to be shared with the group after each person has had time to think independently (Delbecq & VandeVen, 1971). This allows everyone to think through ideas on their own without being biased or persuaded by those speaking up the loudest in the group.

Third, do not just share the group's decision with others, but also explain *why* the group made the decision when presenting solutions to those outside of a group. If the group has followed a systematic decision-making process, the explanation should be able to be shared easily. When steps in the process are skipped or rushed, it may be more difficult to provide a rationale for the decision made. Also, this is also an opportunity to give credit to those involved in the decision-making process. Finally, by providing an explanation of how and why the decision was made, it also highlights the communication that occurred so any errors may be corrected, and strengths can be noted for future interactions.

A well-cited research study from 1983 provided insight into role of communication in decision-making groups. In this study, six groups considered "effective" and five groups considered "ineffective" were observed an analyzed with respect to their communication.

Nominal Group Technique (NGT)

a form of structured brainstorming where group members write down individual ideas to be shared with the group after each person has had time to think independently

Effective Decision-Making Groups	Ineffective Decision-Making Groups
1. Spent time discussing and analyzing all opinions presented.	1. Glossed over and rarely challenged ideas presented; accepted options as facts often with no or little analysis.
2. Spent much time testing alternatives using pre-determined criteria.	2. Used pre-determined criteria to test alternatives but did not do so thoroughly.
3. Conclusions based on reasonable facts, assumptions, and inferences.	3. Conclusions based on questionable facts, assumptions, and inferences.
4. Highly influential group member(s) exerted positive influences and guided the group to a high-quality decision.	4. Highly influential group member(s) exerted negative influences and inhibited the group from making a high-quality decision.

Source: Hirokawa, R. Y., & Pace, R. (1983). A Descriptive investigation of the possible communication-based reasons for effective and ineffective group decision making. *Communication Monographs*, *50*(4), 363. https://doi-org.proxy.library.ohio.edu/10.1080/03637758309390175

SUMMARY

After studying problem-solving processes in chapter 4, it is clear that in order for groups to make effective decisions, they must work systematically and not jump to conclusions. There are several models of decision-making, including well-known stage models by Fisher and Tubbs, that suggest groups must first get oriented with one another, constructively work through conflict, and then continue on to effective decision-making. In addition, we learned that, in line with the Standard Agenda, in each phase of the decision-making process groups must work together to fully analyze the problem, set forth viable criteria, brainstorm ideas and draw reasonable conclusions.

If problem-solving phases are skipped (intentionally or unintentionally), they may face challenges to problem-solving that can negatively impact decisions made. Barriers in the group can be alleviated, however, by engaging in open communication, encouraging creativity, and modeling effective groups. Problem-solving is not always easy and can be even more difficult in a group setting. Nevertheless, the process will always go more smoothly and effectively when communication is strong from the start. Fully understanding the problem is an important first step. As Dorothea Brande said, "A problem clearly stated is a problem half-solved."

© Tang Yan Song/Shutterstock.com

REFLECTION QUESTIONS

1. What is a stage model? Why is it important to follow steps a particular order?
2. Compare and contrast Fisher and Tubbs' stage models of group decision-making.
3. What is analysis paralysis and why is it detrimental for groups?
4. What are the steps in the Standard Agenda? Provide an example of how groups might set out criteria to evaluate solutions.
5. Why is the solution criteria stage in the Standard Agenda important?
6. For each type of solution selection (minority rule, majority rule, consensus), what are conditions in each one should be used? What are conditions where each should not be used?
7. What is group polarization and how does it differ from the risky shift phenomenon?
8. What are some common barriers to group decision-making? In addition to the barriers identified in this chapter, what other challenges might groups face?
9. What communication practices can help groups make effective decisions?

LEARNING BY ACTION

In small groups of four to five students, have students identify a local organization that is considered a small business. Groups should schedule a time to interview someone employed at (or whom owns) the organization to identify a problem they are currently working to solve. Students must then work together to propose a solution for the organization applying the steps of the Standard Agenda. Students must (in consultation with an organizational member) identify the problem, analyze the problem, identify solution criteria, generate alternatives, and evaluate the solution. Finally, the group must present their solution (as well as an explanation/justification for the proposed solution) to the organizational leaders.

VIDEO CLIP

Based on the real-life story of the Apollo 13 mission, *Apollo* 13 is a 1995 Blockbuster that showed the story of a group of astronauts on a mission to the moon. Following a successful takeoff from Earth, oxygen tanks fail and the astronauts face danger. The movie illustrates how a group must make important decisions and engage in problem-solving in order to survive. In this movie, students should identify effective and ineffective communication strategies used by the astronauts and discuss how it impacted their situation.

CONTEMPORARY COMMUNICATION

For better or worse, technology is large part of our everyday lives. Particularly, there are very few people who do not depend on smart phones and tablets to manage personal and professional needs. For many things we choose to manage, we can find an application that will help us organize, connect with others, or simply provide entertainment. Did you know, there are also applications that help us make decisions? One app, FYI Decision, is a free application that can be used by groups when a decision needs to be made. Through this app, groups can share ideas, distribute information, and vote on ideas using pre-determined templates for decision-making. Therefore, when busy schedules don't permit group meetings, one way to continue the decision-making process "on the go" is by using the FYI Decision application.

CASES IN COMMUNICATION

You are a part of a student organization on campus that is responsible for planning the annual Spring Fling. The event is set to occur in three short months and your student group has yet to develop a theme for this year's event. As a group, you have a maximum of one week left to figure out the theme so that you can start planning the event and setting up activities around campus. Your group meets to discuss possible ideas for the Spring Fling, and after spending some time talking about past events and possible themes for this year, only three ideas have surfaced. As a group, you decide to reconvene in a few days after everyone has had time to think about possible ideas. The next time your group meets, there is quite a debate over two ideas presented. Half the group likes one of the ideas and the other half does not. Therefore, the group decides to continue brainstorming. At the end of the group meeting, 17 ideas in total have been developed. Now, the group must decide between those 17 ideas and choose only one for this year's Spring Fling. Uncertainty is high and many group members feel as if they are at a standstill because no one will budge on their ideas they like. Finally, one person says they will pick one an idea out of a hat and that will be the Spring Fling theme.

1. What step(s) in the group decision making process was (were) skipped by your group?
2. What communication strategies can your group use to narrow down the ideas presented?
3. What mistakes as this group made in the decision-making process that has led them to this standstill?

REFERENCES

Delbecq, A. L., & VandeVen, A. H,. (1971). A group process model for problem identification and program planning. *Journal of Applied Behavioral Science*, 466–491. doi:10.1177/002188637100700404.

Dewey, J. (1910). *How we think*. Lexington, MA: D.C. Heath.

Fisher, B. A. (1970). Decision emergence: Phases in group decision making. *Speech Monographs, 37*, 53-66. doi.org/10.1080/03637757009375649

Graham, E. E., Papa, M. J., & McPherson, M. B. (1997). An applied test of the functional communication perspective of small group decision-making. *Southern Communication Journal, 62*(4), 269. https://doi-org.proxy.library.ohio.edu/10.1080/10417949709373064

Hirokawa, R. Y., & Pace, R. (1983). A Descriptive investigation of the possible communication-based reasons for effective and ineffective group decision making. *Communication Monographs, 50*(4), 363. https://doi-org.proxy.library.ohio.edu/10.1080/03637758309390175

Larson, E. (2017, March). 3 best practices for high-performance decision-making teams. *Forbes*. Available at https://www.forbes.com/sites/eriklarson/2017/03/23/3-best-practices-for-high-performance-decision-making-teams/#26be3f15f971

Mallenbaum, C. (2018, April 25). Why escape rooms have a lock on the U.S. *USA TODAY*. Retrieved from https://www.usatoday.com/story/life/people/2018/04/25/escape-rooms-trend-us/468181002/

Stoner, J.A.F. (1961). *A comparison of individual and group decisions involving risk*. (master's thesis). Massachusetts Institute of Technology.

Tubbs, Stewart. (1995). *A systems approach to small group interaction*. New York, NY: McGraw-Hill.

CHAPTER FIVE

The Good, The Bad, and the Ugly: Power in Groups

After studying chapter 5 you should be able to:

- Define power and explain the five power bases.
- Explain how one gets power.
- Define compliance-gaining and identify compliance-gaining strategies used in groups.
- Identify verbal and nonverbal messages used to communicate power in groups.
- Describe the role of power plays in groups.
- Compare and contrast three types of power plays.
- Explain various communication strategies to balance power in groups.
- Analyze four ways to resist power in groups.

- The World Health Organization (WHO) – over 7,000 members worldwide work to maintain health standards and keep people safe.
- The U.S. Drug Enforcement Administration (DEA) – members work to impose the laws about controlled substances in the United States.
- The U.S. Internal Revenue Service (IRS) – a part of the U.S. Treasury department, this group works to collect incomes taxes and other federal monies.
- The National Collegiate Athletic Association (NCAA) – members work to ensure the well-being and success of college athletes.
- People for the Ethical Treatment of Animals (PETA) – several million members work to protect the rights for animals and safeguard ethical treatment of animals.

Chances are you have heard of some, or all, of these organizations. You may even be a member of one these groups. What is one thing all of these groups have in common? All are regarded as powerful in our culture. The list of powerful groups in the United States goes on and on including student groups, political groups, media groups, and so forth. These groups are quite influential, or powerful, but what makes them so powerful? And, more importantly, how is power communicated in these groups?

In chapter 5, we will take a close look at the role of power in group contexts. Although you may not be part of a large group such as the ones listed above, power is a phenomenon present in *all* groups that must be acknowledged. No matter the size or reach of the group, questions of who has power, how that power is used, and power struggles are common. Perhaps you have experienced, first-hand, power struggles in groups that you have been involved with. If so, you can relate to the importance of communication when such issues arise. If not, it is likely that you will experience the impact of power dynamics in a group setting at some point in your life. To begin, let's take a look at what power is and how we can define the term.

WHAT IS POWER?

Power

the ability to influence another's attitudes, beliefs, values, and communication

Power may be defined as the ability to influence another's attitudes, beliefs, values, and communication. It is important to note that power only exists when people engage in interaction. It is not something that a person "has" or "does not have." Power is something that is granted to another person. In other words, no one may have power, or influence, over another unless that power is conceded to him/her.

Think of the captain of a sports team. Often, team captains have the power to direct others on the team and influence behavior. This power, however, is only possible if team members abide by the request/direction of the team captain. Imagine a team captain directing his/her peers to be suited up and on the court at a certain time. If the teammates do not do so, and do not follow the direction, they are not granting the captain power. Power is a relational concept meaning in order for a person to be influential, he/she must be permitted that ability by others. Power is inherent in all relationships, but how do we decide who in the relationship holds the most power?

WHO HAS POWER?

Take a moment to think about powerful influences in your own life. What kind of characteristics must a person possess in order to be granted power by others? In your own group experiences, who had the power and what qualities did that person (or persons) have that made *you* grant that person power?

There are several characteristics that can impact our willingness to grant others power. The first characteristic is credibility. **Credibility** is the perception that a person is competent, trustworthy, and shows goodwill toward others. We are unlikely to allow a group member the power to make decisions about the group if we feel they are not capable to do so. Moreover, if they cannot be trusted, or do not seem to genuinely care about the good of the group, we may be hesitant to let them exert power.

In addition to being perceived as credible, we grant power to those who are respected. **Respect** occurs when we deeply admire someone for certain qualities, they possess such as expertise, values, or commitment. We are much more likely to be influenced to behave a certain way or enact some direction when respect the person giving the directive. Quality communication is another characteristic important for those in power. Being able to clearly and effectively communicate with others will not only impact who we want to hold power in groups, but also affect our satisfaction with the power exerted.

A person's perceived level of credibility, communication ability, and the respect we hold for him/her may certainly influence to whom we grant power. This list, however, is by no means exhaustive. An article published in *Forbes* magazine addressed 11 traits of powerful leaders and argued that the most powerful leaders are self-managing, act strategically, are effective communicators, are accountable and responsible, set clear goals and accomplish said goals, have a vision for the future, manage complexity well, foster creativity and innovation, create strong relationships with others, and are adaptable to change.

All of these characteristics are ideals that are quite frequently esteemed in the American culture. As a result, we are more likely to grant power to persons with these characteristics. The type of power granted, however, depends on the situation. Power is a multi-faceted concept and can be categorized into various forms.

Credibility
the perception that a person is competent, trustworthy, and shows goodwill toward others

© Rei Imagine/Shutterstock.com

Respect
when we deeply admire someone for certain qualities, they possess such as expertise, values, or commitment

BASES OF POWER

When thinking about types of power in group settings, various things may come to mind. Depending on the situation, we may attempt to influence others in different ways. In 1960, French and Raven advanced five power bases that explain different types of power. The well-documented five power bases include: referent power, expert power, legitimate power, coercive power, and reward power.

Referent power is power that is granted when others look up to you and, in some way, want to be like you. This is often perceived as

Referent Power
power that is granted when others look up to you and, in some way, want to be like you

a form of respect. When you think of groups you have been a part of, there may be someone who sticks out as a great mentor or leader. Upon reflection, maybe you looked up to them in some way. If so, it is likely that had they asked you to do something for them, you would do so. This is an example of referent power.

Others are granted power based on a position they hold. When this is the case, this is called **legitimate power**. For instance, the President of the United States holds a certain amount of power based on his position in the country. Leaders (such as presidents, vice-presidents) in student organizations are granted power due to the position they hold within the group.

Legitimate Power
power granted based on a person's position

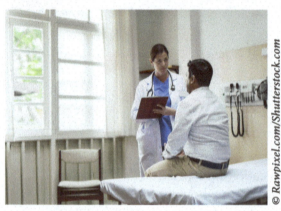

© Rawpixel.com/Shutterstock.com

While some are given power based on their position or role, others are seen as powerful due to their level of expertise, or skill set, in a certain area. This is referred to as **expert power**. When you go to your doctor because you feel ill, if he/she instructs you to take medication or engage in some other behavior, how often do you follow direction without questioning it? Probably often. We give doctors the power to direct us because we perceive them as having knowledge in that area. As a result, we do what we are told often without question.

Expert Power
power granted because of one's level of expertise, or skill set, in a certain area

Perhaps you have been in a group project where you had to complete a large task. If part of that task included work in an area you were not familiar with (i.e., specialized computer software, coding, statistics, etc.). If someone else in the group had knowledge in that area, you might allow then the power to complete that task and/or direct you on how to complete that task. We often grant power to those who are considered expert in an area, especially when we do not have the same skill set.

Reward Power
when power is given to a person based on their capacity to provide reward for a certain behavior or attitude change

Finally, sometimes people who have the ability to reward or punish others have power. When power is given to a person based on their capacity to provide reward for a certain behavior or attitude change, this is called **reward power**. A teacher, for example, may assign extra credit for work done in a college class. If students comply with the request for the work in order to earn the extra credit, they are granting the teacher reward power. If that same teacher announces students will have points deducted if the work is not completed, the teacher is enacting coercive power. **Coercive power** is granted to a person when they have the ability to punish others when a request is not fulfilled. While we may grant different people various types of power depending on the situation, how that power is communicated in an attempt to gain compliance is important to understand.

Coercive Power
power granted to a person when they have the ability to punish others when a request is not fulfilled

Read the following scenario and then test your knowledge on the power bases. Can you identify which types of power are being granted?

Rita recently got hired at the Zeep Company, which is a large retail store in her hometown. Rita is a college sophomore who is taking 15 credit hours and works approximately 25 hours per week. Even though Rita lives at home with her parents, she has financial responsibilities such as a car payment, car insurance, and textbooks that require her to work. In her first month at Zeep, Rita met a lot of new and interesting people. Whether realizing it or not, Rita has granted each person power over her own actions and attitudes in a short period of time. Can you identify which person has which power base?

Phil: College senior who works 30 hours per week at Zeep while taking six college courses. Rita looks up to Phil as he is able to balance his time well and is thriving in school.

Todd: Rita's supervisor at Zeep. Todd has instructed Rita that if she has perfect work attendance for six months, she will receive a bonus.

Laura: Laura is the accountant at Zeep who handles employee payroll. Rita needs help completing her tax forms for payroll, so she refers to Laura for help based on Laura's skill set in that area.

Carly: The store manager at Zeep. Carly holds an all-employee mandatory meeting where she announces anyone who comes in late to work more than two days will have hours cut from their schedule the following week.

Tom: Tom is a trainer at Zeep and is assigned to mentor Rita. Based on Tom's position as mentor/trainer, Rita closely follows Tom's directions and does what he instructs her to do.

ANSWERS:
Phil: referent power
Todd: reward power
Laura: expert power
Carly: coercive power
Tom: legitimate power

COMPLIANCE-GAINING IN GROUPS

Now that we know what power is and understand several different types of power, how do we gain compliance in groups? Compliance-gaining is often the result when a person has been granted some type of power. In past research, compliance-gaining has been defined as, "the communicative behavior in which an agent elicits from a target some agent-selected behavior" (Wheeless, Barraclough, & Stewart, 1983, p. 111).

Compliance-gaining
when a sender verbally or nonverbally sends a message to a received requesting he/she conform to a specific request or behavior

Let's break down this definition a bit before we look at compliance-gaining strategies used in groups. In order to gain compliance from another person, there must be a message communicated. This message may be verbal or nonverbal. An "agent" refers to the sender of the message and the "target" refers to the received of the message. "Agent-selected behavior" refers to the action the sender is requesting from the receiver.

Thus, compliance-gaining occurs when a sender verbally or nonverbally sends a message to a received requesting he/she conform to a specific request or behavior. In 2020, the United States faced an unimaginable pandemic in which the novel Coronavirus (COVID-19) spread at record-pace throughout the country (and globally). During the peak of this pandemic, groups of politicians, doctors, and scientists held daily press conferences urging Americans to stay home in quarantine to halt the spread of the deadly virus. As a group, state and national leaders employed a variety of compliance-gaining strategies to urge people to behave in certain ways during the crisis.

Marwell and Schmitt (1967) developed a list of 16 compliance-gaining strategies people often used when trying to persuade others to comply. Many of these strategies were used in the 2020 COVID-19 Pandemic.

> Promise: the promise to provide a reward for compliance
> Threat: establishing punishment for noncompliance
> Positive expertise: promises of implicit rewards for compliance (i.e., you will feel good about yourself if you comply)
> Negative expertise: implicit punishments for noncompliance (i.e., you will feel horrible about yourself if you do not comply)
> Liking: behaving in a way to increase others' liking of you so that they may subsequently comply to your request
> Pregiving: providing a reward *before* someone complies to a request
> Aversive stimulation: continuous punishments that only end when a compliance occurs
> Debt: requesting compliance as "re-payment" for past favors; paying back debt
> Moral appeal: asserting that one will be perceived as sinful or not moral if they do not comply to a request
> Positive self-feeling: assurance that one will feel better about themselves if they comply with the request
> Negative self-feeling: communicating that one will feel worse/badly if they do not comply with the request
> Positive altercasting: asserting that a "good person" would comply with the request

Negative altercasting: asserting that only a "bad person" or a person with negative qualities would not comply with the request

Altuism: asserting that if one complies with a request it would be helpful to others

Positive esteem: communicating that others will think highly of you if you comply to the request

Negative esteem: communicating that others will think badly of you if you do not comply to the request

When Marwell and Schmitt reviewed the underlying factors of all 16 items, they found five categories of compliance-gaining strategies: rewarding activity, punishing activity, expertise, activation of impersonal commitments, and activation of personal commitments. Think of groups you have experienced. When one member tries to gain compliance from another member, what strategies have been used? Are more positive or negative?

Compliance-gaining may be used to get others to agree to small task or larger undertakings. One study investigated college student use of compliance-gaining strategies to persuade others to drink alcohol. The strategies most likely to be used were positive self-feeling, negative self-feeling, and positive expertise (Wagner & Punyanunt-Carter, 2009). Just as this study is specific to college students, there are many group factors that can impact what group members use compliance-gaining in groups and how effective those strategies may be.

First, the number of group members can play a role in compliance-gaining. It is easier to get one or two people to comply with a request as opposed to a large group of people. The gender of the group member employing a compliance-gaining strategy as well as the gender of the target can influence the effectiveness of the communication (see Hertzog & Scudder, 1996). Power differences among group members can influence attempts at compliance-gaining. Depending on one's position within the group, he/she may be more likely to get others to comply and/or use differing strategies to achieve compliance.

COMMUNICATING POWER IN GROUPS

In group settings, there are several ways members can communicate power. To start, power may be communicated nonverbally or verbally. Nonverbally, we can use behaviors to request and/or declare power in an interaction. For instance, we can adjust our poise, or the way we hold our body, to communicate confidence and a "take charge" attitude.

Poise
the way we hold our body

Touch communication can also be used to communicate power. We know from research that higher-status and lower-status people often use differing types of touch. Those with higher status often feel free to use localized types of touch (i.e., touching another's arm, shoulder), but those whom have lower status typically stick to more formal types of

Table 5.1: Compliance-Gaining Strategies in Groups

COMPLIANCE-GAINING STRATEGY	EXAMPLE
Promise	"I will treat everyone in the group to ice cream if you all submit your project parts by Monday."
Threat	"If someone doesn't submit their part of the group project by Monday, I will tell the professor."
Positive Expertise	"I know you don't want to work with everyone in the group, but in the end, you will be glad you did!"
Negative Expertise	"How do you think you are going to feel about yourself if you let the rest of the group down?"
Liking	The group leader was overly nice to all group members all day. Later that evening, he asks everyone if they can pitch in and loan him money to get his car fixed.
Pre-giving	After proofreading the entire group project without being asked, Kristen asks the group if it is okay if she skips the group presentation.
Aversive Stimulation	Burt consistently sends annoying text messages to the group text and when people comment he says he will stop sending non-stop messages when others have completed their part of the group project.
Debt	"Abby, can you cover for me in class today? I *did* help you write up your summary for the group paper."
Moral Appeal	"Wow! Are you really going to skip out on the group presentation? Everyone is going to really be mad if you do that."
Positive Self-Feeling	"Trust me, if you ignore all the issues and help others finish the group project, you will feel better about yourself."
Negative Self-Feeling	"Trust me, you are going to feel badly about yourself if you don't finish your part of the project by Monday."
Positive Altercasting	"You know, good group members show up for all meetings; not just some of them."
Negative Altercasting	"Only bad group members skip meetings and don't complete their tasks on time."
Altuism	"You know Suzy has trouble with PowerPoint. It would be so helpful if you could help her out with that."
Positive Esteem	"Professor Brown will be so happy with you if you show up and help out the group."
Negative Esteem	"Professor Brown is going to be super disappointed with you if you don't show up and help the group."

touch (i.e., handshakes) (Hall, 1996). If you think of it, in a classroom group, it is not uncommon for the instructor to pat a student on the back or shoulder to communicate praise for good work. Conversely, however, when is the last time you patted your professor on the back and said, "Good class today!"? Probably not too often.

Eye communication can also be used to communicate power nonverbally in groups. There is a theory of eye communication referred to as **visual dominance behavior**. Visual dominance behavior suggests that when communicating power, or dominance, in an interpersonal interaction, we alter our normal eye contact behaviors (see Dovidio & Ellyson, 1985). Specifically, in typical interactions, we engage in more eye contact when listening as opposed to speaking. The listener engages in eye contact in order to show respect for the speaker. When engaged in visual dominance behavior, however, the listener does not engage in much eye contact. This behavior indicates dominance or power and communicates a message that due to the higher status; he/she does not have to engage in extended eye contact when listening.

In a group setting, the group members may often make eye contact when interacting. When the leader takes on the listener role, however, it is possible he/she can communicate power by not engaging in eye contact. As you can see, a variety of nonverbal behaviors can communicate power in groups. In addition, power may be communicated verbally. One strategy often used to assert power or dominance is via the use of power plays.

POWER PLAYS

Power plays are patterns of communication used repeatedly by an individual to manipulate them in some manner (Steiner, 1981). Claude Steiner suggested three power play types often used: you owe me, nobody upstairs, and yougottobekidding power plays. The **"you owe me" power play** is similar to the pregiving compliance-gaining strategy reviewed earlier in this chapter. In this power play, one person does something (a task, favor) for another and subsequently request something in return. What makes this a form of power is that the person does the initial task strategically and purposefully so that he/she can then use it a collateral to demand a favor in return. A lot of times, when we feel like we owe someone something, we are more likely to comply with their request.

The next power play is called the **"nobody upstairs" power play**. When using this strategy, the person essentially ignores a request repeatedly. By acting as if they don't know common social rules, they simply ignore requests for compliance; thus, asserting power in a situation. For instance, if the group is working on the project and input is needed from one group member, yet that person consistently refuses to

Visual Dominance Behavior

the theory that states when communicating power, or dominance, in an interpersonal interaction, we alter our normal eye contact behaviors; when listening we engage in less eye contact to communicate positions of power

Power Plays

patterns of communication used repeatedly by an individual to manipulate them in some manner

"You Owe Me" Power Play

when one person does something (a task, favor) for another and subsequently request something in return

"Nobody Upstairs" Power Play

when the person essentially ignores a request repeatedly: by acting as if they don't know common social rules, they simply ignore requests for compliance

share his/her input, they may be practicing the "nobody upstairs powerplay." Acting as if he/she didn't realize it was an important request and not responding is an attempt to assert power within the group.

The third power play is "yougottobekidding." Have you ever suggested what you thought to be a great idea to someone, and they responded with, "Are you kidding me?!" or a similar response? If so, how did that make you feel? You likely felt embarrassed, or even angry that the person essentially put down your idea in a single sentence. If that person did not agree with your idea, there are other ways to communicate their perspective.

For instance, they could acknowledge the idea and then propose something new. They can praise one part of your idea (i.e., the creativity behind it), yet politely disagree. Yet, when a person effectively attacks your idea verbally with comments such as, "You got to be kidding me!" this is considered a power play. This power play can be particularly tough to handle in group contexts. It is bad enough if you feel like your communication is attacked in a private conversation, but if this occurs in front of others in a group, it can really sting.

"Yougottobekidding" Power Play

responding to communication in a way that puts down the other persona and makes them feel stupid or embarrassed for presenting an idea or opinion

Power Play Examples in Groups

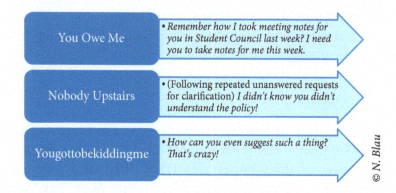

© N. Blau

OTHER POWERFUL MESSAGES

Power plays *are* ways to communicate power, but most would argue they are not effective strategies. There are more *abuses* of power, rather than effective ways to send powerful messages and persuade others to comply. Another, more ethical, way to communicate power is via the use of verbal immediacy behaviors.

To begin, the term **immediacy** refers to perception of physical or psychological closeness between persons (Andersen, 1979). Therefore, **verbal immediacy** may be defined as using words to create perceptions of physical and/or psychological closeness. Verbal immediacy behaviors can include calling people by name, praising others, and using inclusive language such as "we," "us," and "our," instead of "me," "you," or "mine."

Immediacy

the perception of physical or psychological closeness between persons

Verbal Immediacy

using words to create perceptions of physical and/or psychological closeness

Using verbal immediacy behaviors in group contexts can lead to a number of positive effects. First, the use of immediacy behaviors can help create the perception that power within the group is shared. By referencing group decisions and solutions in terms of "we" as opposed to "me" (i.e., "We can solve this problem together." versus "I will solve the problem.") is empowers other group members to work together.

Next, as the definition of immediacy states, using verbal immediacy behaviors can create perceptions of physical and psychological closeness. This is important when creating cohesion within the group. And, as we have already learned, group cohesiveness is strongly related to group member satisfaction. Finally, the use of verbal immediacy behaviors can positively impact the use of nonverbal immediacy behaviors in the group.

Nonverbal immediacy is when we create the perception of psychological and/or physical closeness via the use of nonverbal behaviors. Common nonverbal immediacy behaviors variety in vocal pitch, volume, smiling, and leaning in toward a person (Andersen & Andersen, 1982). We know that in the classroom settings, groups are more motivated to learn when nonverbal immediacy behaviors are present (Mottet, Parker-Raley, Cunningham, & Beebe, 2005). In terms of athletic groups, we know that verbal and nonverbal immediacy behaviors correlate with increased group cohesion and social attraction to the group (Turman, 2008). Similarly, the use of immediacy behaviors in other types of groups may be a way to motivate group members to participate and achieve group goals.

When those whom have power in groups communicate their power in an effective manner, such as through the use of verbal and nonverbal immediacy behaviors, it is more likely the group will be cohesive and productive. We now know that groups vary in terms of whom is granted power, what type of power is granted, and how that power is communicated. These fluctuations can make achieving group goals difficult at time. Thus, it is important that we understand how to communicate in a way to balance power within group contexts.

BALANCING POWER IN GROUPS

Power struggles, or competition for the ability to assert dominance over others, occur in groups. Some struggles may be small and others large. Nevertheless, power struggles will arise, and we must have tools to face such issues effectively. One way to balance power within groups, and remedy power struggles that may exist, is to communicate assertively.

Assertiveness has been defined as "the ability to communicate the full range of your thoughts and emotions with confidence and skill" (Adler, 1977, p. 6). As opposed to aggression, which includes communication that attacks a person's message and/or character, when one

Nonverbal Immediacy
the perception of psychological and/or physical closeness via the use of nonverbal behaviors

Power Struggles
competition for the ability to assert dominance over others

Assertiveness
"the ability to communicate the full range of your thoughts and emotions with confidence and skill" (Adler, 1977, p. 6)

is assertive, he/she is able to send messages directly without attacking others, yet not feeling the need keep their opinion to themselves.

Assertive messages are frequently considered to be superior other types of powerless language in most instances. Powerless messages include verbal messages that are less direct and are less likely to persuade others to comply with a request. Hesitating when making a statement, adding on tag questions at the end of a statement, or being too critical of oneself are examples of powerless language.

POWERLESS VERBAL MESSAGES	
POWERLESS VERBAL MESSAGES	EXAMPLE
Hesitations	I, um, would like to, eh possibly schedule a group meeting for next Monday.
Tag questions	We really need to finish the report by Friday, don't you think?
Disqualifiers	I wasn't there in the beginning of the group meeting, but I'm sure it was great.
Self-criticism	I know you all appointed me the leader of this group, but I am not very good at making decisions.

In situations where a group member is trying to use a power play or communicate power unfairly, an assertive voice can help minimize those attempts. In addition, when group members see others communicating assertively, they may be empowered to, also, communicate in strong, yet appropriate, manner. If most group members communicate assertively, this will help balance power within the group.

Tips of the Trade: Communicating Assertively

- Voice your opinion directly.
- Use a conversational (not controlling) tone of voice.
- Be concise and clear in your message.
- Avoid attacking another person or message.
- Make eye contact when speaking to others.
- Be honest.
- Do not be manipulative.
- Be confident and firm.
- Be collaborative when working with others.

Another way to balance power within groups is to always keep in mind that power is fluid. In other words, the power we grant to others can always be increased or decreased. Thus, if we grant a group member power, but then that power is being used inappropriately, the power can be decreased. Group members can take some of that power away.

Power can also be increased for those who do not seem to have enough power within the group. Perhaps there are a couple of group members that don't speak up often, or who have had their voice muted by others in the group. People have the ability to grant them power and encourage them to communicate their thoughts and feelings. You can simply ask them questions, give them the "floor" to speak during meetings, or even ask others to pull back and let others share the spotlight. No matter the method, we can increase or decrease power as needed in an attempt to balance power within groups.

When there appears to be power differences among group members, we often see the members whom hold more power taking advantage. In fact, when it comes to rules (social norms, group norms, or explicit rules), those with power often are afforded more freedom to break the rules, whereas those with less power must abide by the rules.

In an effort to balance power in groups, groups must set out rules and guidelines early in the forming stages. Clear rules that are applicable to all group members will be useful later on when power struggles arise. If the guidelines created apply to all group members, and a person with more power is found breaking the rules, it is much easier to "call them out" or question the abuse of power when there is a clear set of rules to which others may refer. In other words, reminding a group member about the rules for meeting attendance that all agreed to (including the transgressor) is a much more effective means to gain compliance than urging him/her to stop being late to meetings when no rules have been established.

Think of your own history in groups. What rules were set in place? What happened when the rules were broken? Were more exceptions made for broken rules depending on how much power the group member held? If one group member is attempting to exert too much power, or using power unfairly, a strategy to balance out power is to simply resist his/her efforts at influence.

In 1980, a research study identified four ways to resist influence: negotiation, justification, identity management, and non-negotiation (see McLaughlin, et al.). **Negotiation** includes offering a compromise and attempting to comply with part of the request, but not all of it. **Justification** occurs when an individual resists compliance by providing reasons whey he/she cannot or will not comply. **Identity management** is when a compliance request is resisted by manipulating the identity of the person initiating the request. This may be done positively or negatively. **Positive identity management** is when one resists power by making the requestor feel positive, or good, about him/herself. An example may be if the group leader told you to complete the entire report on your own. You may say, "You are a much better writer than me, so I think the entire group would benefit if you wrote up the report." **Negative identity management** is essentially the opposite. This is

Negotiation

offering a compromise and attempting to comply with part of the request, but not all of it

Justification

when an individual resists compliance by providing reasons whey he/she cannot or will not comply

Identity Management

when a compliance request is resisted by manipulating the identity of the person initiating the request

Positive Identity Management

when one resists power by making the requestor feel positive, or good, about him/herself

Negative Identity Management

when one resists power by making the requestor feel negatively, or bad, about him/herself

where one resists power by making the requestor feel negatively, or bad, about him/herself. Again, if the group leader instructs you to writeup the entire group report, you may try to manipulate his/her identity in a negative manner to resist the request for compliance. You may say, "It is really an unfair thing to do by asking me to write the entire group report solo. No good leader would ask one member to do something like that."

Non-Negotiation

one's outright refusal to comply with a request

Non-negotiation is one's outright refusal to comply with a request. In non-negotiation, a person straightforwardly refuses to do what is asked. An example may be, "No, I will not write the entire group report." In non-negotiation, no justification is provided, nor offer to compromise made.

Finally, keep in mind that power imbalances in groups are not just uncomfortable for those members with less power, but holding a large amount of power can also be difficult. Many times, the most powerful person in the group also has the hardest job. It is that person who often makes the difficult decisions. It is that person who takes the "heat" when the group faces external criticism. It is that person who may be viewed as not popular when forced to do something no one else in the group likes, even if it is best for the group in the long run.

In 2020, Dr. Amy Acton, Ohio Director of Public Health, led a group of doctors, scientists, and politicians who teamed up to make state decisions centered around the novel Coronavirus Pandemic. Similar to other directors of public health in other states, Dr. Acton held a lot of power within this specialized team. With that power, came a lot of hard work.

In mid-March 2020, Dr. Acton made a decision to sign a legal "stay-in-place" order for Ohio residents for a period of time in an effort to slow down the spread of this deadly virus. Ohioans were instructed to stay home unless working a job deemed as essential by the State of Ohio, traveling to care for family members, get food, or see a doctor. Restaurants, bars, hair salons, non-essential stores, and more were shut down.

Initially, this decision was a shock to many in the state. In addition, Dr. Acton's decision to sign this order was not very popular. Several people believed it was an overreaction and were unhappy when they found themselves out of work and kids home from school. Nevertheless, Dr. Acton had been granted the power and made the difficult decision. Only time would tell that this decision was likely to credit for thousands of lives saved from this deadly virus. In the moment, however, having the power meant that tough decisions needed to be made and implemented.

Most of us will never face that type of power imbalance. We may, however, find ourselves in a group where others have graciously granted us power; thus, creating a similar imbalance. This may make us uncomfortable. One solution to balance out power is to practice empowerment. **Empowerment** is when we share power; we grant others power over a certain domain. Often, empowerment is when we relinquish power so that others may make their own decisions and choose their own behaviors. Sharing power with other group members not only takes the burden off of the person with more power, it may motivate those with less power to make decisions and take action they may, otherwise, had not done. When people feel empowered, less focus is on the imbalance of power, and more focus is on the task at hand.

Empowerment
when we relinquish power so that others may make their own decisions and choose their own behaviors

> *The purpose of getting power is to be able to give it away.*
>
> —*Aneurin Bevan*

SUMMARY

In chapter 5, we have learned a lot about the role of power in groups. To begin, we reviewed the concept of power and that power is something that is granted by one person to another. In addition, we have learned that there are five bases of power and each type is distinct. In group situations, it is common for some members to attempt to gain compliance from others. In doing so, they may use one of many compliance-gaining strategies to persuade another and communicate power.

No matter the group size or mission, there are always going to be power imbalances among members. It is impossible for every member to have exactly the same amount of power. This is not necessarily an issue, however. It is okay for some people to hold more or less power than others, and in some instances, it is necessary to meet the goals of the group. When power imbalances become too pronounced, it is possible for power struggles to arise.

In this chapter, we have addressed various communication strategies to balance out power in groups such as resisting power, communicating assertively, and empowering others. Power is an interesting concept no matter the context. It is a phenomenon we will face in every relationship we have, including group relationships. Learning how to communicate power effectively and face challenges related to power in groups will not only help in particular situations but will ultimately help us better enjoy group dynamics.

REFLECTION QUESTIONS

1. What is power? How does a person get power?
2. What are the five bases of power? Provide an example for each type.
3. How do we use compliance-gaining in groups? What is the best compliance-gaining strategy? The worst strategy?
4. How can we nonverbally communicate power in groups?
5. What is visual dominance behavior? Explain how this may be illustrated in group situations.
6. What are power plays? Explain three types of power plays.
7. How can we verbally communicate power in groups?
8. Imagine you are in a group that is experiencing many power struggles. What communication strategies can you use to balance power in the group?
9. What is empowerment? Why is it important to empower group members?

LEARNING BY ACTION

All communities, large or small, are governed a by a group of elected officials. Typically, the mayor of the city in which we live is considered the person with the majority of the power in the group. For this activity, students should (individually or in groups) set up a time to interview the mayor or a council person of the city in which they live, work, or attend school. The student(s) will have to contact the city office, request an appointment, and set up a date and time for the brief interview. Students should then prepare interview questions that will be reviewed by the instructor prior to the interview. Interview questions should include the following topics:

1. Who holds the most powerful position in the group (government/city council) and why?
2. Does the group ever face any power struggles?
3. If so, ask for an example.
4. How are power struggles handled in the group?

Students may also include additional questions of their choosing. The point of the interview is to learn about the group dynamic sand power differences among group members. Following the interview, the student(s) will write up a report of the interview results and report their findings to the class.

VIDEO CLIP

Airing on television from 2005-2013, *The Office* remains one of the most watched shows today. All of the episodes are on Netflix and this show continues to be popular year after year. The show is about a group of co-workers at Dunder-Mifflin Paper Company in Scranton, Pennsylvania and their everyday trials and tribulations in the office. Most episodes show some power struggle among the cast. A good episode to view is the pilot in which the characters are introduced, and various types of power are illustrated. After watching the pilot, identify types of power seen in the show, as well as strategies used to communicate power. Which strategies were effective, and which were not?

CONTEMPORARY COMMUNICATION

When we find ourselves in a position of power – whether it be referent power, expert power, or some other form of power – we have choices on how we may communicate. While some may abuse power that has been granted to them, a more effective use of power is motivating and empowering others to be their very best. Instead of taking advantage of power, using power to inspire others is a superior strategy. There are several applications we can use to find daily quotations and mantras that can inspire ourselves and others. For instance, "Daily Fix Me – Motivation" is a free app that provides daily quotes, sayings, tips, and goal setting to motivate yourself to be your very best. These tips and inspiring messages may be shared with others as a form of empowerment.

CASES IN COMMUNICATION

You decide to go on a weekend camping trip with four of your friends. The location is approximately three hours away. As a group, you decide everyone must be responsible for bringing certain supplies the group will need to get through the entire weekend, as the locale is too far from home or stores. Once the group arrives at the camping spot, everyone begins getting set up. Friends are setting up tents, wood to make fires, and organizing food. The person who organized the trip, Todd suddenly comes over to you and says, "Are you kidding me? You brought two packages of hot dogs and thought that would be enough for all of us? You are crazy!" You were not sure how to reply, and shortly you see Todd approach another friend and say, "Hey Kate, you were in charge of bringing water bottles, but you must have forgotten. It's a good thing I brought some! Since I did that, you need to come over here and pitch my tent for me." It is clear Todd is attempting to communicate power within the group.

1. What power play(s) does Todd attempt to use on the others?
2. What communication strategy might have Todd used to communicate power in a less aggressive manner?
3. How would you respond to Todd in this situation (or how would you suggest Kate respond?)

REFERENCES

Adler, R.B. (1977). Confidence in communication: A guide to assertive and social skills. New York, NY: Holt, Rinehart, & Winston.

Andersen, J. F. (1979). Teacher immediacy as a predictor of teaching effectiveness. In D. Nimmo (Ed.), *Communication yearbook 3* (pp. 543-559). New Brunswick, NJ: Transaction Books.

Andersen, P., & Andersen, J. (1982). Nonverbal immediacy in instruction. In L. L. Barker (Ed.), *Communication in the classroom: Original essays* (pp. 98-120). Englewood Cliffs, NJ: Prentice-Hall.

Deep, P. (2017, March). 11 powerful traits of successful leaders. *Forbes.* Available at https://www.forbes.com/sites/deeppatel/2017/03/22/11-powerful-traits-of-successful-leaders/#76894f93469f

Dovidio J.F., Ellyson S.L. (1985) Pattern of visual dominance behavior in humans. In Ellyson S.L., Dovidio J.F. (eds). *Power, Dominance, and Nonverbal Behavior.* Springer Series in Social Psychology. Springer, New York, NY.

Hall, J.A. (1996). Touch, status, and gender at professional meetings. *Journal of Nonverbal Behavior, 20,* 23–44. https://doi.org/10.1007/BF02248713

Hertzog, R. L., & Scudder, J. N. (1996). Influence of persuader gender versus gender of target on the selection of compliance-gaining strategies. *Howard Journal of Communications, 7*(1), 29–34. https://doi-org.proxy.library.ohio.edu/10.1080/10646179609361711

Marwell, G., & Schmitt, D. R. (1967). Dimensions of compliance-gaining behavior: An empirical analysis. *Sociometry, 30,* 350-364.

McLaughlin, M. L., Cody, M. L., & Robey, C. S. (1980). Situational influences on the selection of strategies to resist compliance-gaining attempts. *Human Communication Research* 1, 14–36.

Mottet, T.P., Parker-Raley, J., Cunningham, C., & Beebe, S.A. (2005). The relationship between teacher nonverbal immediacy and student course workload and teacher availability expectations. *Communication Research Reports, 22,* 275-282.

Steiner, C. (1981). *The other side of power.* New York, NY: Grove.

Turman, P. D. (2008). Coaches' immediacy behaviors as predictors of athletes' perceptions of satisfaction and team cohesion. *Western Journal of Communication, 72,* 162–179. https://doi-org.proxy.library.ohio.edu/10.1080/10570310802038424

Wagner, T. R., & Punyanunt-Carter, N. (2009). Come on… have another drink! College students' perceptions of compliance-gaining strategies used for drinking alcohol. *Human Communication*, *12*(4), 477–483.

Wheeless, L. R., Barraclough, R., & Stewart, R. (1983). Compliance-gaining and power in persuasion. In R. Bostrom (Ed.), *Communication Yearbook 7* (pp. 105–145). Beverly Hills: Sage.

CHAPTER SIX

We Don't Always See Eye to Eye: Managing Conflict in Groups

LEARNING OBJECTIVES

After studying chapter 6 you should be able to:
- Define conflict.
- Articulate the difference between functional and dysfunctional conflict.
- Explain various types of conflict including task, relational and value conflicts.
- Classify five conflict management styles.
- Distinguish three conflict resolution strategies.
- Identify variables that impact group conflict.

Imagine you are out having a fun evening with a group of friends. All of a sudden, a few people you do not know approach your group and start an argument. They claim you are at their table and they want you to leave. After a few of your friends refuse to leave, an argument begins. What do you do? How might you react in this situation?

- If you decide it's time to take a restroom break and leave while the conflict goes on, you might be an avoider.
- If you feel like you would agree to just leave to make peace, you may be an accommodator.
- If you are one of the people who are refusing to leave and arguing your point with the other group, you may have more of a competitive style of conflict.

In chapter 6, we will examine interpersonal conflict that often arises in group situations. All relationships, including groups, face conflict at one point or another. It is important that we understand what conflict is, as well as how to effectively manage conflict when it arises. In order to prepare ourselves to handle group conflict, it is necessary to understand various types of conflict as well as various conflict management styles. To begin, let's analyze the term conflict.

WHAT IS CONFLICT?

If you turn on Netflix and choose a television show to watch, chances are, it includes some type of conflict. From the show *Friends* to *Game of Thrones*, and more, we see groups engaging in conflict in the main storylines. Conflict is inevitable in life, and this includes groups to which we belong.

Conflict has been defined as "an expressed struggle between at least two interdependent parties who perceive incompatible goals, scarce resources, and interference from the other party in achieving their goals" (Wilmot & Hocker, 2011, p. 11). At first glance, this definition may be confusing. In order to really understand the various parts of this definition, let's take a closer look.

The first part of the conflict definition refers to "expressed struggle". **Expressed struggle** suggests that the conflict must be openly communicated in some way. Imagine you are part of group at school and you feel frustrated with a few of your group members. Until you express your frustration, this is not considered interpersonal conflict. You may feel conflict within yourself, which is referred to as **intrapersonal conflict**, but in order to meet our definition of conflict, your frustration must be communicated to the group. We may express our frustrations in many ways including direct communication, expressing it in writing, or even nonverbally. Nevertheless, in order to be considered conflict, it must be stated in some way.

The next part of the conflict definition states that the conflict must occur between two interdependent parties. **Interdependence** happens when one's behavior influences that of another person. As you know, when working in groups, the behavior of one group member frequently impacts everyone in the group. If a group member fails to complete a task, for example, the whole group may suffer as a result. This is interdependence.

In groups, we are especially dependent on others. If we did not need anything from groups members, we would have no reason to be a part of the group. Sometimes, we are in groups to achieve a task and we depend on others to help do so. Some groups are for enjoyment purposes only, but we still depend on other group members to accomplish the happiness we get from the enjoyable activities. If we did not depend on our group members in some way, we would likely not be a part of the group and would never experience group conflict.

Continuing our analysis of the conflict definition, it states that in order for conflict to exist, at least one member must believe his or her goals are not compatible with those of other group members

© UKRAINE/Shutterstock.com

or have **perceived incompatible goals**. In other words, this is the idea that at least one group member believes that his/her goals contradict the goals of other group members and/or the overall group goal.

It is important to take note of the word "perceive" in the definition. In reality, it may be *possible* for the goals of all group member to be met, but when at least one member believes it is *not possible*, such a perception can lead to conflict. If I am part of a group and I believe that I cannot meet my goal if others in the group are able to meet their goals, I may get upset or angry. These feelings may lead to conflict within the group (assuming I express my feelings).

In addition to the perception of incompatible goals, we sometimes feel that there are not enough resources for everyone in the group. The **perception of scarce resources** arise when one believes that there is not enough means to meet all needs/desires. Keep in mind a **resource** is an asset, or something valued by a person. Examples may be time, materials, or anything important to achieving group goals.

Money, for instance, is a common cause of conflict in groups. Suppose a group has a certain amount of money and group members have different ideas of how to spend the money. Maybe some members want to use the money for supplies and others want to spend the money on entertainment. If at least one group member perceives there is not enough money to go around, conflict may arise. Again, remember the key word is "perception." There very well could be enough money to obtain needed supplies and pay for entertainment, but if one or more group members believe there is not enough for everyone, conflict can occur.

Finally, the last part of the conflict definition mentions perceived interference by others in achieving goals. **Interference** occurs when there are impediments from other group members in achieving one's goals. Just like with perceived incompatibility and scarce resources, even the perception, or belief, of interference can cause conflict to arise in groups.

All of the components of this definition are applicable to various types of interpersonal relationships such as friendships, romantic relationships, family relationships, and others. In addition, we can easily apply all parts to group dynamics. When adapted in the group context, **group conflict** may be defined as expressed struggles between two or more group members where in at least one group member perceives incompatible goals, scarce group resources and interference from other group members when working to attain goals.

Now that we have fully reviewed what group conflict is, it is notable that not all conflicts are alike. Based on your own experiences in groups, have all group conflicts been the same? More importantly, what was the outcome of those conflicts? Was it positive or was it negative? Just like most things in life, conflicts come in many forms. This means

Perceived Incompatible Goals

at least one group member that his/her goals contradict the goals of other group members and/or the overall group goal

Perceived Scarce Resources

when one believes that there is not enough means to meet all needs/desires

Resource

an asset, or something valued by a person such a time, materials, or money

Interference

when there are impediments from other group members in achieving one's goals

Group Conflict

as expressed struggles between two or more group members where in at least one group member perceives incompatible goals, scarce group resources and interference from other group members when working to attain goals that we will experience many different types of conflicts as we engage in different groups in our lifetime. Therefore, let's turn to a review of types of conflict evident in groups.

TYPES OF GROUP CONFLICT

Just like most things in life, group conflicts are not all the same. We see variations based on the type of groups, group missions, tasks, and even group members themselves. At the most basic level, group conflict can occur internally or externally.

Inter-group conflict occurs when one group engages in conflict with other (external groups). For instance, high school cliques often argue with other cliques or groups. When it becomes one group versus another, that is inter-group conflict. Conversely, sometimes groups experience conflict amongst their own group members, or internal to the group. This is called **intra-group conflict**. If those same clique members begin to fight with one another, this would be an instance of intra-group conflict.

In 2006, a group of researchers asked college students to report on types of groups that engage in conflict, and reasons for intergroup conflict based on their own experiences (see Cargile, Bradac, & Cole, 2006). After receiving all the responses, 87 reasons for intergroup conflict surfaced. Based on those results, multiple reasons for intergroup conflict emerged and including deep fundamental differences, economic issues, the nature of the group being disposed to engaging in conflict, being greedy, communication problems, and others. Examples of each can be seen in Table 6.1. Depending on how each group managed the conflict, there could be negative or positive outcomes, making the conflict functional or dysfunctional.

FUNCTIONAL vs. DYSFUNCTIONAL CONFLICT

Knowing that group conflict may occur within the group or between groups, we can now look a bit more specifically at types of group conflict. Although the word, conflict, is often perceived negatively, not all conflict is bad. Some conflict can be beneficial to group contexts. Several years ago, two communication scholars identified two types of conflict: functional and dysfunctional (Canary & Messman, 2000).

Functional conflict includes conflict that ultimately results in a positive outcome and sometimes even strengthens the relationship among group members. Communication during functional conflict includes using verbal and nonverbal messages that are cooperative, confirming, agreeable, focused, and helps to de-escalate the situation.

Unfortunately, as you have probably learned, not all conflict is functional, or useful. From time to time, group conflict results in negative

Inter-Group Conflict

when one group engages in conflict with other (external groups)

Intra-Group Conflict

when groups experience conflict amongst their own group members, or internal to the group

Functional Conflict

conflict that ultimately results in a positive outcome and sometimes even strengthens the relationship among group members

Table 6.1

GENERAL REASON FOR INTERGROUP CONFLICT
1. Deep differences (i.e., beliefs, values, religion, and other core ideas)
2. Economic factors
3. Natural disposition (i.e., natural tendency to fight with others)
4. Greedy domination (i.e., being selfish, desire more power)
5. Communication problems
6. Countering injustice (i.e., the group feels it has been wronged in some way)
7. Fear
8. Need for independence (i.e., groups want to win or protect their autonomy)
9. Following others
10. Other problems (i.e., self-esteem or other psychological issues)
11. Prejudice (against other groups)
12. Stubborn superiority (i.e., the group feels they are the best)
13. Narrow-minded ignorance
14. Emotional reaction

Cargile, A. C., Bradac, J. J., & Cole, T. (2006). Theories of intergroup conflict: A report of lay attributions. *Journal of Language & Social Psychology, 25*(1), 47–63. https://doi-org.proxy.library.ohio.edu/10.1177/0261927X05284479

outcomes. This is called dysfunctional conflict which includes conflict that has a damaging effect on the group members, or even the group as a whole. As opposed to functional conflict, communication patterns inherent in dysfunctional conflict often are viewed as oppositional, disconfirming, coercive, unfocused, and often escalate the conflict interaction.

In the 2000 Blockbuster film, *Remember the Titans*, we saw how two football teams were merged following years of segregation in Virginia. The two groups were united, but conflict ensued. Much of the conflict centered on issues of race and did nothing to help the integrated football team unite and accomplish their goal. In other words, most of the conflict among the group was dysfunctional. It was not until the group learned ways to effectively manage conflict that they were able to truly become a team.

Think back on your own group experiences. Now, can you remember a time when the group (the entire group or certain members) engaged in conflict? What was the outcome of that conflict? If, as a result, the group benefitted, it can be considered functional conflict. If not, it was likely dysfunctional conflict.

Dysfunctional Conflict

conflict that has a damaging effect on the group members, or even the group as a whole

FUNCTIONAL V. DYSFUNCTIONAL CONFLICT IN GROUPS			
FUNCTIONAL CONFLICT EXAMPLES		**DYSFUNCTIONAL CONFLICT EXAMPLES**	
Cooperation	"Let's all work together to get the paper edited for the class project so that we all end up with a good grade."	*Oppositional Communication*	"If you want to edit the paper that way, go ahead. I will do it my own way and ask for a separate grade."
Confirmation	"I see your point, Susie. That is not how I was thinking we would approach this project, but I do see where you are coming from."	*Disconfirmation*	"I'm not really sure what is going on with this project, but how about we just go get lunch instead of having this meeting?"
Agreement	"Okay, I agree that we need to talk through this more before we split up jobs for the group project. It makes sense that we are all on the same page."	*Coercion*	"I have had this instructor before, and I know what she wants. If you all do not want to do what I am suggesting, I will go tell Dr. Smith that you have not helped at all on this group project."
Focused Communication	"I'm glad everyone had such a fun weekend, but let's try to stick to the task and tackle this group project."	*Unfocused Communication*	A: "How about we start of discussing who will complete each part of the group paper?" B: "Okay, but first, I really need to tell you what happened this weekend!"
De-escalation	(speaking in a calm voice) "Everyone is clearly getting frustrated. Let's take a moment to re-group, take a deep breath, and then all take turns sharing our suggestions to the group."	*Escalation*	"I wouldn't be frustrated if you would just let everyone speak their minds and stop being so bossy! Maybe I don't want to take a deep breath!"

TASK, RELATIONAL, VALUE

Task Conflict

when group members perceive incompatibilities with regard to the achievement of group tasks

Task conflict arises when group members perceive incompatibilities with regard to the achievement of group tasks. This may involve group conflict surrounding availability of resources to achieve tasks, as well as differing opinions on how to reach goals. For instance, think of a group that must complete the semester project which includes creating a video public service announcement.

Two group members want to get started on the project right away, but the other two members think they have plenty of time and do not want to start working on the video for another week or so. In other words, the group members are choosing to manage time differently. One of the project requirements is that all group members be a part of the video, but only two members are willing to get together to film at the time. Thus, conflict emerges on *when* and *how* to finish the project. This is an example of task conflict in the group.

Relationship conflicts within groups occur when interpersonal relationships experience strains. For example, if two group members disagree on an issue, they may feel a strain on their working relationship. Moreover, let's assume the group includes two friends. The two get into an argument (about something unrelated to the group), but it still impacts the group dynamic. Because relational issues are so personal, relationship conflicts can be very stressful. For this reason, relational conflicts can also be the most difficult to resolve.

One study focused on feelings of inequity among group members. Researchers found that when group members perceived inequity, relational conflict increased (Wall & Nolan, 1987). Feelings of inequity are difficult to overcome not only because they impact relationships, but because this taps into our core attitudes, beliefs, and values.

When two or more group members find themselves disagreeing on fundamental attitudes and beliefs, they may face **value conflicts**. Some examples on value conflicts include differences of opinion with respect to things such as religion politics, ethics, and other deeply held beliefs.

Relationship Conflicts

conflict that occur within groups when interpersonal relationships experience strains

Value Conflicts

when two or more group members find themselves disagreeing on fundamental attitudes and beliefs

© N. Blau

Whether the group members engage in conflict about how to achieve a task, due to some relational issue, or even argue about value differences, all three types of conflict can impact the entire group. If you have ever been involved in a group where two members argued, it likely impacted the entire group. Group members may "take sides" or be sidetracked by the conflict situation. Because group conflict is inevitable, it is extremely important to find ways to effectively manage conflict in groups. To begin, we should investigate individual conflict management styles that may be seen in group interactions.

CONFLICT MANAGEMENT STYLES

We do not all manage conflict in the same way. While some people may shy away from conflict, others are entertained by conflict and really enjoy it. Moreover, we may use different conflict management styles in various contexts. As an example, you may use a more accommodating style in your personal life, but a more assertive style at work.

The same holds true in group situations. One group member may employ one style which may be different than others in the group. Thus, the first step in managing conflict effectively in groups is to understand different conflict management styles so that we can approach conflict in a productive way. There are five common conflict management styles: avoidance, accommodation, compromise, collaboration, and competition. Let's take a look at each style individually.

Avoidance

Avoidance

characterized by not engaging in the physical, psychological, or communicative functions of conflict

The avoidance **conflict management style** is characterized by not engaging in the physical, psychological, or communicative functions of conflict. The "avoider" is the person who does anything possible so as to not participate in conflict. For many people conflict situations are uncomfortable. This can be especially true in group interactions. Thus, they avoid topics, people, or situations altogether in which conflict may arise.

Last Christmas, I was at a family gathering when a political topic was raised. In the group of eight family members sitting around the living room, conflict quickly arose. While I am typically not one to avoid conflict situations, this was one where I chose an avoiding management style. I chose to stay out of the conflict because I knew that jumping in on one side or the other would not help the situation and could potentially damage my relationships with those in this particular group.

AVOIDANCE CONFLICT MANAGEMENT STYLE

PROS:
- Can provide time to think about the issue
- Can salvage relationships within groups
- Can save time

CONS:
- Can be viewed as "weak"
- Can be perceived as not caring about the group conflict
- May not be helpful in finding a resolution

A study conducted in 2017 showed that when it comes to political groups and conflict via social media, many users will selectively avoid the conflict, whereas they may be more willing to engage in conflict if centered on a different topic (Zhu, Skoric, & Shen). So, even if you typically do not avoid conflict, in some situations or when conflict is focused on specific topics, you may try to avoid the conflict altogether.

Accommodation

In some ways, similar to the mindset of the avoider, those with accommodating conflict management styles often feel uncomfortable with conflict. Accommodation may be defined putting another's needs ahead of your own. This can also include putting the needs of the *group* before your own personal needs.

When we accommodate, we often "give in" and do what another person has asked. In a group, sometimes conflict may arise, and one member wants the conflict to fizzle, so he/she just agrees in order to end any arguments. In groups, it is fairly common for group members to accommodate others at some point in time. Sometimes it is just easier to agree with what others in the group want in order to achieve a task or just avoid awkward conflict. For instance, if the conflict is over an issue that is small or trivial, then we may choose to accommodate others' wishes. There certainly can be, however, negatives to the accommodation conflict management style.

Accommodation
putting another's needs ahead of your own

> ### ACCOMMODATING CONFLICT MANAGEMENT STYLE
>
> PROS:
> - Can provide time to think about the issue
> - Can salvage relationships within groups
> - Can allow more experience group members to take lead
>
> CONS:
> - Can lead to decreased power in the group
> - Can lead to less solutions offered for consideration
> - May not be helpful in finding a resolution

Compromise

Next, some people favor a compromising **style** of conflict management. When we compromise in conflict, we work with others to get part of what we want, and they also get part of what they want. No one gets *all* of what they want, but all parties get *some* of what they want.

Compromising
when we work with others to get part of what we want, and they also get part of what they want

It is pretty common in our culture to hear people advocate for compromise among people. We learn from a young age that compromise is good and refusing to compromise with others is bad. Compromise *can* be a good thing – in certain situations. For instance, if the stakes are not high and each party giving up some of what they want is not a huge deal, compromise can work well.

Picture two group members who disagree about where the group should meet for the weekly meeting. One wants a quite spot and suggests the library, while the other prefers somewhere the group can have dinner while they work. Who should get their wish? If the group chooses to meet at a small diner that is typically quiet (but not as quiet as a library) that has food (but not the same type of food some wanted), both get *part* of what they want, but not *all* of what they want. This is compromise.

The decision of where to meet is likely not the most important thing for this student group. Therefore, the compromise on location was not high stakes and the decision was efficiently made. This is a clear circumstance where compromise can be beneficial. If the decision to be made is more important – or more impactful – compromise may not be the best management strategy to choose. Compromise can be negative to those losing part of what they want or need. Thus, collaboration may be a superior strategy in some instances.

**COMPROMISING CONFLICT
MANAGEMENT STYLE**

PROS:
- Everyone gets at least part of what they want/need
- Can help to balance power among group members
- Can save time; efficient

CONS:
- Everyone may lose part of what they want/need
- Does not help to think about new, creative solutions
- Solutions may only be short-term

Collaboration

Collaboration

when group members work together through conflict to ensure the needs and/or wants of all members are met

There are many people who argue that collaboration is the best conflict management style possible. Collaboration occurs when group members work together through conflict to ensure the needs and/or wants of all members are met. Collaborative conflict management can be very difficult and requires "thinking outside of the box" for ideas on how to encompass all ideas and opinions. It is easier to simply pick on possible solution without trying to satisfy all group members, but this does not necessarily always result in the best possible outcome.

Using the previous example of the group meeting location, what if the small diner had an unusually high number of customers on that particular evening of the group meeting? In that case, it may not have been quiet enough for the group to focus on their work. In that instance, perhaps the compromise was not reflective of the best possible outcome.

Some view collaboration as the process of "expanding the pie" to increase ways of thinking to include all ideas and needs. It is clear that if all group members get what they want, they will likely be satisfied, and collaboration may be seen as a positive management strategy. Collaboration, however, is difficult to maintain and often takes longer than any other conflict management strategy. Thus, once again, we find that the conflict itself should dictate the management strategy needed.

In some situations, group members may choose to accommodate others, compromise, or take the time to engage in collaboration. In other situations, group members may find themselves in competition with one another.

COLLABORATING CONFLICT MANAGEMENT STYLE

PROS:
- Can satisfy all group members
- Can be used to generate new, innovative ideas
- Can positively impact group relationships

CONS:
- Can be extremely difficult
- Can be extremely time-consuming
- May not be worth the time depending on the conflict

Competition

The competing **conflict management style** is evident when group members disagree with other viewpoints and do not necessarily attempt to see things from a different point of view. Competing management styles are often dysfunctional in nature. When group members compete with on another the goal is for one side to "win," while the other side "loses" something.

Group members can solve problems competitively by asserting thoughts and opinions. Think back to chapter 5 where we learned that assertion includes communicating thoughts and feelings with confidence, but not by attacking another person. Unfortunately, competitive

Competing

when group members disagree with other viewpoints and do not necessarily attempt to see things from a different point of view

communication is not always assertive, but can be aggressive. Some-times group members get confrontational and the communication style can be harsh. For example, placing blame, criticizing others, and even threats can creep up when group members solve conflict in a compet-ing manner. These are all aggressive message types.

Even if the communication is not one of these damaging types, the group members that lose are often disappointed. As a result, it is diffi-cult to achieve group satisfaction when applying this conflict manage-ment style. Moreover, group member relationships can be broken if the competition is destructive.

In some cases, group competition can lead to positive results. For instance, if the competition leads to increased motivation to com-plete a task, this would be beneficial to the group. Let's imagine you are part of a recycling group that meets every Tuesday to clean up local neighborhoods. If your group breaks into teams and competes to see which team can clean up their assigned neighborhood the best, or the fastest, this type of competition could be viewed as positive.

COMPETING CONFLICT MANAGEMENT STYLE

PROS:
- Can be useful when on a time crunch
- Can generate innovative ideas
- Can be useful for a short-term solution

CONS:
- Can harm relationships among group members
- Can lead to destructive communication among group members
- Can negatively impact the group long-term

As with other conflict management styles address in this chapter, competition can produce positive or negative effects within the group. Although conflict management styles we use are dependent on many factors such as the topic of conflict, group goals, and group member personalities, research indicates that more integrative types of con-flict management such as collaboration and compromise lead to better group decisions as compared to competitive, avoidant, and/or accom-modating styles (Kuhn & Poole, 2000).

Further, think back to chapter 2 when we focused on two impor-tant dimensions of groups – task and social dimensions. Depending on which dimension the group emphasizes, one conflict management style may be favored over another. For example, if a group is competi-tively managing conflict, they are likely not centered in on the social dimension of the group, and not as concerned about the relationships that could be damaged as a result of competition. Like many things in life, how we choose to manage our conflicts can directly impact the outcome. Conflict management strategies correlate with specific resolution strategies used in groups.

CONFLICT MANAGEMENT STYLE	TASK DIMENSION	SOCIAL DIMENSION
Avoidance	Low	Low
Accommodation	Low	High
Compromise	Moderate	Moderate
Collaboration	High	High
Competition	High	Low

CONFLICT RESOLUTION STRATEGIES

Conflict resolution strategies are ways that we can solve conflict within groups. The resolution strategies used in groups are reflective of the conflict management strategies adopted by group members.

Win-Win

A win-win resolution strategy is when the goal is to satisfy the needs/wants of all group members. Although it may not always be possible to make everyone happy, but when the intent is to do so, this is a win-win mentality. As you can see, when practicing a collaborative conflict management strategy, the aim is typically a win-win resolution tactic.

Lose-Lose

When no group members are happy with the decision or group outcome, this can be considered a lose-lose situation. You might be wondering *why* any group would actually choose a lose-lose resolution strategy. In most cases, this is not an obvious choice, but rather an outcome when group communication is ineffective. When groups are dysfunctional in conflict management, it could end up that no one is satisfied with the result and everyone is disappointed.

Win-Lose

A win-lose resolution strategy is where some group members are satisfied, while others are dissatisfied. This strategy is indicative of the "I win, you lose" mentality that is often associated with a competitive conflict management style. When groups are split in a conflict

Conflict Resolution Strategies

ways that we can solve conflict within groups

Win-Win Resolution Strategy

when the goal is to satisfy the needs/wants of all group members

Lose-Lose Resolution Strategy

when no group members are happy with the decision or group outcome

Win-Lose Resolution Strategy

where some group members are satisfied, while others are dissatisfied

situation, if members are set on getting what they prefer, rather than creating a solution that benefits everyone in the group, a win-lose strategy may be used. As with the conflict management strategies reviewed in this chapter, resolution strategies will differ based upon the group situation.

GROUP CONFLICT RESOLUTION STRATEGY EXAMPLES		
WIN-WIN	*LOSE-LOSE*	*WIN-LOSE*
A group of friends decide to go on a spring break trip. Half want to visit a beach, and the other half want to check out an amusement park. The group researches vacation spots that include both types of locations within 25 miles of one another and choose a hotel in the middle of the beach and park.	A group of friends decide to go on a spring break trip. Half want to visit a beach, and the other half want to check out an amusement park. Group members begin arguing about where to go, and as a result the entire trip gets cancelled. No one goes anywhere on spring break and everyone loses.	A group of friends decide to go on a spring break trip. Half want to visit a beach, and the other half want to check out an amusement park. Group members decide to research options and go with the least expensive option. In the end, the group ends up heading to the beach for spring break. Although the trip is fun, some are still bummed they don't get to the amusement park.

WHAT IMPACTS GROUP CONFLICT?

Culture

Think back to chapter 3 when we learned about culture and diversity in groups. We reviewed various types of group cultural orientations such as individualistic and collectivist cultures, high versus low-uncertainty avoidance cultures, and masculine versus feminine cultures. Often, groups include members from various culture types, and this can result in differences in perceptions.

As we know, differing perceptions can often lead to conflict and can also complicate conflict management. One study looked at differences between Turkish and American college students and their propensity toward arguments. The results of the study showed that Turkish students are more likely to approach arguments than are Americans (Demier & Hample, 2019). This is only one example of cultural differences, but if group members vary in terms of argumentation and conflict, such differences will surely impact the group overall.

Further, cultural variations in groups can cause conflict on certain topics (i.e., how to handle a situation with an outside group), as well as impact how groups communicate about the conflict (i.e., aggressively versus calmly). As Ting-Toomey and Oetzel argue in their book on intercultural conflict, if groups approach conflict in an ethnocentric manner, the conflict situation will only worsen. It is important to acknowledge culture as it impacts the group and work together to overcome cultural barriers for a productive outcome. In addition to cultural diversity, gender can impact group conflict.

Gender

Gender refers to masculine or feminine roles enacted by people. Masculine gender roles are often thought of in terms of competitiveness, aggression, and independent, while feminine roles are considered more cooperative, nurturing, and interdependent. As you can imagine, and have probably experienced, when two group members encompass different gender roles, conflict may arise.

Moreover, those who are masculine may approach conflict management different than a more feminine group member. Considering task, relational, and value conflict types covered earlier in this chapter, one gender type may be better suited in conflict management than another. As with other characteristics, there is no one right or wrong way to approach conflict but being respectful to dissimilar opinions is always necessary to effective communication, especially in times of conflict.

Gender

masculine or feminine roles enacted by people

Power

In chapter 5, we learned about different types of power bases. Some people are granted legitimate power, while others are granted expert power. We not only know that people hold various types of power, but that there are often power imbalances within a group. Such power struggles can certainly lead to conflict within a group. Avoiding powerless language, asserting your thoughts and opinions, and empowering others is one way to better manage conflict even with power issues within the group.

Environmental Factors

Have you ever just woken up on the wrong side of the bed? Feel your mood has been affected by the weather, or had some event just cause you to feel negatively? Environmental factors are components outside of us that impact our communication with others. Examples include things such as gray skies, traffic, time changes, and even other people around us. Certain factors in the environment can certainly impact group conflicts, including the medium groups use to communicate.

© fizkes/Shutterstock.com

When virtual groups began growing in popularity, researchers thought there might be a difference in groups that meet face-to-face versus online. Though they found more conflict in groups meeting online relating to group processes and relationships initially, after some time, there was no difference (Hobman, 2002). These findings, however, may not be the same for all groups and some may engage in more conflict in one channel versus another.

We cannot control for all the variables that may impact group conflict, but we can be aware that conflict does not happen in a vacuum. We must recognize that there are so many things that play a role in group conflict, so focusing in only one component may not permit us to view the big picture. When we enlarge our "window to the world" and acknowledge other factors, we have a better opportunity to manage group conflict effectively and efficiently.

TIPS FOR GROUPS IN CONFLICT

As we wrap up chapter 6, let's turn to a few tips on how handle group conflict effectively when it arises. Although there is no exhaustive list on how to manage conflict, and solutions are context-based, there are some communication strategies that are helpful in most situations. Empathy has been defined as seeing things from another's perspective. We know that empathy is important in our interpersonal relationships, but it is also important when we are facing intergroup conflicts. When investigating psychological processes associated with intergroup conflict, Stephan (2008) argued that emotional empathy is valuable in order to let the other groups know that there is concern for the welfare of both groups. This can be very useful when trying to effectively resolve conflict between groups. Furthermore, groups can be trained in emotional empathy to better learn how to look at things from the perspective of another and resolve conflict.

Another key communication behavior that is important when trying to resolve group conflict is to engage in listening. Listening involves more than just hearing. Hearing is physiological in nature and is much less involved than listening, which is more psychological. When we engage in true listening, we pay attention to the message and we try to process that message, as opposed to simply letting the sound waves bounce off of our eardrums. When we engage in active listening, we will be better able to understand the perspective of others and respond appropriately.

Finally, if we want to effectively manage conflict within group situations, one way to do so is to create a communication climate that is positive. Group communication climates are essentially the tone or the feeling within the group. When the climate is tense, people might feel less obliged to communicate effectively with one another. In situations that are uncomfortable some people may shut down and

Empathy

seeing things from another's perspective

Group Communication Climates

the tone or the feeling within the group

avoid communication altogether, while others might get competitive in nature. To create positive communication climates, groups should be open to new ideas and perspectives, welcoming, empowering, and inclusive. When the communication climate is positive and welcoming, more group members might feel comfortable sharing their thoughts and feelings which may ultimately lead to better conflict resolution.

SUMMARY

Every day we see groups in conflict. Some conflict is inter-group, while some is intra-group. From hockey players during a game to political groups, we see the inevitability of group conflict. In this chapter, we have reviewed several different conflict management styles, as well as how those styles manifest in resolution strategies.

Further, we have learned that conflict can be functional or dysfunctional, often depending on how it is managed. Conflict is impacted by several variables, and sometimes that can be difficult to manage. As we conclude this chapter, think about group conflicts you have experienced first-hand. How did you manage the conflict? How was it resolved, if at all? What could have been done differently to more effectively help the group reach goals?

REFLECTION QUESTIONS

1. What are the five components of conflict? Illustrate each component in the setting of a group conflict.
2. What is the difference between inter-group and intra-group conflict?
3. How can group conflict be functional?
4. Explain task, relational, and value group conflicts. Provide an example for each.
5. Which conflict management style is the best? Worst? Defend your answer.
6. How can each conflict management style be positive for group outcomes? Negative?
7. What are three conflict resolution strategies and how do they relate to the five conflict management strategies?
8. What influence does culture have on group conflict? What about gender?
9. What are other variables that impact group conflict?

LEARNING BY ACTION

We know that all groups – no matter the type – engage in conflict. Some conflicts are minor, and others are significant. Nevertheless, the way in which groups manage conflict can create long-lasting implications. In small groups (four to five students), have them identify a group on campus. This could be student senate, a fraternity/sorority, or any other structured group on campus. Groups should identify one or two members to meet with the identified group to discuss one conflict the group faced. This may be a past or present conflict. In addition to learning about the group conflict, they should discuss what strategies were used (or are currently being used) to manage the group conflict. If dealing with a conflict that has already been resolved, have students evaluate the strategy utilized. If the group is facing a current conflict, students may analyze the conflict situation and propose a strategy to help the group effectively resolve the issue. The students may then present their solutions to the group (if, and only if, the group would like the suggestions). Upon completion, all groups may present their conclusions to the rest of the class. With all of the shared information, the class can compare and contrast various conflict types and management strategies, as well as the effectiveness of each.

VIDEO CLIP

In 2020, *Trolls World Tour* was released. The second film in the hit animated series features a beloved group of trolls who live in harmony and love. One day, however, the group of trolls find out that they are actually not the only group of trolls and there are other groups (called tribes) who live in a different land. Each tribe is devoted to a different type of music, and the rock group is planning to take over the world and destroy other music types. In the film, two tribes clash and engage in conflict. While this film is clearly fictional, many of the concepts covered in chapter 6 are illustrated in the film. After watching the film, students may identify several types of conflicts shown between the tribes. In addition, students can analyze and evaluate the conflict management strategies used, as well as suggest techniques that may have been more effective.

CONTEMPORARY COMMUNICATION

When engaged in conflict with others, communication can be difficult. The difficulty is escalated when the conflict is a group conflict and many people are involved. In order to effectively resolve conflict, we often have to engage in crucial conversations that can sometimes be uncomfortable or tough to have with others. There is an application available on most smartphone platforms, called "crucial confrontations." This application helps people work through difficult topics to help resolve conflicts. Many times, our conflicts are a result of expectations that were violated, differences of opinion, or instances of bad behavior. This application helps the user discover skills to resolve conflict in any type of situation, including group situations.

CASES IN COMMUNICATION

You work at the local sporting goods store. New owners recently bought the store and decide to host a "Grand Re-Opening." The owners would like to host an event on an upcoming Saturday where local community members are invited to the store to see all that the store has to offer. Specifically, they want to fill the parking lot with new sports equipment for customers to check out, have food and drink, and hire a band for entertainment. You, along with four of your co-workers, have been assigned to the "food and drink" committee. As a group, you must decide what food to serve, how to serve it, and from where to order the food. This must be done within an assigned budget of no more than $500. At the committee's first meeting, the initial conversation goes as follows:

You:	I am so excited for the grand re-opening! Let's start with ideas on what food to serve.
Dana:	I'm excited also! I was thinking if the weather is nice, we could grill hotdogs.
Bill:	Wait a minute… who is going to stand behind a grill all day? I'm surely not! That idea is dumb.
Dana:	Thanks for calling my idea dumb, you jerk! Do you have a better idea?
Bill:	Yes, I do. We can just have bottles of water and chips. Easy!
Dana:	Well, that's not a lot of food. I don't think that's what the owners imagined. What do you think, Angela?
Angela:	I'm okay with whatever… Just tell me what to do and I will do it!
Dana:	That's not very helpful. What about you, Len?
Len:	Ummm, I'm not sure yet. Please excuse me – I need to take this call (exits room).
You:	Okay, we are not makei. So far, we have chips and hotdogs as ideas. Why can't we just have both and that's a great little lunch for the customers! Also, then both Bill and Dana are happy.
Bill:	Fine, but I will not be helping with the grilling at all. I will only put out the chips. Dana can grill all on her own!
You:	Okay, we can talk about jobs later. How about we move on to drinks for now?
Bill:	I already suggested water. What else could we possibly need?
Dana:	Water is okay, but a little boring. Maybe we can have a few other drink options also.
Bill:	Sounds like too much work for me! Another dumb idea…

1. What conflict management style does each character in the story illustrate?
2. Is this conflict functional or dysfunctional? Why? Defend your answer.
3. What communication strategies might you use to help resolve the conflict in the group?

Conflict Management Styles Assessment

Directions: Please CIRCLE ONE response that best describes you. Be honest, this survey is designed to help you learn about your conflict management style. There are no right or wrong answers!

	RARELY	SOMETIMES	OFTEN	ALWAYS
1. I discuss issues with others to try to find solutions that meet everyone's needs.	1	2	3	4
2. I try to negotiate and use a give-and-take approach to problem situations.	1	2	3	4
3. I try to meet the expectations of others.	1	2	3	4
4. I would argue my case and insist on the advantages of my point of view.	1	2	3	4
5. When there is a disagreement, I gather as much information as I can and keep the lines of communication open.	1	2	3	4
6. When I find myself in an argument, I usually say very little and try to leave as soon as possible.	1	2	3	4
7. I try to see conflicts from both sides. What do I need? What does the other person need? What are the issues involved?	1	2	3	4
8. I prefer to compromise when solving problems and just move on.	1	2	3	4
9. I find conflicts exhilarating; I enjoy the battle of wits that usually follows.	1	2	3	4
10. Being in a disagreement with other people makes me feel uncomfortable and anxious.	1	2	3	4
11. I try to meet the wishes of my friends and family.	1	2	3	4

12. I can figure out what needs to be done and I am usually right.	1	2	3	4
13. To break deadlocks, I would meet people halfway.	1	2	3	4
14. I may not get what I want but it's a small price to pay for keeping the peace.	1	2	3	4
15. I avoid hard feelings by keeping my disagreements with others to myself.	1	2	3	4

Source: Reginald (Reg) Adkins, Ph.D., Elemental Truths. http://elementaltruths. blogspot.com/2006/11/conflictmanagement-quiz.html

Scoring the Conflict Management Styles Assessment

As stated, the 15 statements correspond to the five conflict management styles. To find your most preferred style, total the points for each style. The style with the highest score indicates your most commonly used strategy. The one with the lowest score indicates your least preferred strategy. However, all styles have pros and cons, so it's important that you can use the most appropriate style for each conflict situation.

Style Corresponding Statements: *Total:*

Collaborating (questions 1, 5, 7):   _____

Competing: (questions 4, 9, 12):   _____

Avoiding: (questions 6, 10, 15):   _____

Accommodating: (questions 3, 11, 14):   _____

Compromising: (questions 2, 8, 13):   _____

REFERENCES

Canary, D.J., & Messman, S.J. (2000). Relationship conflict. In C. Hendrick & S. S. Hendrick (Eds.), *Close relationships: A sourcebook* (pp. 261-270). Thousand Oaks, CA: Sage.

Cargile, A. C., Bradac, J. J., & Cole, T. (2006). Theories of intergroup conflict: A report of lay attributions. *Journal of Language & Social Psychology, 25*(1), 47–63. https://doi-org.proxy.library.ohio. edu/10.1177/0261927X05284479

Demir, Y., & Hample, D. (2019). A cross-cultural study of argument orientations of Turkish and American college students: Is silence really golden and speech silver for Turkish students? *Argumentation*, *33*(4), 521–540. https://doi-org.proxy.library.ohio.edu/10.1007/s10503-019-09483-1

Hobman, E. V. (2002). The expression of conflict in computer-mediated and face-to-face groups. *Small Group Research*, *33*(4), 439–465.

Kuhn, T., & Poole, M. S. (2000). Do conflict management styles affect group decision making? *Human Communication Research*, *26*(4), 558. https://doi-org.proxy.library.ohio.edu/10.1111/j.1468-2958.2000.tb00769.x

Stephan, W. G. (2008). Psychological and communication processes associated with intergroup conflict resolution. *Small Group Research*, *39*(1), 28–41.

Ting-Toomey, S., & Oetzel, J. G. (2001). *Managing Intercultural Conflict Effectively*. Thousand Oaks, CA: Sage.

Wall, V. D., & Nolan, L. L. (1987). Small group conflict: A look at equity, satisfaction, and styles of conflict management. *Small Group Behavior*, *18*(2), 188-211. https://doi.org/10.1177/104649648701800204

Wilmot, W., & Hocker, J. (2011). *Interpersonal Conflict (8th ed.)*. New York, NY: McGraw Hill.

Zhu, Q., Skoric, M., & Shen, F. (2017). I shield myself from thee: Selective avoidance on social media during political protests. *Political Communication*, *34*(1), 112–131. https://doi-org.proxy.library.ohio.edu/10.1080/10584609.2016.1222471

LEARNING OBJECTIVES

After studying chapter 7 you should be able to:

- Define leadership.
- Differentiate the three primary leadership styles.
- Explain the trait, situational, and contingency theories of leadership.
- Summarize telling, selling, delegating, and participating leadership styles.
- Outline the steps need to emerge as leader.
- Analyze the difference between leaders and managers.
- Recognize communication skills need to effectively lead groups.
- Explain why it is important to lead ethically.

George Washington – *First President of the United States*
Phil Jackson – *Former NBA player and coach*
Margaret Thatcher – *Former U.K. Prime Minister*
Neil Armstrong – *Astronaut, first to walk on the moon*
Condoleezza Rice – *Former U.S. Secretary of State*
Winston Churchill – *Former British Prime Minister*
Michelle Obama – *Former First Lady*
Nelson Mandela – *Former President of South Africa*
Martin Luther King, Jr. – *Activist Civil Rights Movement*

What do the people listed above all have in common? If your guess is that they are all leaders, you are correct! In any group situation, it is important to have strong leaders. All persons listed above were regarded as great leaders in their own right. This list, of course, is not exhaustive, but does include examples of leaders from various sectors.

In chapter 7, we will focus on the role of leadership in groups. A good leader can be the cornerstone of a productive groups, while a bad leader can destroy a group. Leadership is a multi-faceted concept that is central when studying group processes. In this chapter, we will define leadership, types of leadership, examine various theories about leadership, and address the way in which group members may become leaders. To begin, we must define the term leadership.

© donskarpo/Shutterstock.com

WHAT IS LEADERSHIP?

Leadership is an important part of group communication. Similar to "communication," leadership has been defined in several ways. In 2018, Johnson and Hackman defined leadership as "human (symbolic) communication that modifies the attitudes and behaviors of others in order to meet the shared group goals and needs" (p. 12). Others has defined leadership in terms of specific behaviors or personality characteristics. Further, some define leadership in terms of roles people play within groups. Nevertheless, in order to be a leader, one must effectively communicate. For that reason, communication is an integral part of leadership and, should be explicitly included in its definition.

As a result, the definition of **leadership** we will use in this text is the communication process used by persons in an attempt to influence followers to meet group goals. Leadership is not a simple concept. Rather, leadership is a *process* of communication where communicators can simultaneously exchange messages (called **transactional communication**). In other words, leadership is not a one-way street.

When communication is transactional, this means that both sender and receiver can simultaneously send messages and mutually influence one another. One cannot lead without followers, and one cannot follow without a leader (see Platow, Haslam, Reicher, & Steffens, 2015).

All of the leaders listed at the start of this chapter had a significant number of followers. Many followers did not know the leader personally, yet still were influenced by their leadership. Without their followers, near and far, they would not be leaders. As much as the followers

Leadership

the communication process used by persons in an attempt to influence followers to meet group goals

Transactional Communication

when communicators simultaneously exchange messages both verbally and/or nonverbally

were persuaded to behave a certain way or believe in something, the leaders were influenced by those whom chose to follow. As with any role in life, not all leaders are the same. There are various types of leadership styles present in groups.

LEADERSHIP STYLES

A psychologist named Kurt Lewin worked with colleagues to develop a typology (or classification) of leadership styles in 1939. The researchers identified three primary leaderships styles: democratic, authoritarian, and laissez-faire styles.

Typology
classification

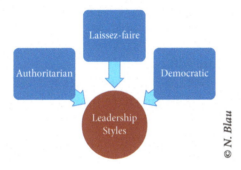
© N. Blau

Democratic Leadership

The democratic leadership style includes shared power and governance among group members. Rather than the leader using power to control other group members, power is more evenly distributed among the group. When it comes to decision-making, democratic leaders include group members in the process and value their input. In fact, instead of the leader making the decision unilaterally, often the group votes on decisions.

In addition, democratic leaders often share responsibilities with other group members. For this reason, when others in the group participate in tasks and decision-making, this style of leadership is sometimes referred to as participatory leadership. When group members perceive the leader is sharing control, this often results in increased satisfaction and commitment (see Puni, Ofei,& Okoe, 2014).

Democratic leadership is often regarded positively, but there can also be negatives. For instance, if group members do not have the knowledge and/or skill set to accomplish goals or complete tasks, this leadership style may not be ideal. While empowering others and providing members a voice is always "good," it is not always the best way to attain goals. This may especially be true if time is a factor. If the group is on a short time limit, there may not be enough time to take all opinions and ideas into consideration. In instances such as this, a more authoritarian leadership style may be needed.

Democratic Leadership style

shared governance and power among group members

PROS & CONS OF DEMOCRATIC LEADERSHP	
PROS	*CONS*
Leaves room for creativity & innovation	Can take more time to make decisions
Works well when the problem is complex	Not all group members may participate
Provides satisfaction for group members	Feelings can get hurt if ideas are not adopted by the group

Authoritarian Leadership

Authoritarian Leadership Style

leadership style in which the leader typically seizes control within the group and does not often relinquish such control

Often thought of as the opposite of the democratic leadership style is the authoritarian leadership style. An authoritarian leader (sometimes called an autocratic leader) typically seizes control within the group and does not often relinquish said control. In a group led by an authoritarian leader, there is often a very clear hierarchy between those with power and those without power.

Unlike groups with a democratic leader, authoritarian leaders do not let others in the group share in decision-making. Because the authoritarian leader likes to maintain control within the group, the communication differs in this type of group. Instead of using empowering and open communication, direct orders are typically used by authoritarian leaders. Authoritarian leaders make expectations very clear and allow little room for group members to "think outside the box" or come up with novel solutions.

Employee Burnout

when an employee becomes disengaged with their work often showing signs of exhaustion and apathy

When this leadership style was studied in the workplace, research showed that the authoritarian leadership style related to increased employee burnout (Kelly & MacDonald, 2019). Employee burnout occurs when an employee becomes disengaged with his or her work, often showing signs of exhaustion and apathy. Employees can easily get burned out when working to meet leader expectations.

© Grindstone Media Group/ Shutterstock.com

Vince Lombardi was a famous coach for many years in the National Football League. Lombardi was the head coach of the Green Bay Packers where he won six NFL championships, two Super Bowls, and was named the NFL Coach of the Year not once, but twice. Coach Lombardi was considered an authoritarian leader. It was no secret that he valued discipline and believed that if the team won or lost, it was due to his own decisions. In his quest to win, he instituted a military-type style when leading his team to victory. He had very high expectations for his players and made all team decisions and laid out every task. The players – Lombardi's followers – were obedient and listened to their leader. In this case, the authoritarian leadership style was effective.

Groups led by authoritarian leaders are usually very structured and controlled. Even though this leadership style is seemingly negative, if group members do not have the proper expertise to attain the group goals, this type of leadership may be necessary. Similarly, if group members are not motivated to complete tasks, the authoritarian style can be useful.

Some democratic leaders will change over time and become authoritarian. It is much more difficult, however, for authoritarian leaders to convert to a more democratic leadership style (Lewin, Lippitt, & White, 1939). It would be even more difficult for an authoritarian leader to relinquish all control as in laissez-faire leadership.

PROS & CONS OF AUTHORITARIAN LEADERSHP	
PROS	*CONS*
Efficient; good when time constraints are present	Discourages creativity and innovation
When groups are not cohesive and need strong leadership, a clear authoritative leader can help provide direction	Group members feel they do not get a voice
Provides structure for group members	Can lead to decreased satisfaction of group members

Laissez-faire Leadership

Different from both democratic and authoritarian leadership styles is the laissez-faire style. Loosely translated, laissez-faire means "hands off." Keeping this meaning in mind, the laissez-faire leadership style is one in which the leader provides very little structure for the group. There is very little control from this type of leader.

The laissez-faire leader allows group members to act as they wish. In addition, this type of leader typically does not make decisions, but lets the group make decisions. There is very little overt action taken by this type of leader. Because the laissez-faire leader is so hands off, research indicates that often groups with this type of leader are not very productive (Anbazhagan & Kotur, 2014).

Now, this may not be true in highlight motivated groups. When group members are skilled and motivated, they may not necessarily need a leader dictating every move. A leader may leave the group members to their own devices and the group may be able to accomplish the group goals effectively. For instance, Paul Allen, one of the co-founders of Microsoft, was a hands-off leader. Allen was passionate about creativity and desired to empower his followers to believe in their own talents and figure out how to get the job done well. Many of Allen's employees appreciated his leadership style and were motivated to be productive.

If group members, however, are *not* motivated, then this type of leadership may result in less productivity. In fact, sometimes a laissez-faire leadership style is perceived by group members as the leader not caring or not being involved with the group. If this is the case, this may lead to a decrease in group member satisfaction.

Laissez-faire Leadership Style

the leader provides very little structure for the group

PROS & CONS OF LAISSEZ-FAIRE LEADERSHP	
PROS	**CONS**
Allows group members to be creative	Group members may lose confidence in the leader
Can provide feelings of independence for group members	It can take longer to accomplish group goals with little structure
Group members learn to build their own leaderships skills	Group members can break into smaller groups or cliques impacting group cohesion

WHICH LEADERSHIP STYLE IS IT?	
1. Suzy is the leader of a local group that walks dogs for community members that need assistance. For next week, they have requests from 50 clients, but only have five group members available to walk dogs. They need to decide how many clients they can service and whom (if any) they must turn down. Suzy holds a group meeting and asks for everyone's opinions. After all ideas have been shared, the group votes on the best option.	ANSWERS:
2. Jim is the leader of a student service organization that must provide service within the local community at least seven times per year. Jim calls a meeting at the start of the year an announces the group must come up with seven service commitments for the upcoming months. Jim then tells the group he has another meeting to attend, and that they can decide on the commitments as they please. The group members are asked to email Jim when they have "mapped out" their year of service.	1 = democratic; 2 = laissez-faire; 3 = authoritarian
3. Tina is the team leader of five employees in the student affairs office at her university. The team will be hosting a new student orientation later in the week where they will provide new students important information, as well as provide a campus tour. Tina needs to decide the best way to present the information and schedule tours, but instead of asking for input from her team members she solely decides on the schedule. She then types up the orientation schedule, who will be doing what, and emails her team. They are simply told to be on time and ready to work.	

THEORIES ON LEADERSHIP

Now that we know the definition of leadership as well as the three primary classifications of leadership, we can turn to the various perspectives on leadership. There are many different ideas of what makes an effective leader. Some believe certain people possess specific traits that make a good leader. Others believe quality leadership is contingent on the situation. Thus, let's look at common leadership perspectives.

Trait Theory of Leadership

Trait Theory of Leadership

the idea that leaders are born with certain traits that make them an effective leader

Originally developed from Thomas Caryle's "Great Man Theory" and later advanced by Ralph Stogdill in 1948, the first theory is called the **trait theory of leadership**. As the name suggests, this theory is based on the idea that leaders are born with certain traits that make them an effective leader. Some people are born with these traits, and others are not.

A trait is a distinct quality or characteristic a person has that is relatively stable over time. Traits that make a good leader can include physical traits, such as physical appearance and vocal qualities, or personality traits. Physical traits often associated with great leaders include things such as stature, height, and attractiveness levels. While we know that being an attractive person may not necessarily make you a great leader, it is also known that people like to be around those who are considered attractive by cultural standards. Thus, we often grant power to those who are physically attractive and allow them to lead.

The trait theory of leadership, however, is most known for the idea that leaders exhibit certain personality characteristics or traits that make him or her an effective leader. Positive personality traits such as being perceived as intelligent, competent, trustworthy, and credible are typically associated with great leaders. In addition, some researchers found that emotional stability, or one's ability to remain emotionally in balance when necessary, makes for a strong leader (see McCall & Lombardo, 1983).

Trait

a distinct quality or characteristic a person has that is relatively stable over time

Emotional Stability

one's ability to remain emotionally in balance when necessary

SAMPLE OF TRAITS ASSOCIATED WITH LEADERS	
TRAIT	**DESCRIPTION**
Confidence	Leaders must feel and act as if they are equipped to handle the situation faced; this also builds confidence in followers.
Motivated	Leaders must not only be able to lead but feel passionate to do so.
Trustworthy	Leaders must be perceived as honest; followers need to trust a leader.
Knowledgeable/Intelligent	Leaders must know how to lead and have the intellect to lead.
Assertive	Leaders must be able to communicate their opinions and instructions without being aggressive or attacking others.
Dependable	Leaders are people followers need to be able to rely on; they must "show up" for their followers.
Tolerant	Leaders must be accepting of others; not everyone will follow automatically, so leaders must be able to work with various types of people and situations.
Perseverance	Leaders must be able to "stick it out" even when situations are difficult.

In a well-known research study that explored the "big five" personality traits and employee satisfaction with leadership in the workplace, researchers found that when leaders exhibited high levels of emotional stability, extraversion, and agreeableness, subordinates reported greater satisfaction. This, in turn, leads to lower turnover rates (see Smith & Canger, 2004).

When this theory was initially created, it made sense to a lot of people. In fact, it still does to some extent. Thinking back on great leaders in history, we see certain traits that are common among all of these people. For instance, John F. Kennedy was not only smart, but motivated, trustworthy and related well to his followers. These types of traits inherently seemed to fit the idea of an effective leader. To this day, this theory still holds up and most people believe that leaders must exhibit certain personality traits in order to communicate effectively with followers.

Our Nation's President

Our Nation's President Think of our current President of the United States. Being our nation's leader, do you feel this person is a good or bad leader? What traits does this person have the directly impact their ability to lead others?

The trait theory of leadership, however, indicate that these traits must be innate. A person may have certain traits listed above, but still not make a good leader. Moreover, the theory suggests that these traits cannot be learned, or that they're *just there* and will work in every type of situation. Therefore, over the years, researchers have begun to question this theory and look at other perspectives that make leaders effective. For instance, the context may play a role in the success of a leader.

Situational Theory of Leadership

Situational Theory of Leadership

appropriate leadership is determined by the situation; different situations call for diverse leadership styles

Unlike the trait theory that assumes leaders have certain traits which help them successfully lead others, the situational theory of leadership states that appropriate leadership is determined by the situation. Specifically, different situations call for diverse leadership styles. When you are placed in a group during class to complete an activity, the situation may look very different than a major group project for which you will be graded. Thus, the leadership for the smaller, in-class group activity will not be the same type of leadership needed for the larger project.

According to this situational perspective, leaders must be willing and able to adapt to the situation. Think of those working in law enforcement. When called to investigate a situation they could face anything from helping a child find a lost dog to a murder scene. Clearly, flexibility to respond appropriately to the situation is needed.

A well-known model of situational leadership was developed by Dr. Paul Hersey and Ken Blanchard. This model classified four leadership styles: telling, selling, delegating, and participating.

Telling Style

the group leader "tells" or instructs followers on what to do as well as how to do it

The telling style occurs when the group leader "tells" or instructs followers on what to do as well as how to do it. Recently, a group of high school students were working on building a retaining wall in my backyard. There was only one student who knew the steps to properly construct the wall, so he explicitly directed the others on what to do when and how to do it. This leader enacted a telling style of leadership.

Next is the selling style where a leader tries to "sell" his or her ideas to the group and negotiate with group members in an attempt to get them to follow their lead. Consider a group situation where the leader presents an idea, but other group members have different ideas on how to accomplish the goal. If the leader is using a selling style, he or she might try to persuade the other group members that their idea is the best idea. They may go back and forth and communication with other group members in order to sell their idea or persuade others to follow.

As the name suggests, leaders utilizing a delegating style divvy up tasks and "hand out" jobs to group members. Group members take most of the responsibility for any decisions made as the leader is very hands off with this type of style. The delegating leadership style is often used by laissez-faire leaders.

Finally, the participating style is one in which leaders relinquish some control and allow group members to actively play a role in decision-making and problem-solving. The leader participates in group tasks, as do other group members. The participating style is a more democratic form of leadership.

Leaders practicing a situational style, must first analyze the situation, take inventory of the skills of the group members, and then choose a leadership style that will work. Any sports-related move always has some leader (whether it be a captain of the team or the coach) who must size up the group he/she is leading in order to effectively lead them to a victory. Often, the leadership style he or she begins with is not the leadership style that is most appropriate for that team. Often, it depends on the maturity level of the team that needs to be led.

In their work, Hersey and Blanchard also investigated the maturity level of leaders as it relates to their leadership style. They found that leaders who are low in maturity are more likely to employ a telling style. Those whom showed moderate maturity, but limited skill sets, were most likely to use these selling leadership style. Those with moderate maturity, but more of a skill set, used more of a participatory style. Finally, leaders who were considered high in terms of maturity often used a delegating style. Not every leader who is low in terms of maturity will use the telling style and not every leader who has high maturity levels will use the delegating style. These are trends, but there are always exceptions to every rule.

Think back to chapter 2 when we learned about the task and social dimensions of groups. Whereas the task dimension refers to functionality of the group (the outcome is productivity), the social dimension centers on relationships formed among group members (the outcome is cohesiveness). With regard to these dimensions, various leadership styles lend themselves more to one dimension or another. Just as we

Selling Style
a leader tries to "sell" his or her ideas to the group and negotiate with group members in an attempt to get them to follow their lead

Delegating Style
the leader simply divvies up tasks and "hands out" jobs to group members

Participating Style
leaders relinquish some control and allow group members to actively play a role in decision-making and problem-solving

learned earlier in this text, some group situations require more of a task, or productivity, orientation and others allow for more relationship building.

	TASK DIMENSION	
	Low	High
SOCIAL DIMENSION High	Participating Style	Selling Style
Low	Delegating Style	Telling Style

© N. Blau

As with the trait perspective, the situational leadership style has both positives and negatives. On the positive side, this leadership style allows the leader of the group to employ a strategy that will work best in a particular context or group. Group tasks, relationships, and even membership can change over time, and this leadership styles allows flexibility as those changes arise.

While this style allows for flexibility, the group leader needs to be aware of a plethora of information such as the disposition of the group members, the complexity of the group task, and maturity levels within the group. For these reasons, being able to adapt to all the group nuances can be challenging.

Contingency Theory of Leadership

Contingency Theory of Leadership

the belief that the best leadership style in a group situation is dependent on specific variables

From time to time, particular group variables necessitate a specific leadership style. The belief that the best leadership style in a group situation is dependent on specific variables is the contingency theory of leadership. Now, this leadership theory may sound very much like the situational leadership style. If you thought that, you are correct. They are similar. They are also dissimilar in some ways.

Unlike a situational style wherein the leader assesses the situation and then chooses a style, the contingency theory states leaders don't apply a certain style, but rather can adopt leadership behaviors depending on the variables needed. Thus, the leader may start off focused on the task and less on the social dimension, but this may quickly change as the situation changes.

There are several contingency theories, but they are all alike in that the common idea is that there is not one "best" or "right" leadership style. The best style is the one that suits a given group, task, and variables facing the leader. You may have a leader who is intelligent, likeable, assertive and have many other positive traits, but still struggle to lead a certain group. In this case, it is not the leader traits, but other variables influencing leader behaviors.

So, what type of variables impact leadership style according to the contingency theory? Environmental factors impacting group problems and decision-making can impact leader behaviors. For instance, in 2020, most of the United States shut down for a period of time due to the global coronavirus pandemic. College students enrolled in face-to-face classes had to suddenly transition to an online format. In one class, groups were working on a large class project and their work had to change as they could

© SergioVas/Shutterstock.com

no longer meet in person to work. Due to the circumstances, group leaders had to adapt to this "new normal" and adjust accordingly.

Similarly, variables, such as group member beliefs, work ethics, motivation, and organizational cultures can impact leadership styles. Think about a group to which you belong. What variables impact the leadership within that group? Now, how might that leadership style change if those variables were modified?

Leadership is often regarded positively in our culture. In fact, many people strive to earn leadership roles within groups. Not everyone, however, wants to become a leader. Others desire to lead but may not ever become a leader. In the next section of this chapter, we take a look at how people become leaders within groups.

BECOMING AN EFFECTIVE LEADER

Perhaps you are a part of a group and you believe you could serve as a great leader. Maybe you aspire to be a leader in the future. How does one become a leader? In this section, we will explore ways leaders emerge in groups. Before looking at the process, it is important to note what leaders are *not*.

© Vitalii Vodolazskyi/Shutterstock.com

Leaders are not managers. Too often, we see these terms used interchangeably and the two are not the same. A **manager** is someone who is assigned authority within a group to administer group functions and maintain the current state of the group. Leaders, in contrast, can be appointed, but this is not always the case. Leaders can emerge naturally from group processes.

Manager

someone who is assigned authority within a group to administer group functions and maintain the current state of the group

If you think back to the stages of group development reviewed in chapter 2, we learned that many group members do not know one another when the group is initially formed. It is through communication that some roles are defined, and this may include leadership. Thus, unlike managers who are often hired into the position of authority, leaders emerge as the group develops.

If you have ever worked in the retail field, you have likely witnessed a manager first-hand. Managers are responsible to keep order over their group and make sure tasks are accomplished. This may even be the same task day after day and the manager is charged with keeping everything in order – not necessarily making changes. Leaders, on the other hand, strive to bring about change. Moreover, leaders are often passionate about making the group better in some way and leading others to change positively.

Transformational Leadership

leaders who bring about change

Leaders are transformational. **Transformational leadership** refers to those who bring about change (see Bass & Bass, 2008). True leaders transform situations and groups for the better. Mangers simply focus on using communication that keeps things (or groups) operating as they should. Some managers can be leaders, but this is not true all of the time. The two roles are seemingly similar, but they are also different. As Peter Drucker once said, "Management is doing things right; leadership is doing the right things."

Like managers, some leaders are appointed (or designated) to or from the group. For instance, each year our campus student senate appoints a new president to lead the group. This is an example of a **designated leader**. Other times, leadership emerges from the group dynamics. I recently watched a group work together to plan a disc golf tournament to raise money for a local charity. At the start, the students had no designated leader, so they just began sharing ideas. As time went on, however, a certain group member began communicating in a manner that not only managed the group, but also empowered group members to put their effort into the project. By the time the event occurred, all group members agreed that this person was the leader of the group. There was no election or appointment – it happened organically.

Designated Leader

leaders are appointed to or from the group

As with the group planning the disc golf tournament, leadership emerged as a *process* – it took time. As indicated in the definition of leadership provided earlier in this chapter, leadership is a progression where one person persuades others to follow. Until group members begin following, the person is not a leader.

So, what does this process look like? First, group members need to decide on the group goal. Often, the goal impacts who may be chosen as a leader. Sometimes, this goal is chosen for the group, other times it is chosen by the group. Either way, the group must know their goal.

Next, group members who are unwilling or unable to lead are excluded. Some members may not have the appropriate skill set or knowledge base to lead. Others may have the skills, but not the desire to lead. In order to be an effective leader, one must both have skills and motivation to do so. If not, it is not likely he/she will be a good leader.

Third, leader skills must be assessed with the group goal(s) in mind. For instance, one group member may be skilled when it comes to technology, but the group goal has nothing to do with that skill set. Thus, they may not be chosen as the best person to lead the group. Once leader candidates have been evaluated in terms of skills, traits, and motivation, a leader can emerge.

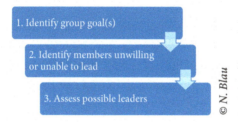

These steps in the process may occur overtly and a leader is chosen specifically by the group members. Alternatively, via group communication, it may become clear who is willing and able to lead the group. Often, the leader will send messages clearly indicating knowledge and passion to lead the group. As a result, a leader may emerge.

Like other processes, this process may take time. The leader, however, may not truly be considered a leader until he/she begins communicating in a way that group members follow. When the group begins effectively working toward its goal, the leader has emerged. Once a leader is acknowledged – via designation or emergence – he or she must communicate effectively. Thus, we turn to a review of communication skills leaders must practice in order to be successful.

EFFECTIVE LEADER COMMUNICATION

Leaders Must Be Emotionally Intelligent

Emotional intelligence is one's ability to consciously control emotions and the communication of those emotions. We all get angry, upset, and frustrated from time to time. This is normal and leaders experience these emotions as well. As we all know from personal experience, it can be difficult at times to control our feelings. Now, consider a leader

Emotional Intelligence
one's ability to consciously control emotions and the communication of those emotions

who is frustrated with group members. If that leader is not able to control his/her emotions, something may be communicated that they later regret. If the leader is able to control his or her emotions and communicate appropriately, this is going to be better for the group in the long run. Thus, being able to self-monitor emotions is a necessary communication skill for leaders.

Leaders Must Be Good Listeners

By this point, we know the importance of listening in groups. It is even more important for leaders to engage in quality listening behaviors. Leaders who do not listen to group members can easily miss pertinent information, fail to understand the feelings of the group, or face other issues. It is not only imperative that leaders listen to followers, but group members also need to know the leader is listening to their thoughts and ideas.

Therefore, leaders should practice active listening. **Active listening** occurs when a person concentrates on the message being received, works to process the information, and then provides noticeable feedback to the speaker. The feedback may be verbal or nonverbal, but it is imperative that the speaker sees this feedback. Some ways leaders can send active listening cues include asking questions, paraphrasing, head nods, and sending back channeling cues (i.e., "uh-huh," "keep going").

Leaders Must Empower Followers

If you recall from chapter five, empowerment happens when we share power and motivate others. Good leaders realize that by empowering followers, group members are more likely to work toward group goals. If group members are motivated, it is likely the group will be more productive. Thus, it is important for leaders to help others see their own potential and create positive change.

Leaders Must Engage in We-Orientation

We-orientation is the tendency to be inclusive of others and focus on the group (we) instead of the self (me). A good leader cannot only be focused on him/herself. To be effective, a leader must also be concerned about the good of the group overall as well as members individually. When the focus is inclusive, the group will increase chances of being successful. When the focus is exclusively on oneself, chances of achieving group goals may be diminished.

Leaders Should Practice Ethical Leadership

Ethics is the study of beliefs of what is right or wrong, good or bad, moral or immoral. Ethical principles guide behaviors. The more ethical a person is, the more they will engage in behaviors that are good or

Active Listening

when a person concentrates on the message being received, works to process the information, and then provides noticeable feedback to the speaker (verbal or nonverbal)

We-orientation

the tendency to be inclusive of others and focus on the group (we) instead of the self (me)

Ethics

the study of beliefs of what is right or wrong, good or bad, moral or immoral

moral. Ethics are subjective. This means that what one person might think is good behavior, another may regard as bad, or unethical. This being said, there are many behaviors that most people consider "ethical" or "unethical." For instance, most of us would agree that murder is not ethical. Providing help to a friend or family member, however, is often consider ethical.

Keeping in mind that leadership involves working toward positive changes, if a leader transitions a group in a way that is unethical, there may be change but it will not be positive. As a result, group members may be persuaded to engage in behavior that could ultimately hurt them or others. Let's imagine a group of swimmers who are attending a week-long swim camp. The swim captain (the leader) is in charge of pushing her team to do well in their upcoming season. It is the expectation that the swim captain will work with the team during camp to train and get ready to perform their best when the season begins.

One evening, the swim captain talks the team into sneaking out past curfew and going to a local bar for some fun. She promises the group that they will only stay for one hour, drink only water, and watch the band. They will then go back to camp and get their rest for practice the next day. Once they arrive at the bar, she then decides to buy everyone a round of drinks. Stating that "one drink won't hurt anyone," the night of fun begins. Before they know it, they are out until 2:00 a.m. and no one will feel up to practice the next day. Further, when the coaches found out they snuck out to a bar, everyone on the team was issued punishment.

The unethical behavior by the team captain may change the dynamic of the group, but surely not in a positive manner. Had the swim captain not persuaded the team to break the rules and risk their health, they would have performed better and not suffered any consequences. Strong leaders lead others in ways that are ethical. They lead followers in ways that are best for the group. One form of ethical leadership that is called servant leadership.

Servant leadership occurs when a leader shares power with group members and provides service in an effort to create positive change. Rather than our conventional thoughts on leadership, the leader serves the followers – as opposed to the follower serving the leader. A good example of servant leadership was that of Dr. Martin Luther King, Jr.

Martin Luther King, Jr. had a vision to end segregation and reunite a broken nation. He believed that he could lead others to share his vision by providing service to those in need in various communities. He believed in helping others by listening to their needs and working to address those needs. He was genuine, caring, and trustworthy. He was truly an ethical leader.

Servant Leadership

when a leader shares power with group members and provides service in an effort to create positive change

Life's most persistent and urgent question is, 'What are you doing for others?'

—*Martin Luther King, Jr.*

Leaders Must Be Transformative

Transformational leaders help groups change in positive ways. These leaders do not simply manage groups but inspire others to also work toward goals. In 2019, three researchers interviewed employees on preferred traits of organizational leaders. The results show the followers preferred leaders that are transformational. They reported transformational leaders are more positive, and significantly impact their work performance (Maizan, Florianna, & Hamidi). Transformative leaders are energetic, open, supportive, and inspirational. These are the types of leaders that others like to follow. These are the leaders that make groups not just good, but excellent.

SUMMARY

In chapter 7, we have examined at the role of leadership in groups. By reviewing the definition of leadership, we can now understand why it is such a complex concept. Not all leaders are the same, and not all leaders practice the same style. While leaders can take on several different forms, there are three common leadership styles including authoritarian, laissez-faire, and democratic leadership styles. In addition to reviewing different styles of leadership we also looked at three different perspectives of leadership including the trait theory, situational theory, and contingency theories of leadership. Becoming an effective leader of a group is not an easy task. In order to be a true leader, you have to have strong communication skills, and be willing to put the good of the group ahead of your own. Good leaders are transformative in nature, ethical, and motivational.

1. What is leadership? Provide examples of good leaders.
2. Describe and provide an example of authoritarian, laissez-faire, and democratic leaders.
3. Why do different leadership styles work well in different groups?
4. What traits make for a good leader, according to the trait theory of leadership?
5. What is the difference between situational and contingency leadership theories?
6. What is the difference between a leader and a manger? How are they similar?
7. What is transformational leadership?
8. How does one become a leader of a group?
9. Why are ethics important in leadership?

LEARNING BY ACTION

There are many online quizzes, questionnaires and assessments designed to help identify leadership styles. Students can be asked to search for a leadership style questionnaire (or one can be assigned by the instructor) to be completed individually. Moreover, students can complete a personality assessment (such as the Meyers-Briggs) to discover potential leadership traits they may possess. After completing the assignment, in groups have students share their assessment results with their classmates. Ask students what type of leadership style resulted from their questionnaire, as well as their feelings about the results. Were they surprised? Does their style change in different groups? Taking action to learn more about ourselves can be an effective learning activity. Taking time to reflect on our own skills and values often results in more successful group communication.

VIDEO CLIP

The Way Back (2020) starring Ben Affleck is about the life of a former star basketball player that fell on hard times ending his career. After fighting his own demons, he takes the position of head coach of an ethnically diverse high school basketball team whom is in desperate need of leadership. As students watch this film, have them analyze Affleck's leadership style. Does his style change from the start of the film to the end? If so, how? Also, have students identify variables that influenced the coach's leadership style and communication with the players.

CONTEMPORARY COMMUNICATION

In today's age, leaders often work with more than one team simultaneously. Especially in the corporate world, leaders often juggle many different projects and groups. An application called Dapulse can help leaders collaborate with group members and stay "up-to-date" with various project. Not only does this app help keep things organized, leaders may use this app to show group members the bigger picture on how all of their work comes together. This is one job of the leader to show the way for followers and this app helps create that picture.

CASES IN COMMUNICATION

In the Department of Communication at your university, there are two student groups. One group is the Communication Club and the other is called COMRades. Both groups have recently lost members due to students graduating and have decided to join forces and merge into one group. They are going to retain the name "Communication Club." Both groups previously had leaders and other defined roles. They now need only one group leader and have designated the previous leader of the COMRades group to lead the newly formed Communication Club. When meeting for their first time, Beth, the new leader instructs the group members that she has compiled a list of group rules that everyone will follow. Further, she informs the group that she will make all decisions on events they will plan and how the group will function. A few group members get together after the meeting and agree they do not want this type of leader for their group. They agree that they would prefer a leader who listens to input from the rest of the group members and takes their opinions into consideration. They would like a leader who participates in group functions but does not dictate everything that happens in the group. They plan to discuss thief feelings with other group members via group text and will hopefully be able to elect a new leader soon.

1. What leaderships style does Beth practice in this case?
2. What leadership style do the other group members prefer?
3. How can the group communicate their preferences and elect a new leader without causing permanent damage to group relationships (and the level of cohesion in the group)?

REFERENCES

Anbazhagan S, & Kotur, B.R. (2014). Worker productivity, leadership style relationship. *Journal of Business and Management, 16*, 62-70. doi:10.9790/487x-16846270

Bass, B.M., & Bass, R. (2008). *The Bass handbook of leadership: Theory, research, and managerial applications.* New York, NY: Free Press.

Hersey, P., & Blanchard, K. H. (1969). *Management of Organizational Behavior – Utilizing Human Resources.* New Jersey/Prentice Hall.

Johnson, C. E., & Hackman, M. Z. (2018). *Leadership: A communication perspective (7th ed.).* Long Grove, IL: Waveband Press, Inc.

Kelly, S., & MacDonald, P. (2019). A look at leadership styles and workplace solidarity communication. *International Journal of Business Communication, 56*(3), 432–448. https://doi-org.proxy.library. ohio.edu/10.1177/2329488416664176

Lewin, K., Lippitt, R., & White, K. (1939). Patterns of aggressive behavior in experimentally created "social climates". *The Journal of Social Psychology, 10*, 271-299.

Maizan, C., Florianna, L.M. & Hamidi, H. (2019). Preferred leadership traits by employees: A case study in telecommunication organization. *Journal of Cognitive Sciences and Human Development, 5*, 53-65.

McCall, M.W. Jr., & Lombardo, M.M. (1983). *Off the track: Why and how successful executives get derailed.* Greensboro, NC: Centre for Creative Leadership.

Platow, M.J., Haslam, S.A., Reicher, S.D., & Steffens, N.K. (2015). There is no leadership if no-one follows: Why leadership is necessarily a group process. *International Coaching Psychology Review, 10*, 20-37.

Puni A., Ofei S. B., Okoe A. (2014). The effect of leadership styles on firm performance in Ghana. *International Journal of Marketing Studies, 6, 177-185. doi:10.5539/ijms.v6n1p177*

Smith, M. A., & Canger, J. M. (2004). Effects of supervisor "big five" personality on subordinate attitudes. *Journal of Business & Psychology, 18*(4), 465–481.

Stogdill, R. M. (1948). Personal factors associated with leadership: A survey of the literature. *Journal of Psychology, 25*, 35–71.

Onward and Upward: Evolving from Group to Team

LEARNING OBJECTIVES

After studying chapter 8 you should be able to:

- Define team.
- Differentiate between group and team.
- Explain how groups become teams.
- Identify communication behaviors of effective teams.
- Classify ways teams can establish identity.
- Classify skills needed for strong team leadership.

Mac is a sophomore in college, and he is taking a course in small group communication which is required for his major. This class meets two afternoons per week and every week the professor allows an entire class period for groups to work on the class project. Mac has been assigned to a group which includes two males and three females. In only two weeks, Mac and his group must present their project to the course for a grade. Things are coming down to the wire, so each meeting it is important that the group is productive so that they will be prepared for the presentation. Mac enjoys the group to which he has been assigned and they all seem to work well together. He does not know the other members very well, but for purposes of the class, all is going okay.

Every day after class, Mac goes straight to baseball practice. He plays shortstop on the school baseball team. Baseball is Mac's passion. No matter how badly his day has been, when he arrives at baseball practice his mood instantly lifts. Mac sees his coach and teammates as family members who he can lean on no matter what. When on the field, Mac is not concerned about earning individual accolades (even though he has earned many) but plays his best for the good of the team.

In the scenario above, we learn about two groups to which Mac belongs: his class project and the group of baseball players. Both are groups, but they are different. One is clearly more meaningful to him. In fact, one is a team, whereas the other is simply a group. Can you guess which is which?

In chapter 8, we will examine the difference between a group and a team. More specifically, the process of moving from "group" to "team" will be addressed. Not all groups will become teams. All teams, however, are groups. The difference is important to understand as we continue our studies of small group communication. In addition to differentiating between the two, this chapter will provide insight on communication behaviors of teams including team identity and leadership in teams.

GROUPS vs. TEAMS

It is not uncommon to hear the words "group" and "team" used interchangeably. Although this is common, the two are not necessarily the same. From time to time, we can learn about a certain phenomenon by understanding what it *is not*. In this case, it might be helpful to learn what a team is by looking at what it is not.

To begin, not all groups are teams. Although the term group can be defined in several different ways, one way to think of a group is a gathering of persons. As defined in chapter 1, a **group** includes three or more people brought together by a common goal who depend on one another to achieve their goal. When a group of people are together engaged in group communication, they are frequently working toward a specific goal.

We know that some groups are created externally while other groups are created by group members themselves. In Mac's case that started this chapter, he was a part of two groups. The group that he was working with on the class project was formed by the professor of the class. Mac had no choice but to participate in that group for class credit. The second group, the baseball group, was one in which Mac voluntarily participates. As we can tell from the mini case study, Mac feels differently about each group. He seemingly is much more passionate about the baseball group than the class project group, even though he enjoys being part of the group he is in for his course. This leads us to our first significant difference between groups and teams: the passion one has toward the group.

Passion is Stronger in Teams

Normally, a person has much more passion about a team than an ordinary group. **Passion** is a strong emotion or feeling one has for others or a phenomenon. Mac was passionate about playing baseball. He loves the game and his team. Even

Group

three or more people brought together by a common goal who depend on one another to achieve their goal

Passion

a strong emotion or feeling one has for others or a phenomenon

© zsolt_uveges/Shutterstock.com

though he liked the group he was a part of for his class, I don't think he would say that he *loved* the project or felt strongly for his fellow group members. In fact, he referred to his teammates as family, which is stronger than his feelings for his group members in the class. The next difference between groups and teams is the one's level of commitment toward the group.

Commitment is Stronger in Teams

Commitment may be defined as one's dedication to a goal, person, or group of people A person's commitment may differ with regard to feelings toward the group members generally as well as commitment to be a part of the group. Many groups are short-term situations. There is a clear-cut beginning and ending for the group. For instance, a class project or a work group might consist of people working together to complete a task knowing the group will disperse when that project is finished.

> **Commitment**
>
> one's dedication to a goal, person, or group of people

When it comes to a team, however, commonly the commitment is much stronger (and longer) than that toward a group. In terms of relationships, teams are often committed to long-term relationships and are motivated to make said relationships last. In a group, we know the relationships may end when the task is complete, so the commitment does not need to be as strong.

In terms of time, typically a person is committed to be a part of that team for a longer period of time than in a group. Sometimes the commitment is even an indefinite period of time. Think of professional sports teams. Those players commit to a team possibly hoping to spend an entire career with the same group of people. This is a much longer and stronger commitment than most groups. In addition, players on sport teams are typically very dependent on one another.

Interdependence is Stronger in Teams

Interdependence occurs when group members depend on one another for tangible or intangible things. Some examples of tangible things we depend on others for include money, clothing, and other material resources. Intangible items include assistance, reassurance, and motivation.

> **Interdependence**
>
> when group members depend on one another for tangible or intangible things

When we are part of a group, we regularly depend on others. The degree to which we rely on others, however, may differ between groups and teams. If you have ever worked in any type of group, it is likely you have had to depend on others to do their assigned tasks. If your own task was dependent on others, then you experienced interdependence. From time to time, however, one person in a group chooses to take on all the tasks so he/she does not have to rely on others to accomplish the goal. Thus, the level of interdependence is minimal.

In a team setting, however, team members must depend on one another to accomplish their goal. It is not possible for only one team member to do all the work to be successful. Imagine a relay race where one person completes a part of the race and hands off the next portion to a teammate. In this type of team situation, the members are highly interdependent as they must rely on one another to compete in the race. One member cannot compete alone, and his or her chances of winning are dependent on those he or she is teamed up with.

Because teams are typically longer in terms of commitment, the members are often more interdependent than in other group types. This is not to say groups are not at all interdependent, but teams may experience stronger reliance than groups. Being dependent on one another may also relate to team cohesion.

Cohesiveness is Stronger in Teams

Think back to chapter 2 when task and social dimensions were first introduced. From that, we know that the main output of the social dimension in groups is cohesiveness. As a reminder, the social dimension includes the relationships formed among group members as a result of their communication.

© fizkes/Shutterstock.com

Relationships among team members are often stronger than other groups for a few reasons. First, teams often last longer than groups as mentioned earlier. This time allows for relationships to develop and strengthen. Relationships formed in teams may also be stronger due to a common passion. Teammates often choose a certain team based on the focus of the team, as opposed to being grouped together with others. For example, players on sports teams *choose* to join the team due to their passion for that particular sport. This is very different than a group that is formed in the workplace in order to complete a specific task. For this reason, there is similarity from the very beginning in the relationships among teammates, whereas that similarity might not be as strong in other types of groups.

Shared similarity and shared passion are factors that facilitate strong relationships. When these relationships grow strong, levels of cohesiveness increase. This, of course, is not to say that relationships cannot be formed in all types of groups. Relationships can – and do-form in all types of groups. The relationships formed in teams, are typically often stronger than the relationships in groups.

In addition to the total time the group stays together, the time spent in the group activities may relate to the strength of her relationships that may be formed. Often, group members spend more of their time (on a daily basis) with teammates than they do group members in other types of groups. Many times, teammates spent every day together as opposed to meeting once or twice a week. Due to the close proximity and large amounts of time spent together, it is natural for strong relationships to develop. As the relationships strengthen, the group cohesion will also strengthen. Along with cohesion, group identity in teams is important.

Group Identity is Stronger in Teams

If you have ever watched the reality television show *Survivor,* you have seen teams whom have united to accomplish a goal: earning a very large cash prize. The teams, or tribes as they are called on the show, must work together to stay alive on a secluded island. They must work to protect one another so no one gets voted off the island. As soon as you are voted off the island, you are no longer eligible to win the cash prize. As time goes on, the teammates develop strong ties to one another and begin to form a group identity.

A **group identity** consists of anything that will unify or unite a group together. As we will examine further later in this chapter, this can include team mottos, team names, and other communication indicating who they are as a team. Group identities are important for several reasons. First, group identities help members feel a sense of belonging within the group. When group members can identify with the group as a whole, they feel included and feel as if they are important to that group.

In addition, group identities help the group realize what binds them together. When group members can clearly see that they are bonded together, they may be more motivated to work toward achieving group goals. Finally, group identities are important as a sign of solidarity to those outside the group. When people outside of the group see the identity of a certain group, they are more likely to respect that group and acknowledge them as being a united entity.

Thus, group identities are important for the individual group members, the group as a whole, and to those outside of the group. In teams, having the opportunity to identify with other group members and be seen by others as a unified group is typically more important than it is in other types of groups. In groups (that are not necessarily teams), members are less likely to be concerned with how outsiders view them as a group. In addition, while their role in the group might be important, because it is often a short-term role, they are not as reliant upon that as part of their identity.

In teams, often a person's individual identity is at least in part shaped by their group identity. Now that we know some ways in which groups and teams differ, let's turn to a focus on what a team *is*, as opposed to what it is not.

Group Identity

anything that will unify or unite a group together

© N. Blau

WHAT IS A TEAM?

Now that we have identified several differences between groups and teams, we can now define "team." A **team** may be defined as a cohesive group of two or more people who are interdependent, committed to a common goal with similar passion and a shared identity. If group members are **independent**, meaning they do not rely one on another, they do not meet this definition of team. Further, the group members must be connected in some way, by a strong commitment to the goal or passion for something that binds the group together. Teams can be as small as two persons or as large as is possible and still work together.

Teams are a special kind of group. Most people work in groups at some point in their life. This work can be very valuable, but typi-cally team activities are a bit more meaningful. When phenomena are meaningful in life, we tend to remember them. As I think back to all the groups to which I have belonged in my life, I can only recall a hand-ful. On the other hand, as I think of my debate team in high school and the volleyball team I was on in college, I recall many more details. Those groups were more special to me.

Take a moment to think about groups you are a part of currently or have been a part of in the past. Which of those groups were teams? What do you remember about those teams? Now that we know all teams are groups, but not all groups are teams, how does a group become a team? The answer lies in communication.

DEVELOPING INTO A TEAM

Communication behaviors are key determinants when examining how groups become teams. Specifically, the *quality* of the communication matters if a group is to evolve into a team. Not all groups will become teams, nor should they. Those that hope to gel as a team, however, must exhibit quality communication in order to make that happen. There are several communication behaviors that must be considered when identifying a team. To begin, let's review the stages of group development covered in chapter 2.

Stages of Group Development

As we know, groups develop in stages (Tuckman, 1965). This is also true for teams. The first stage is the forming phase wherein group members are placed together in a group either by assignment or choice. In teams, this often includes both choice and assignment. If you think back to high school when you tried out for a sports team, you did so by choice. You wanted to join the team. That being said, you may have been assigned

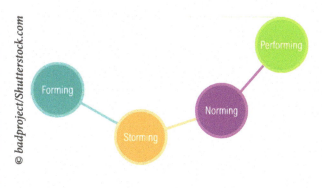

© badproject/Shutterstock.com

to a team, or even a sub-team, by the coach. Either way, you were placed with other group members that you may not have known very well. The group was formed.

The main difference in this phase is the factor of choice. A group formed for purposes of a class project is very different than one formed from student trying out for the volleyball team. You may have little to no choice in the class project, but a lot of choice in whether or not to join the volleyball team.

The second phase, storming, is the phase in which conflict and disagreements often arise. At this stage, group members are just getting to know one another and trying to figure out group roles, which frequently results in confrontation. Also, subgroups may form in this phase.

To assume that teams "skip" the storming phase and automatically get along and work together would be naïve. If you have seen the movie *Remember the Titans,* you saw this is not always the case. In the film, two high school football teams (one with all white kids, the other all black kids) were merged together into one team. The two teams did not get along at all at the start. There was a lot of conflict and dislike for one another. The new team had been formed, but the group was certainly not performing as one team. At the start, it was a large group—not a team.

In phase three, the norming phase, power struggles and other issues begin to get resolved and group members begin to understand what is "normal" for their group. As with any group, all teams must create their own norms and rules. The norms within a team may differ from other types of groups due to the common goal of all team members, but nevertheless norming is a process that must occur in teams.

Next, groups enter the performing phase where all the "kinks" are worked out and the group is positively working toward the goal. Not all groups make it to this phase. Teams, however, often do make it to this stage. I recall many group projects in college where I was the only one carrying most of the burden. I was concerned about my grade, so I did the majority of the work to ensure we earned a good grade. This is possible in group projects but indicates the group (as a whole) is not performing together. In contrast, in order for a team to be successful, one or two people cannot carry the load. The entire team must perform well. Thus, this phase is not optional for teams. If teams do not perform, it is unlikely they will be effective, and may not last together very long.

The final phase, adjourning, also occurs in both groups and teams, but may differ somewhat. The main difference is timing. Many groups are formed to achieve a specific goal, and once that goal is achieved, the group adjourns. Although teams are also formed to achieve a specific goal, they may realize that goal and remain a team much longer. For instance, if a professional football team wins the Super Bowl one year, this does not mean the entire team will adjourn. The team will come together and try again the following year. Unlike other groups that meet their goals professionally or personally and leave the group, teams often remain in-tact much longer.

Inclusive Language and Verbal Immediacy

In chapter 5, we learned about the concept *verbal immediacy*, which was defined as using words to create perceptions of physical and/or psychological closeness. Further, we know that by using inclusive language such as "we," "us," and "our," instead of "me," "you," or "mine" we can create perceptions of closeness among group members. The use of inclusive language is imperative in teams.

In a research article published by Joyce Thomas and Deana McDonagh in 2016, the authors argue in order for a group be really behave as a team, it is necessary that they have a "shared language" that all team members understand and may identify. Further, they reason that a shared language is critical to collaboration. Collaboration, of course, is an essential component in teamwork. Therefore, a shared language that is inclusive for all team members, is important to create collaboration among group members.

In fact, in a research study on verbal immediacy behaviors with athletes, Turman (2008) found that when coaches used verbal immediacy behaviors with athletes, the team members reported greater levels of satisfaction and cohesion. Coaches, or team leaders, are not the only people who should use verbal immediacy behaviors, however. Teammates can also increase satisfaction by being immediate when communicating with one another.

When teams practice using inclusive language, victories become "our victories," instead of his or her victory. In the same vein, mistakes or failure are also "our mistake" as opposed to his or her mistake. When groups begin using inclusive language consistently, this may indicate that they have evolved from "group" to "team." When team members feel included and feel close to other members as a result of language use, we can often attribute that to verbal immediacy. Immediacy, however, includes nonverbal communication as well and is equally important.

Nonverbal Immediacy

Typical nonverbal immediacy behaviors include using variety in vocal pitch, volume, smiling, and leaning in toward a person (Andersen & Andersen, 1982). In addition, other nonverbal behaviors such as a pat on the arm or a hug can are immediate and may increase perceptions of closeness.

© kiuikson/Shutterstock.com

Similar to research conducted on verbal immediacy, past research studies support the idea that when coaches are nonverbally immediate with athletes, there are positive results. Particularly, a study conducted in 1998 by Kelly Rocca, Matt Martin, and Mary Toale showed that when coaches used nonverbally immediate communication behaviors with their players, the players reported the coaches as being more responsive.

Both verbal and nonverbal immediacy behaviors are important in teams. Any communication that is positive and increases perceptions of closeness will aid in the development of teams. This is not to state that immediacy is not important in groups, as well, but rather to indicate the importance of positive communication when creating a team atmosphere. It is important that all team members feel included and important so that they in turn want to contribute to the success of the team. When team members practice inclusive and immediate language, it is likely that they will feel more cohesive and engage in what is called we-orientation.

We-Orientation

Earlier in this textbook we reviewed different cultural orientations of groups. One cultural orientation we learned about is collective/ individualistic cultures. If you recall, a collective culture is one in which the members put the needs of the group ahead of their own needs or desires. In this type of culture, group members exhibit what is called we-orientation.

We-Orientation

when group members are more concerned with the needs of the group as opposed to their own needs

We-orientation arises when group members are more concerned with the needs of the group as opposed to their own needs. In more individualistic cultures, such as the United States, members are often more **me-oriented**. Me-orientation often arises when group members are more concerned about their self (or immediate friends/family) as opposed to the greater group.

Me-Orientation

when group members are more concerned about their self (or immediate friends/family) as opposed to the greater group

Consider the example provided earlier in which I often volunteered to do the majority of group projects in order to earn a good grade. I did not necessarily do the work for the good of the group, but to ensure that my own grade was safe. In that instance, I was engaged in me-orientation as opposed to we-orientation. We can sometimes get away with we-orientation in groups depending on the group goal and/or task. This is not true, however, in team settings.

When working as a team, the entire team must put the good of the group ahead of their own needs or desires. If this does not happen, the team will not be effective. Imagine a baseball team where each player performs a different role. If one person is playing first base and is only concerned about their own statistics and achievements, they may not be looking out for other team members when necessary. Thus, while he/she may excel in that position, the team may end up losing the game.

Sometimes when we work in teams, we have to give up things we want or designer in order to benefit the greater group. When we do this, and we engage in we-orientation, the group will often benefit. When a team is, we-oriented, they will often engage in communication that is positive, or confirming, on a regular basis.

Confirming Communication

When groups operate as a team, we often see confirming communication taking place. **Confirmation** may be defined as communication that acknowledges the other person's message and feelings. When we confirm another's message, we must not necessarily *agree* with their message, but we do *acknowledge* their communication. Sometimes, it is easier to understand a term by defining what it is not.

Confirmation

communication that acknowledges the other person's message and feelings

Disconfirmation

when we verbally ignore another person's message

Rejection

when we openly acknowledge another person's message but quickly reject or disagree with it

When people communicate with us, we have different response options we can choose. Sometimes we choose to essentially ignore the message being delivered. This is called **disconfirmation**. Disconfirmation occurs when we verbally ignore another person's message. For instance, let's say that a friend of yours brings up a topic that you are not interested in discussing. You might quickly change the topic; thus, verbally ignoring the message that was communicated by your friend.

In other situations, we engage in what is called **rejection**. Rejection is when we openly acknowledge another person's message but quickly reject or disagree with it. Both disconfirmation and rejection messages can be harmful to relationship building in teams. Even though we may not agree with everything our teammates say, when we can acknowledge the importance of their feelings behind their communication, this will enhance cohesion within the group.

Examples of Confirmation, Disconfirmation, and Rejection

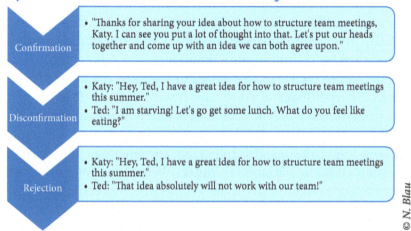

Confirmation
- "Thanks for sharing your idea about how to structure team meetings, Katy. I can see you put a lot of thought into that. Let's put our heads together and come up with an idea we can both agree upon."

Disconfirmation
- Katy: "Hey, Ted, I have a great idea for how to structure team meetings this summer."
- Ted: "I am starving! Let's go get some lunch. What do you feel like eating?"

Rejection
- Katy: "Hey, Ted, I have a great idea for how to structure team meetings this summer."
- Ted: "That idea absolutely will not work with our team!"

© N. Blau

Positive Communication: Avoiding Communication Pitfalls

Verbal immediacy, nonverbal immediacy, and confirmation are all positive communication behaviors that are often evident in team settings. It is clear how positive communication can benefit teams. Moreover, positive communication within groups can help a group evolve into a team.

In addition, other positive communication behaviors are helpful when trying to establish a strong team mentality. For instance, avoiding cynical communication is important when establishing a positive team climate. Cynicism may be defined as a negative attitude whereas one communicates doubts in the team's ability to achieve goals and be effective.

Although sometimes, in our interpersonal communication, it is important to play the role of "devil's advocate," being cynical consistently will not be helpful in teams. Even if a team is struggling to overcome a challenge, constant negativity does nothing to boost morale or enhance relationship building. Moreover, when cynicism comes into play, team member motivation may decrease.

One way to combat cynicism in teams is to engage in effective listening. By listening to an entire message before casting doubt or distrust may provide time for you to think through what is being said. Next, appreciation is a form of positive communication that can be very helpful in team settings. When we show appreciation for another team member, we are showing that we are grateful for their work and

Cynicism

a negative attitude whereas one communicates doubts in the team's ability to achieve goals and be effective

Appreciation

showing that we are grateful for another's work and efforts in the team

efforts in the team. A simple "thank you" can go a long way. When a team member does something positive for the group, simply saying thanks can really help them feel better about the work or effort they put into the team.

Have you ever heard of the term paralanguage? **Paralanguage** is *how* we say something, as opposed to *what* we say. In other words, paralanguage includes the way in which we say something. More specifically, often paralanguage is thought of in terms of the tone of voice we use when we communicate a message.

Paralanguage

how we say something, as opposed to *what* we say

We can use the very same words or message, but deliver that message in different tones of voice, and it will result in different perceptions of that message. If anyone is ever heard of the saying, quote it is not important what you say, but how you say it, they were referring to paralanguage. In teams, it is important to watch our tone of voice we use when communicating with others. When we come off as angry, frustrated, or even sarcastic at the wrong time, this could be detrimental to team communication. As a result, paralanguage plays an important role in communicating within teams. Making sure that our tone, pitch, and other components of verbal delivery are appropriate for the situation can either help or hurt team cohesion.

Finally, another form of positive communication needed in teams is open communication about one's commitment to the team. We have already addressed the importance of commitment in teams versus groups, but openly and positively communicating your commitment to the group may ultimately benefit the group as a whole.

When group members hear others voice their commitment to the team, those feelings may become contagious. This may make others commit more strongly to the team effort. The stronger the commitment, the stronger the team. Positive communication within teams not only enhances relationships and potentially strengthens motivation but helps build the team's identity.

TEAM IDENTITY

If someone were to ask you what your favorite sports team is, how would you describe the team? Would you provide the name, type of sport, or other information unique to that team? In all likelihood, you would include descriptors that tie into the team's identity. When in teams, it is important that all members identify as a part of the team. If group members do not identify (at least in part) as being an important part of the team, they may be less motivated to work hard for the team. There are several ways we can build team identity via communication. Some of these ways include the identification of a team name, team logo, and team motto.

Team Names

If you have ever watched a team-based reality television show, such as *Amazing Race* or *Big Brother*, you know that as soon as teams were created a team name was quickly established. Team names are important when creating a team identity, so group members have a way to describe the team and even introduce themselves to other groups. When groups create identifiers, such as a team name, they may feel more bonded together. As we know, when we can create a name or label to any type of phenomenon, it becomes more of a reality for most people. When choosing a team name, however, teams must be careful and strategic. Many times, team names have been considered offensive by some outside of the team, even when the name was chosen with no ill intention. For instance, many professional sports teams have had names that have been at the center of controversy for offending various groups.

The Washington Redskins (NFL) and Kansas City Chiefs (NFL) have faced issues due to their team names being considered offensive to many Native Americans. In fact, in 2020 FedEx, the company that sponsors the Redskin's stadium, threatened to revoke all sponsorship money if the team did not change its name. As a result, in July 2020 the Washington Redskins announced they are officially dropping "redskins" and filing for a team name change. Team names often go hand-in-hand with team logos, which are another way to form team identity.

Logos

A **logo** is a symbol used to represent or help identify team characteristics. Like team names, team logos are quite common. In fact, it is not likely you can name one well-known team without a name and a logo!

Most team logos are closely intertwined with the team names. Because they are so closely related, like with team names, some logos have been the cause of controversy. For example, the Cleveland Indian's (MLB) mascot for many years was Chief Wahoo. This particular logo received much criticism due to perceptions of racial stereotyping of Native Americans.

More recently, product logos such as Aunt Jemima (pancake mix) and Uncle Ben's (rice) have been retired due to criticism of perpetuating racial stereotypes. Team names and logos are integral forms of communication that help team members identify with the group, as well as help the group crate an identity for outsiders to view.

When choosing names and logos, however, it is important that team members carefully think about the message being created. The name and

Logo

a symbol used to represent or help identify team characteristics

© ChicagoPhotographer/Shutterstock.com

logo must realistically characterize the group and its mission but must do so without being offensive and/or hurtful to others.

Team Mottos

"OH-IO" – The Ohio State Buckeyes
"Whatever it takes" – U.S. Marines
"Like a good neighbor, State Farm is there" – State Farm Insurance
"The only easy day was yesterday" – U.S. Navy Seals
"Talent wins games, but teamwork and intelligence wins championships." – Michael Jordan

© dustin 77a/Shutterstock.com

Logos and mottos identify teams.

Motto

a word, phrase, or even a sentence that adequately depicts the character of an individual, a team, group, or product

In addition to creating team names and logos, a third way teams can establish identity is by implementing a team motto. A **motto** may be a word, phrase, or even a sentence that adequately depicts the character of an individual, a team, group, or product.

At Ohio University, for instance, the well-known motto is "OU, OH YEAH!" This motto is known by all people associated with the university and often bonds people together. Recently I was traveling and wearing an Ohio University sweater. As I walked through the airport, a person I do not know called out, "OU, OH YEAH" to which I replied the same. By sharing the school and team motto, we were able to relate to one another.

Mottos can be used for all types of team, including families and companies working together to sell a product. When organizations use mottos in mainstream media, it is a way to identify a product quickly. Nike has used "Just Do It" as their motto for years. This motto is well-known and always associated with the Nike product.

A good team motto can serve a variety of functions. First, team mottos help build team identity. A good motto is catchy and memorable. When others begin to remember the motto and refer to the group or team in terms of that motto, it serves as a form of identification for that team. In many instances, you do not even need to hear the team name but can identify the group being referred to by the motto itself.

Second, the motto may help build team cohesion. It is something all members know and internalize which helps the team bond. They share a common attitude and mission, as communicated via the motto, which helps connect the group. Moreover, if coaches can create a team motto that encourages members to appreciate one another, research indicates that this may result in increased team cohesion (Robbins & Madrigal, 2019).

Finally, team mottos can be informative. Team mottos inherently include information about the group which is represented. Consider the motto, *"Winners train, losers complain."* Whether or not you know which group created this motto, what might you think about the characteristics of that group? Based on this motto alone, we can imply that the group is hardworking, motivated, and feel complaining is a waste of time an energy. The motto itself provides information about the group that created it. In other words, mottos provide insight to the group attitudes and beliefs.

Knowing the functions of team mottos help explain just how important it is to create an appropriate motto. Team mottos should be memorable, informative, and closely tied to the mission and attitude of the group. When we join a team, we often experience positive feelings of pride and inclusion. Being able to identify with others is favorable for most people. In order to continue the positive experience long-term, it is imperative team members engage in productive communication.

PRODUCTIVE TEAM COMMUNICATION

As we know, not all communication is productive. Some communication can be destructive, meaning messages demolish team cohesion and prevent teams from achieving goals. In order to prevent destructive team communication and enhance cohesion and productivity, teams must practice communication that will be beneficial long-term. When looking at major corporations, many are now team-based. Teams are designated within companies to achieve specific goals. Taken together, the company is aimed at a larger objective.

Destructive Message
a message that demolishes team cohesion and prevent teams from achieving goals

An article published in INC. Magazine (2016) highlighted the five dynamics illustrated by the five most productive teams at Google. The five characteristics included psychological safety, dependability, structure and clarity, meaning, and impact.

These working teams employed by Google made team members feel *safe*. The team was a safe place for employees to openly share ideas, as well as concerns. This is important for teams to create an atmosphere where they can trust one another. In addition, strong teams know they can *depend* on one another. This, unfortunately, does not always occur in other types of groups. In fact, some groups are not together long enough to develop a sense of dependability on one another. Teams, however, must depend on one another to be effective.

As with other types of groups, a quality team will have a *clear structure* (defined roles) and clear norms. These things enable the team to focus on the goal or mission rather than consistently wondering who is doing what at any given point in time. Teams are *meaningful* to its members. Teammates feel that their contribution to the team matters. They are important.

Finally, good teams believe that the work they do will ultimately produce a positive *impact*. This impact may be on the greater community, outside groups, or some other organization. Nevertheless, a motivating factor for the team is the ability to be impactful

Complementary Skills

Complementary Skills
abilities that match up well with the talents of others

Further, when team members exhibit skills that are complementary, effectiveness can be increased. **Complementary skills** are abilities that match up well with the talents of others. For instance, imagine the following case. Tommy and Sarah whom are on the same team formed to create a dynamic marketing campaign for their local Mayor who is running for re-election. Tommy knows very little about branding and political messaging, but Sarah is an expert in that area. Sarah has the necessary skills to create the perfect campaign slogan but lacks the ability to use technology to disseminate the message. Tommy, however, is very talented when it comes to technology.

When they pair their skill sets together, they complement one another. This allows them to pull their resources and achieve their goal when launching the campaign. In order for Tommy and Sarah to effectively work together, it is also important that they both contribute to the goal.

Equal Contributions

Social Support
providing assistance to another person

Even though team members may have different skill sets, what matters most is how those talents are used for the good of the group. Productive teams encourage and welcome equal contributions of effort from all members. Relying on only a small percentage of team members is not the most effective strategy to successfully meet goals.

Emotional Support
performing some behavior to make another feel valued and cherished

Even if a particular task can be achieved using only some resources available, when all members contribute, the product is almost always likely to be better. Therefore, teams practicing productive communication behaviors strongly encourage each other to capitalize on skills and equally contribute to the team. When this happens, accomplishing goals is more possible.

Social Support

Instrumental Support
aid that is given in the form of tangible items such as providing resources or assisting with tasks

Although it seems logical that communicating in a supportive manner would be more productive than not, it is always a good thing for teams to remember the importance of social support. **Social support** can be defined as providing assistance to another person. Social support can take on many forms, specifically three: emotional support, instrumental support, and informational support.

Emotional support is when is performing some behavior to make another feel valued and cherished. **Instrumental support** occurs when aid is given in the form of tangible items such as providing resources (money/supplies) or assisting with tasks (housekeeping/running errands).

© Monkey Business Images/
Shutterstock.com

Examples of Social Support

Emotional Support	Instrumental Support	Informational Support
A teammate, Sally, missed a deadline and feels very deflated. You try to talk to Sally and assure her that everyone makes mistakes, but the team still values her and her contributions to the team.	Sally is having a tough time completing her task because she needs to print out flyers but also needs to be in a meeting in five minutes. You tell Sally you can print the flyers and organize them while she attends her meeting.	Sally informs you that she is feeling frustrated because in order to complete her task she needs to see the team budget, but she does not have that information. In order to provide support, you go to the team captain and secure a copy of the budget to provide to Sally.

© N. Blau

Informational support includes providing information to someone that assists them in some way (explaining how to solve a math problem).

Social support can be difficult to provide for others. Sometimes providing resources or being there emotionally can take a toll on us personally. Even providing information can be difficult at times. There are days when it is challenging to find a way to cope with our own problems let along support others when they need assistance.

Productive teams, however, find ways to provide support for one another. According to the Mayo Clinic, social support can reduce stress levels and improve physical health. For those reasons, healthcare experts suggest people create social support systems even when not experiencing large amounts of stress so that when the support is needed, it is in place. Teams are social support systems in place and ready to be used when needed. Providing support for teammates may, in fact, be the most rewarding communication possible in a group setting.

Informational Support
providing information to someone that assists them in some way

TEAM LEADERSHIP

As defined in chapter 7, leadership is the communication process used by persons in an attempt to influence followers to meet group goals. While some leaders are chosen, others emerge as communication evolves. No matter the matter in which one becomes a leader, leading a team is often challenging.

Leading a team is an undertaking that requires motivation, compassion, and diligence. A good team leader must not only focus her or his sights on the team goals, but also ensure the entire team understands the team mission. In other words, leaders must provide informational support to team members to guarantee they understand the goal as well as what is needed to accomplish that goal.

There is a popular television show centered on a team that is responsible for hosting guest on charter yachts. The team works together to make sure the guests that come aboard enjoy the experience they expect. While all teammates have different roles, the ultimate goal is to provide a safe and pleasurable experience for the guests whom pay a high price to charter the yacht. Considering every group of guests want a different experience, the leader must ensure that the team understands the goal of the specific charter each and every time. It is up to the leader to help the team members understand the mission as well as how to accomplish the goal.

Good leaders do not assume that the team will "figure it out" or find their way. Rather, effective leaders provide the information needed and support the team through the process. With information, the team will learn how to handle various situations and achieve goals.

Empowerment

While it is important for team leaders to ensure members have the information needed to carry out the team mission, leaders cannot do it all on their own. They need to learn to relinquish control when appropriate. This is called empowerment.

We learned in chapter 5 that when we empower others, we provide them autonomy to make decisions on their own. A good leader need not make all team decisions unilaterally, but rather help others believe that they can make a meaningful impact individually. Not only will team members be more motivated to work toward goals, they will respect the leader even more when they feel empowered.

Bob Iger, former CEO of The Walt Disney Company, was a dynamic team leader in the company for 15 years. Iger outlines core principles of effective team leadership:

- Optimism
- Courage
- Focus
- Curiosity
- Decisiveness
- Fairness
- Authenticity
- Integrity
- Thoughtfulness
- Relenting pursuit of perfection (not necessarily perfection itself)

Denning, S. (2019, December). Ten leadership lessons from Disney's Bob Iger. *Forbes Magazine*. Retrieved from https://www.forbes.com/sites/stephaniedenning/2019/12/28/ten-leadership-lessons-from-disneys-bob-iger/#2cfdb5e726fc

If you have ever been a part of a team where the leader tried to control (or micro-manage) every move of the team, you may have felt trapped or even resentful that you could not think for yourself to solve problems. When a leader actually *leads*, as opposed to simply manages, team members can feel confident they have help when needed, but freedom to demonstrate their own talents and abilities freely.

Leaders must discipline when necessary but show compassion consistently. Some of the best team leaders in sports or major organizations, were seen as strict leaders with very high expectations of the members. The best leaders, however, also have compassion and provide support for team members.

The role of a good team leader is multi-faceted. This means that leaders must "wear many hats" and do multiple jobs. They must lead the team in the right direction while balancing discipline and compassion. They should also empower team members to do their best, which will ultimately benefit the entire team. In addition, because we know cohesiveness is important in team settings, a good leader should work to encourage relationships among teammates. When the leader encourages strong, support relationships team satisfaction may increase.

Last, but not least, teams need to have fun! An effective team leader will not only ensure necessary work is being done, but that teammates enjoy themselves. Teams need to celebrate victories. Not every team you will ever join will be a ton of fun, but many teams are filled with potential for fun. Like everything else in life, teams need balance. They need to work hard, but also have fun along the way. As quoted by Andrew Carnegie, *"There is little success where there is little laughter."*

SUMMARY

In this chapter, we have learned a lot about teams. First, groups and teams are not necessarily the same. All teams are groups, but not all groups are teams. In order for groups to become teams, there must be a strong team identity. There are many ways team identity can be established including via the formation of team names, logos, and mottos.

Just because a team has been formed, however, does not guarantee it will be successful. In order for teams to achieve goals, they must engage in productive communication behaviors, equally contribute to the group, and provide social support for one another. Another key component of teams is the leader. Strong leaders need to support the team overall yet empower members to live up to their own potential. Being a part of a team can be an awesome experience. Developing an effective team involves hard work but will also be rewarding in the long run.

REFLECTION QUESTIONS

1. What are some ways we can distinguish groups and teams?
2. Why is commitment important in teams? Provide an example.
3. What is interdependence? Why is this key in team communication?
4. What is verbal immediacy? Nonverbal immediacy?
5. How are confirmation, disconfirmation, and rejection different? How do each contribute to team communication?
6. What are some productive communication behaviors teams may use to build cohesiveness?
7. Identify ways in which teams may use names, logos, and mottos to create identity.
8. Why is it important for teams to be strategic when selecting a name, logo, and/or motto?
9. What is social support? Which type of social support is most important in teamwork?
10. Imagine you have been appointed the leader for your team. What communication behaviors will help you be effective in your role?

LEARNING BY ACTION

As a service-learning assignment, have students work in teams to create a fundraiser for a local non-profit organization. Students may choose the organization, or the instructor may assign students to a particular organization. Possible organizations include the local Red Cross, Big Brothers Big Sisters, or Wildlife Conservation. Students must develop a team name and logo prior to starting. Once that has been established, student groups should meet with an organizational leader to identify a potential fundraiser. Fundraising activities may include a 5K walk or run, a golf outing, or any type of even that will work for the organization. Teams must work together to decide on the logistics of the event as well as carry out the event. After the event has been completed, students should report back on the team communication and its effectiveness.

VIDEO CLIP

Survivor (1997 - present) is a popular reality television show in which teams are created on a deserted island. The teams must figure out how to provide themselves with food, water, shelter and other necessities – they must find ways to work together to survive. The teams work together to win challenges and prevent members from being eliminated from the show (and kicked off the from the island). Students may choose any season of the show and analyze the team communication illustrated. Specifically, analysis should center on team names chosen, the type of team leadership and its effectiveness, as well as types of productive communication used while fighting to survive.

CONTEMPORARY COMMUNICATION

More often than not, we have consistent access to smartphones and computers and use technology to communicate with one another. When we are a part of a team (or perhaps multiple teams), the ability to efficiently communicate with teammates is important. Team App is a free application to help manage team communication. Using this application, teams of all sizes can message each other, post videos, photos, and even run quick surveys to vote on issues and gather information. Moreover, team schedules and contact info can easily be organized using this application.

CASES IN COMMUNICATION

You have recently graduated from college with a degree in communication with a minor in sports and lifestyle studies. You have accepted a position at your local high school where you are tasked with the creation of a new school lacrosse team. You have marketed the new sport and have already held tryouts. You have selected the students that will be part of the team and must begin leading this team.

1. How can you turn this group into a team?
2. What leadership characteristics will be needed to help create the team?
3. What team guidelines will you create to guide student communication in an attempt to help them build relationships and become a unified group?

REFERENCES

Andersen, P., & Andersen, J. (1982). Nonverbal immediacy in instruction. In L. L. Barker (Ed.), *Communication in the classroom: Original essays* (pp. 98-120). Englewood Cliffs, NJ: Prentice-Hall.

Buchanan, L. (2016, April). The most productive teams at Google have these 5 dynamics. *INC. Magazine*. Retrieved from https://www.inc.com/leigh-buchanan/most-productive-teams-at-google.html

Denning, S. (2019, December). Ten leadership lessons from Disney's Bob Iger. *Forbes Magazine*. Retrieved from https://www.forbes.com/sites/stephaniedenning/2019/12/28/ten-leadership-lessons-from-disneys-bob-iger/#2cfdb5e726fc

ESPN. (2020, July). Stadium sponsor FedEx asks Redskins to change nick-name.Retrievedfromhttps://www.espn.com/nfl/story/_/id/29401445/stadium-sponsor-fedex-asks-redskins-change-nickname

Mayo Clinic. (2018, June). Stress management. Retrieved from https://www.mayoclinic.org/healthy-lifestyle/stress-management/in-depth/social-support/art-20044445

Robbins, J.E., & Madrigal, L. (2019) Team cohesion: Demonstrating one team's strong bonds in relation to environment, leadership and atti-tude. *Strategies, 32,* 36-40, do: 10.1080/08924562.2018.1538833

Rocca, K.A., Martin, M.M., & Toale, M.C. (1998). Players' percep-tions of their coaches' immediacy, assertiveness, and respon-siveness. *Communication Research Reports, 15*: 445-450, doi: 10.1080/08824099809362144

Thomas, J., & McDonagh, D. (2013). Shared language: Towards more effective communication. *The Australasian medical journal,* 6(1), 46–54. https://doi.org/10.4066/AMJ.2013.1596

Tuckman, B. (1965). Developmental sequences in small groups. *Psycho-logical Bulletin, 63,* 384-399.

Turman, P. D. (2008). Coaches' immediacy behaviors as predictors of athletes' perceptions of satisfaction and team cohesion. *Western Journal of Communication, 72*(2), 162–179. https://doi-org.proxy.library.ohio.edu/10.1080/10570310802038424

CHAPTER NINE

Work Hard, Play Hard: Group Communication in Context

LEARNING OBJECTIVES

After studying chapter 9 you should be able to:

- Explain why it is important to understand group communication in various contexts.
- Define health communication and the importance of patient-centered communication.
- Describe the importance of transparency in health contexts.
- Recognize how a person's needs may be met in workplace groups.
- Analyze the role of social influence in workplace groups and public advocacy groups.
- Identify the importance of strong communication skills in the workplace.
- Explain why social groups are important.
- Define bullying and address ways to cope with bullying groups.

Landon (age 22) and Sandy (age 21) are studying abroad for the semester in Italy. They are working for an Italian agency that plans events for wealthy clients all over Italy. As Communication Studies majors, they are placed in a group with students also studying communication from other American universities. All students are working together for the first time and are all very far from home. Over time, however, the group members became friendly with one another. Landon has the most experience in event-planning, so he is the group lead. Sandy is new to the business and has a lot to learn. After approximately one week of working together, Landon and Sandy have become romantically involved.

The group is working on planning a large-scale event to launch a new shoe line for an up-and-coming shoe designer. The event will be formal and will consist of a five-course meal as well as a runway show to introduce the shoe line. In a group meeting, Landon announces that he needs someone to go with him to meet with the client. Sandy is expecting him to choose her based on their new relationship, but Landon announces he will be taking Kate (another inexperienced student) to the meeting. He states that he feels Kate is the most professional; thus, she will accompany Landon in the meeting while the others stay behind to clean the venue for the event.

Sandy is notably upset. Before the meeting has ended, in front of the group, Sandy communicates her frustration with Landon in his decision to take Kate to the meeting. Landon simply replies, "Sandy, it's not personal, it's business." This upsets Kate even more and makes everyone else in the group feel uncomfortable.

Is this setting social, or is it strictly business? What is the situation impacting this group communication? What may have happened if this conversation took place in private, as opposed to *during* the group meeting? Would this situation have occurred at all if Landon and Sandy were not in a romantic relationship? In chapter 9, we will take a closer look at the impact of a given situation on group communication. The entire dynamic may change based on the context in which the communication occurs. In this chapter, we will take a look at common themes of group communication in health, organizational, political, and personal contexts.

WHY STUDY GROUPS IN CONTEXT?

Think of all the groups to which you belong currently. Now, consider all the groups and teams you have experienced in your entire life. Are they all the same? Are some *groups* while others may be defined as *teams*? In all likelihood, you are a part of groups at work (professionally), at school, and personally. You have groups of friends, family, and many more.

As you consider all of the groups in your life, you will note that the function and purpose of the groups all vary. Some groups are voluntary, others are not. Some are purely for entertainment and others may be necessary to accomplish as specific goal. Groups differ with regard to communication depending on the context in which the group operates.

Context

the situation in which the communication takes place

A **context** can be thought of as the situation in which the communication takes place. This includes the location, members, timing, and other circumstances that influence the group. Because group communication is impacted by the situation, it is important to explore group communication in diverse contexts. While it is not possible to cover every context in one chapter, and although each group is unique in its own right, we can examine a few contexts that play a significant role in our everyday lives. To begin, let's examine group communication in health contexts.

HEALTH CONTEXTS

Recall the last time you were in a health setting. This may have been a doctor's office, dental office, hospital, or even a health spa. Chances are you did not interact with only one health professional. In many health contexts there is a group of professionals working together. When you go to the doctor, for instance, you often check in with someone working at the front desk upon arrival. Later, a nurse calls you back to take your vitals and additional information. You subsequently see a doctor (or more than one doctor) and may even see additional health professionals if additional services are needed such as x-rays or having blood drawn.

All of these health professionals work together in a group. They perform different, yet related, functions. As a group, they must communicate effectively in order to successfully care for patients. In many health contexts, if the group or team does not effectively communicate with one another it could be a matter of life or death.

Health has been defined by the World Health Organization as "a state of complete physical, mental and social well-being and not merely the absence of disease or infirmity" (WHO, 1948). Health communication, then, can be defined as "the way we seek, process, and share health information" (Kreps & Thornton, 1992, p. 2). Communicating about health issues can take on many forms and happen interpersonally or within groups.

Caregiver Group Communication

If you were to interview any healthcare provider, they would likely tell you that effective communication in a healthcare setting must be patient centered. In other words, the goal is to help the patient and, as a result, the patient must always be the focus of discussion. Patient-centered communication is the type of interaction that occurs among health-care providers and the patient or loved ones of the patient in an effort to help the patient and share concerns (Herbert, 2005).

Patient-centered communication certainly applies when interacting with the patient (or patient's family), but this focus must also apply when communicating with other members of the healthcare team. Typically, there is a group of persons treating a patient. And this group must successfully work together to help the patient.

Often referred to as interprofessional communication, this type of group communication occurs when healthcare providers include the voices of multiple professionals (Clark, 2014). As you can imagine, interprofessional communication must be accurate and efficient. Very often healthcare teams have a very limited amount of time to discuss the patient's case and possible solutions. If you have ever visited a doctor, you may have noticed many doctors do not spend a lot of time in

Health

"a state of complete physical, mental and social well-being and not merely the absence of disease or infirmity" (WHO, 1948)

Health Communication

"the way we seek, process, and share health information" (Kreps & Thornton, 1992, p. 2)

Patient-centered Communication

the type of interaction that occurs among health-care providers and the patient or loved ones of the patient in an effort to help the patient and share concerns

Interprofessional Communication

group communication that occurs when healthcare providers include the voices of multiple professionals

your patient room. They always seem to be rushing from one patient to the next. Caregiver groups must be efficient in order to communicate information that is necessary, yet in a quick manner.

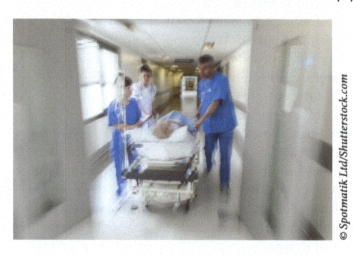

Imagine working in an emergency room. A patient enters the hospital and is not breathing. There is a very narrow window of time the team has to save this person's life. Communicating in an inefficient manner can delay treatment and the patient may not survive.

Another key component of quality group communication within a healthcare team is listening. Earlier in this text, we learned the importance of strong listening skills in group contexts. Listening is especially important in health context groups. One study investigated nurse's perceptions of doctor communication as it relates to job satisfaction. In this study, Melissa Wanzer and her colleagues found that nurses reported greater job satisfaction when doctors engaged in effective listening (2009).

If you recall from chapter 7, **active listening** occurs when a person concentrates on the message being received, works to process the information, and then provides noticeable feedback to the speaker (verbal or nonverbal). Often, active listening can help ensure providers are "on the same page" which is critical in healthcare. In addition to listening, when doctors practice other communication behaviors such as clarity, verbal and nonverbal immediacy, and empathy, nurses are more satisfied in the group. As we know, when satisfaction is increased, so is motivation to achieve goals.

Finally, when communicating within a team of healthcare professionals, transparency is key. **Transparency** is the act of clearly communicating so that group members can easily understand the entire message. When people send a message that is vague or does not include all of the information, they are said to not be transparent. A good metaphor is a window. Glass is considered transparent because you can see right through it very clearly. When the glass is dirty or clouded, it is no longer transparent.

Many groups in health contexts refer to themselves as teams. If the group truly wants to be a team, they must engage in communication that is open and transparent. Concealing details, being strategically vague, or presenting information in a manner that is difficult to understand is not effective. Not only can a patient's health be on the line, there may be other negative consequences such as job dissatisfaction, and a lack of motivation.

Active Listening

when a person concentrates on the message being received, works to process the information, and then provides noticeable feedback to the speaker verbally and/or nonverbally

Transparency

the act of clearly communicating so that group members can easily understand the entire message

Patient-Provider Group Communication

Anytime you, or a loved one, are the patient in a health context, quality communication with healthcare professionals is the top priority. When patients and caregivers view themselves as a group or team, as opposed to being on two opposite sides, collaborative communication is more likely to occur. Collaboration occurs when people work together to meet goals. In health settings, this is working together to solve health issues.

Patient-provider collaboration can result in numerous benefits. The first, and most obvious, is achieving the goal of physically or mentally healing. Healing is typically not immediate. Therefore, during the journey to solve a health issue, there are other benefits possible when patients and families work as a team with health caregivers.

One benefit is stress reduction. A group of researchers recruited patients and families from a Chicago-area children's hospital on an interesting method of communication about health-related issues. They called it the "three-minute mental makeover" where patients (and family members) as well as caregivers engaged in a writing activity to communicate their thoughts, feelings, concerns and questions. This writing was useful to the practitioners who used this information to discuss these issues with the patients and family members. In addition, results indicated that after they engaged in the writing activity and communication, stress levels were reduced (Theoele, et al. 2020).

In addition to mental benefits, such as stress relief, an increase in clarity can result when effective group communication with healthcare professionals occurs. Frequently, caregivers use what is called jargon, which is a specialized language used by a group of people, that is not easily understood by patients. The jargon may include medical terminology or other language not understood by most people whom do not have a background in healthcare.

I have experienced medical jargon many times when visiting a healthcare setting and have had absolutely no clue what the professionals were talking about! If this is information that I need, my lack of understanding can be a big problem. Therefore, finding ways to communicate as a group with health professionals can provide opportunities to ask for clarification or additional information so that we can increase our comprehension, instead of walking away confused.

Finally, just as health professionals need to be transparent when communicating in groups with one another, transparency is also important in patient-caregiver group communication. Willingness to be transparent – on both parts – can positively contribute to the group climate. When we feel as if all available information is shared, as patients we are more satisfied. Even if the information is not good news, such transparency is appreciated.

In addition, healthcare professionals also appreciate transparency from patients or loved ones. Not only will transparency help them do their job, it helps to establish a relationship so that you can work together as a group toward the common goal.

TIPS FOR GROUP COMMUNICATION IN HEALTH CONTEXTS	
CAREGIVER GROUP COMMUNICATION	*PATIENT-CAREGIVER GROUP COMMUNICATION*
• Communicate information efficiently, yet accurately • Keep communication patient-centered • Include multiple voices; consult everyone in the group • Engage in active listening • Practice transparency in communication	• View one another as a team; not opposing groups • Engage in collaborative communication • Avoid the use of jargon • Ask for clarification when needed • Be transparent

Support Group Communication

Social Support Groups

groups that provide emotional, mental, and/or physical support for others experiencing a similar situation

Social support groups are also common in health-related contexts. Social support groups provide emotional, mental, and/or physical support for others experiencing a similar situation. Although social support groups can be focused on any topic, many are created specifically to provide support for health-related issues. For instance, a quick Google search will provide lists of social support groups for those suffering from mental health issues, substance abuse, support of a family member with health issues and a plethora of other health-centered concerns.

Some support group meetings are virtual, others meet in person, and some are a hybrid of virtual and face-to-face meetings. Nevertheless, research has shown that seeking a social support group for health reasons can have positive results. One study found that people who connect with others suffering similar health issues through online social support groups were able to obtain both informational and emotional support (Chung, 2014). People may choose to join a social support group for many reasons, and, over time, the type of support needed may change. Nevertheless, social support groups are nearly always a benefit to those facing health challenges.

According to the Mayo Clinic (2018), support groups can also help some people reduce or manage stress related to health issues. In addition, participating in support groups can help people feel less isolated, reduce depression and anxiety, improve coping skills, and become more empowered.

Different people will have varying experiences with support groups. While many people will benefit from social support groups, there are, too, drawbacks of some support groups (Mayo Clinic, 2018). For example, as with any type of group, sometimes group members may be disruptive. This can cause some members to leave the group or become frustrated increasing stress, rather than reducing stress.

Moreover, if social support groups become "gripe sessions" where people simply complain, this may not be helpful to others in the group. Finally, sharing information among group members is beneficial as long as it is accurate information. Providing and/or receiving unsound or inaccurate medical information can ultimately do more harm than good.

When it comes to social support groups – online or in person – there are both advantages and disadvantages. Each group member will seek out specific support and the benefits will depend on what group members seek from the group. Nonetheless, when people facing health issues are seeking others that share in their experience, social support groups can be easily identified, and connections can be made. For some, knowing others whom face similar challenges make all the difference!

© N. Blau

WORKPLACE CONTEXTS

In this day and age, there are very few workplaces that do not employ groups in some form. Even for people working from home, those employees are often part of a workplace group or team. Chances are, you have worked in a group in the workplace at some point. If you have not, you likely will at some point in your career. Due to the prevalence of groups in the workplace, it is important to take a closer look at group communication in groups at work.

Groups to Satisfy Needs

To begin, if we go back to fundamentals, all employees have certain needs. You may have heard of Maslow's Hierarchy of Needs (1943). Maslow introduced individual needs in the following order from lowest to highest: physiological, security, social, esteem, and self-actualization.

Maslow's Hierarchy of Needs can be applied to workplace contexts. Within the organization, it can be argued that workplace groups can meet social needs for employees. Social needs to include relationships that develop amongst co-workers that can certainly take the form of groups. Quality group communication may indicate acceptance and inclusivity which will positively impact social needs. In other words, if an employee is included in a workplace group, they may be able to use that as an outlet to meet social needs within the organization.

In large workplaces, such as Microsoft, Google, Walmart, Apple, and others, it could prove difficult for many to meet social needs at work. By employing workplace groups, this important need can be met, which can ultimately increase employee satisfaction. Once social needs are met, employees can then work toward meeting higher needs such as esteem and self-actualization needs.

Workplace Decision-Making Groups

In most workplace groups, one goal centers on decision-making. Decision-making in workplaces is often a group or team effort (see Wong, Ormisten, & Tetlock, 2011). A lot of research studies have investigated social influence in workplace groups. **Social influence** occurs when group members agree with others (often the majority opinion) even if they do not agree. This is very similar to the concept of peer pressure when people feel the need to "go along with" the rest of the group.

When it comes to workplace group decision-making, we know that there are two types of social influence: informational and normative (Kaplan, 1989). **Informational influence** includes attempts to influence or persuade others by providing information in the form of facts and evidence and providing logical arguments. At the onset of the COVID-19 pandemic, many workplaces were forced with decision to remain open or close their doors. If a group were designated to make such a decision, one more group member could use data showing the rapid spread of the virus to persuade others in the workplace group to agree to close the business. This would be an example of informational influence.

Normative influence is more social in nature. This type of influence happens when group members attempt to alter attitudes and behaviors of others based on people's desire to "belong" or be accepted

Social Influence

when group members agree with others (often the majority opinion) even if they do not agree

Informational Influence

attempts to influence or persuade others by providing information in the form of facts and evidence and providing logical arguments

Normative Influence

when group members attempt to alter attitudes and behaviors of others based on people's desire to "belong" or be accepted by the group by the group. Essentially, normative influence is used when group members are made to feel shunned when they do not agree with the majority opinion.

Social influence can and does occur in all types of groups. Research has shown that when informational influence is used in workplace decision-making groups, the influence positively impacts quality of decisions as well as group cohesion. Normative influence in decision-making groups, however, negatively impacted the quality of decisions made (Henningsen & Henningsen, 2015).

The type of influence presented in workplace groups can not only impact group and organizational outcomes but can also impact the group climate. In turn, group climates can impact overall organizational culture.

Workplace Groups and Organizational Culture

In addition to workplace groups organized to achieve a specific task, many major corporations organize groups that are ongoing in an effort to better the overall organizational culture. For example, Amazon has what are called "affinity groups" which are resource groups aimed at uniting Amazon employees across departments and locations. Some affinity groups include the following:

© Sundry Photography/ Shutterstock.com

- AmazonPWD – Amazon People with Disabilities – created to support employees and customers with mental and physical disabilities
- Amazon Black Employee Network (BEN) – created to recruit and empower black employees
- Glamazon – created to educate employees about Gay, Lesbian, Bisexual, Transgender, and/or Queer (LGBTQ) issues
- Latinos@Amazon – created to foster a supportive environment for Hispanic/Latino employees

These are just a handful of the affinity groups that are created and supported by a large corporation such as Amazon. Other large organizations create similar groups to support employees as well as customers. While these groups are not considered "working groups" by many, they *do* work to ensure a strong organizational culture. In order for the groups to effectively achieve goals, quality communication is necessary.

Notably each workplace is unique, and groups take on a shapes and sizes. There is no one best way to communicate in workplace groups considering the differences and varying organizational goals, but there are certainly communication skills that can benefit most groups at work, no matter the size or membership.

WORKPLACE GROUP COMMUNICATION SKILLS

Brainstorming

First, groups are often formed in an attempt to pool information and resources to attain a goal. When groups are created for the purpose of problem-solving, it is always a good idea to engage in brainstorming. **Brainstorming** happens when group members communicate as many ideas as they possibly can; the more the better. When ideas are brainstormed, this allows for more potential solutions to be proposed than may have been thought of on an individual basis.

In the brainstorming phase, it is not necessary for groups to spend time evaluating each idea or debating. The goal is to come up with as many ideas as possible that can be evaluated at a later time. In order for brainstorming to be an effective communication tool in workplace groups, it is imperative that group members feel comfortable sharing their ideas. Thus, creating a safe space for group members is necessary. This, however, may be easier said than done!

Workplace groups can practice basic communication behaviors to create such a space where people will feel free to openly share ideas and opinions. One of those fundamental ideas is to engage in listening.

Brainstorming

group members communicate as many ideas as they possibly can; the more the better

© Rawpixel.com/Shutterstock.com

Listening

Listening has been a skill mentioned consistently in this textbook. People want to share ideas when they feel others are truly listening – not just hearing – their thoughts. Even if you do not agree with the ideas presented, providing a professional courtesy by listening is important. When listening, taking an active role can be beneficial. Asking questions, commenting, paraphrasing and sending verbal and nonverbal signals to the speaker to show you are engaged is encouraging. Although some workplace group members will have no trouble voicing opinions, others need a bit of a nudge. When they feel as if their voice is really being heard, they are more likely to participate.

Being Open-minded

Another communication skill mentioned several times previously in this text is one's ability to be open-minded. When a group member is **open-minded**, they are willing to listen and respond to the ideas and opinions of others.

In chapter 3, the advantages of diverse groups were addressed. One positive of having diversity in groups is the likelihood of various group

Open-minded

group members whom are willing to listen and respond to the ideas and opinions of others members share thoughts and ideas from their own culture perspective which may be very different from your own. In order for assorted perspectives to ultimately enhance workplace group communication, however, group members must be receptive to others' perceptions. Thus, group members must be open-minded in order to receive information that may ultimately benefit the group.

In addition to open-mindedness increasing the amount of information collected from others in the group, this communication skill can also benefit working relationships among group members. When group members are not willing to listen to and respect others – or are closed-minded – this can be very off-putting.

Perhaps you have tried to communicate your own perspective and have been quickly shut down by another person or group of people. How did that make you feel? Did you feel satisfied with that interaction? Odds are you did not enjoy having your opinions quickly dismissed while others refused to even remain open for you to explain your position. When people refuse to be open-minded, others can get frustrated or offended. As a result, the working relationship could be strained. Therefore, by remaining open-minded, you leave the door open to a positive working relationship among group members. This does not automatically mean that you must agree with every perspective, but respecting others enough to at least listen to their viewpoint can go a long way to maintain good working relationships.

Empower Group Members

To review, empowerment is possible when group members surrender power so that others may make their own decisions and choose their own behaviors. When workplace groups work to actively empower others, additional skills and talents can be recognized and applied.

Imagine an employee that has a skill set that can really help their workgroup accomplish a task more efficiently. If this person is empowered to make decisions and put his or her talents to good use, he or she is likely to work harder to help the group accomplish goals. If that person's voice is muted, however, his or her skills set may not be utilized to its fullest potential, and, consequently, will not provide much benefit to the group overall.

One way to empower workplace groups is to allow for freedom of speech within the group context (see Haskins, 1996). Specifically, this refers to permitting group members freedom of speech to share ideas and information that may and enhance the group climate. When people are allowed to speak their minds, while continuously respecting others, rich group communication can take place.

Brainstorming, listening, being open-minded, and empowering others are just a few critical communication skills for workplace groups. Every communication skill covered in this class can be useful in workplace groups. Being successful in workplace contexts depends on many variables such as the group members, organizational mission, and specific organizational guidelines and principles. Nevertheless, when you find yourself in a workplace group, no matter the mission, practicing these communication skills can only help you in your quest to be successful.

PUBLIC ADVOCACY CONTEXTS

Public Advocacy

when a group gathers together to engage in some activity intended to raise awareness for some cause or change public policy

Over the years, groups have been created in an attempt to advocate for various issues. When groups engage in **public advocacy**, they publicly gather together to engage in some activity intended to raise awareness for some cause or change public policy. Individuals can certainly advocate for issues, but often public advocacy involves groups in an attempt to create a more noticeable voice by pooling the voices of many. In fact, most times we hear about public advocacy efforts, we see groups, not individuals, leading the cause.

In 2020, an African American male named George Floyd was killed during an arrest by a white police officer when the officer kneeled on Floyd's neck for more than one minute. Subsequently, protests were held all over the United States in an effort to rally against police brutality and advocate for black lives. In fact, the protests led to an entire movement referred to as the "Black Lives Matter" movement. Not all public advocacy groups are as large as the groups that united in response to the George Floyd death, but most public advocacy efforts that raise awareness do include groups of people, as opposed to individuals only.

There are many groups advocating for issues such as children's rights, educational reform, and a large variety of political issues. Similar to support groups, the group members unite as a result of similar interests and passions. While they certainly can and do provide support for one another, social support is not the primary goal for public advocacy groups. Raising awareness and creating change is the primary goal.

Public advocacy groups are not solely focused on human issues. There are numerous groups actively advocating for animal rights, for example. The ASPCA (American Society for the Prevention of Cruelty to Animals) consistently advocates for animal rights and works to create legislative changes to protect animals.

As with other groups, strong communication skills are necessary in public advocacy groups. Not only do the group members need to effectively communicate with one another, quality communication outside of the group is needed in order to create change. One communication behavior necessary to be successful as an advocacy group is persuasive skills.

Persuasion is the process of getting others to comply with a request or change an attitude or opinion. As groups advocate for a cause, they need others to buy into their perspective in order to impact change. In other words, the group must persuade others to make changes or open minds to another viewpoint.

There are several communication techniques groups can use to gain compliance. For instance, appeals to people's emotions (**pathos**) or logic (**logos**) can often be effective when trying to persuade others. Animal rights advocacy groups often appeal to emotions when raising money or seeking policy changes to protect animals. Groups can show how animals are mistreated to tap into emotions and affect change.

Some people are more easily persuaded when presented with a logical argument (logos). Thus, the group may employ logical appeals to make their case and engage in persuasive communication. No single strategy will work for all groups or all issues. There are many variables that impact a group's ability to persuade outsiders. In other words, there is not a "one size fits all" approach to group persuasion.

Establishing credibility can greatly help the group successfully persuade others. **Credibility** is earned when others perceive a person or group of people as being trustworthy, competent, and genuine. If people outside of the group do not perceive the group as credible, advocacy efforts may be useless.

Finally, many public advocacy groups face challenges when fighting for a cause. Depending on the topic and group efforts, groups may face resistance from others and may even be faced with conflict situations. In these cases, strong conflict management skills are helpful.

As we learned in chapter 6, **conflict management** involves using communication skills effectively to manage conflict legitimately and efficiently.

Many communication skills already addressed in this textbook can be used to help public advocacy groups manage conflict. For instance, active listening, confirmation, communicating assertively, and compromise are all skills that public advocacy groups should use both internally and when working with outside groups. Public advocacy groups are common in the United States and will continue to endure. In order to be effective, advocacy groups must engage in clear communication within the group, as well as hone skills for interactions outside of the group. Learning the art of persuasion as well as conflict management can help public advocacy groups carry out meaningful work.

Persuasion

the process of getting others to comply with a request or change an attitude or opinion

Pathos

appeals to people's emotions

Logos

appeals to people's logic

Credibility

when others perceive a person or group of people as being trustworthy, competent, and genuine

Conflict Management

using communication skills effectively to manage conflict legitimately and efficiently

SOCIAL CONTEXTS

To this point we have looked at groups functioning within healthcare organizations, workplaces, and in public advocacy contexts. These contexts are not mutually exclusive. In other words, there is some overlap in various group contexts. For instance, is possible that you are employed in a healthcare field. Thus, your workplace group is situated in a healthcare setting. Perhaps your job is to advocate for public policy issues. Maybe your passion is to publicly advocate or a certain health-related cause.

Even more likely, imagine in any of those contexts you have formed relationships with others that more not just professional, but are also personal. I have several friends that I work with that I feel are more than co-workers. They are true friends that I engage with outside of work.

At any point in our lives, we may be a part of multiple social groups. The family context is a group. We have friendship groups. You may be part of a group that shares a hobby or passion, a church group, or some other group to which your communication is personal (not professional) and voluntary. Social groups are significant in our lives, and worthy of our effort. For many, some of our most important social contexts include our group of friends.

Friendship Groups

Affiliation

connection with others

Throughout our lifetime we develop friendships with others. Friendships can help satisfy interpersonal needs, such as the need for **affiliation** (connection with others) and can genuinely make our lives happier. In fact, among college students, one benefit of friendship groups is feeling a sense of "belonging" that is satisfied by inclusion in a friendship group (Read, Burke, & Crozier, 2018).

© Monkey Business Images/
Shutterstock.com

In addition to meeting needs for affiliation and belonging, according to the Mayo Clinic, membership in friendship groups can improve health. When friendship groups are sources of support and stress relief, this can lead to decreases in health conditions such as stress and depression. When this occurs, we see the correlation between friendship groups and both mental and physical health.

From time to time, we rely on our friendship groups to help us make decisions and solve problems. When it comes to decision-making, one study found that friendship groups (as opposed to acquaintance groups) performed better as a result of commitment to the group and cooperation among group members (Jehn & Shah, 1997). Other benefits of friendship groups include social support and pure entertainment value. Within these social groups we can seek out advice and find people to share fun times.

There can also be drawbacks to friendship groups depending on variables such as group size, commitment level, and membership. A good rule of thumb when it comes to friendship groups is to consistently value quality over quantity. People will come and go throughout life, but a solid group of friends can hard to find.

Family Groups

Sometimes in life, our friends become our family. Families are important groups that impacts many areas of our lives. For many, family groups constitute the most impactful social group to which we will every belong.

Often, when we hear the term "family," we think of our family of origin. The **family of origin** is the family in which we were raised. Families of origin can include biological family members, step-families, extended families, and many any other group types. Families, however, are not just limited to those connected biologically and/or legally. It is very common for family groups to include close friends. You may have an "Aunt" Candice or "Uncle" Ryan. These people may not be your actual aunt or uncle, but a close family friend that has been invited in your family group.

Family groups influence us in many ways. For instance, family groups influence who we interact with, hobbies and pastimes, and even beliefs about what we eat. One study found that families who communicate about cultural beliefs about food impacted healthy food choices (see Hall et al., 2020). Much of the influence of family groups depends on the communication pattern in the family.

Family communication patterns theory (McLeod & Chaffee, 1972) explain various patterns in terms of level of conversation and conformity orientations. A family's **conversation orientation** refers to the level of openness and regularity that a family group discusses topics. A family group high in conversation orientation consistently encourages family members to talk about any topic desired at any level of intimacy, and to share thoughts and feelings openly. In these family groups anything is "fair game" for topic of conversation.

My parents were divorced when I was young, and both of my parents remarried. As a result, I had two families that were very different. When my brother and I were at my mom's house, conversation flowed very openly at the dinner table. Any topic was okay to discuss, and everyone talked very openly. We had a very high conversation orientation in that family group. At my father's house, however, it was a different story. Many topics were considered not appropriate discussions to have, so our dinner table was very quiet. We were afraid to bring up certain topics, so we just reduced the amount of our conversations. This family group was low in conversation orientation.

Conformity orientation is the extent to which a family group encourages family members to adopt similar ways of behaving, feeling, and thinking. In other words, family members are strongly encouraged

Family of Origin
the family in which we were raised

Conversation Orientation

the level of openness and regularity that a family group discusses topics

Conformity Orientation

the extent to which a family group encourages family members to adopt similar ways of behaving, feeling, and thinking to follow along with communication patterns espoused by the family group. Family groups that are high in conformity are often discouraged from expressing their own attitudes and beliefs if they do not align with the overall family values.

Family groups differ with regard to conversation and conformity orientations. Based on those orientations, family groups typically fall into one of four family types: pluralistic, protective, laissez-faire, or consensual. **Pluralistic family groups** are often found to be high in conversation orientation and low in conformity orientation. These family groups feel free to openly discuss many different topics but do not necessarily experience pressure to conform to the shared attitudes and beliefs of other members in the family group.

Protective family groups are typically low in conversation orientation but high in conformity orientation. These family groups strongly encourage family members to conform to the attitudes and communication styles of the family, without necessarily engaging in a lot of conversation about a wide range of topics.

The **laissez-faire family group** is generally low in conversation orientation and also low in conformity orientation. Being a more "hands-off" type of family group entails less conversations as well as less pressure to conform to the values and beliefs of the family unit.

Finally, **consensual family groups** are often characterized as high in conversation orientation and also high in conformity orientation. This means that family members often engage in conversation about a plethora of topics but also feel pressured to conform to the overall beliefs of the family group.

Every family group is unique in some way. The communication pattern of the family group, however, is often a strong influence in one's life. Whether the family is similar to the *Brady Bunch* or the *Kardashians*, often the communication style within family groups is adopted by multiple family members.

Family groups can be a source of support, but they can also be a source of pain for some. Assuming that all family groups are positive influences is a dangerous assumption. This being said, when we are able to choose our own "family" and create a network of support that works in our life, family groups can be one of the best group types you will ever have in your life.

Friendship and family groups are not the only social groups you will ever have during the course of your lifetime. There are many other groups out there that can be considered social groups. For instance, fraternities and sororities, groups centered on some leisure activities such as a sport or a hobby, church groups, or even groups of video gamers can be considered social groups.

If you have ever heard the old saying, "work hard, play hard," then you might understand the importance of social groups. Groups are

Pluralistic Family Groups

high in conversation orientation and low in conformity orientation

Protective Family Groups

typically low in conversation orientation but high in conformity orientation

Laissez-faire Family Group

low in conversation orientation and also low in conformity orientation

Consensual Family Groups

high in conversation orientation and also high in conformity orientation

important in the workplace as well as in our personal lives. Yes, from time to time, some alone time is needed and desired. But very few of us, can spend our entire lives alone. Most of us crave being part of a group and we need the companionship of others. When we work hard, we can reward ourselves with some free time. Reading a good book or taking a walk by yourself can be satisfying, but it is always a good balance to find some time to spend with others in a social group.

Family Types and Communication Patterns

Pluralistic Families	High conversation orientation, low conformity orientation	Brice's family enjoys spending time together daily. Each day they discuss what's on their minds, and no topic is "off limits." One evening, Brice's family even discussed his relationship with his girlfriend to include their intimate relationship. Each family member shared their perspective of the relationship with no pressure to agree with the perspective of other family group members.
Protective Families	Low conversation orientation, high conformity orientation	One evening at dinner, Anna mentioned that they had discussed the Vietnam War in class that day. Immediately Anna's father yelled, "We do not discuss the war in this house. Period!" No one ever mentioned the war again. Every family group member agreed it was not a topic that should be discussed due to the sensitive nature of the topic for Anna's father.
Laissez-Faire Families	Low conversation orientation, low conformity orientation	Billy is wondering if he should take a year off of school to work full time. For a split second, he considers going to his family to talk about this decision, but quickly decides not to engage them. Billy's family typically does not talk about many topics and are very hands off when it comes to share decision-making. Instead, Billy contacts his academic advisor for advice.
Consensual Families	High conversation orientation, high conformity orientation	Erica has been struggling with some personal issues lately and decides to talk to them with her family group one day. In Erica's family, everyone shares their problems very openly. Even though she was considering one possible solution, after talking with her family, she decides to go along with the advice of her family group. Even though she would prefer to go in a different direction, Erica feels that it is in her best interests to heed the advice of her parents.

AGGRESSIVE GROUP CONTEXTS

To this point, we have learned about various groups that we partake in that provide some benefit in our life. Typically, these groups are not considered to be dangerous or unhealthy in most ways. Not all groups, however, are viewed in our society as positive in nature. Some groups are formed with the intent to harm others in some way. One example is bullying groups.

Bullying Groups

Bullying

persistent patterns of physical, emotional, or verbal behaviors used with the intent to harm another person (Olweus, 1993)

Bullying has been defined as persistent patterns of physical, emotional, or verbal behaviors used with the intent to harm another person (Olweus, 1993). Although sometimes used interchangeably, bullying and teasing are not the same communication behavior. Teasing is typically playful and not intended to psychologically or physically harm another person. The intent in the two communication behaviors are not the same.

The reason bullying is often regarded as a group activity is because bullying often includes at least three people: the bully, the person being bullied, and a bystander. A **bystander** is someone who observes the bullying interaction. Some bystanders will take action to stop the bullying from taking place. They may say something or go find help in certain situations.

Bystander

someone who observes the bullying interaction

Many bystanders, however, take no action when observing bullying taking place even if they think that they should do something. When a bystander does nothing, even if they feel as if they should take action, they communicate multiple things. One message that is often communicated when a bystander fails to take action is communicating fear of the bully. The bystander is afraid that if they do something to try to stop the behavior, they will get bullied themselves or make the bully angrier. In addition, research shows that when bystanders take no action A lack of behavior is often perceived as acceptance of the bullies and their behavior (Easton & Aberman, 2008).

Like any other type of group, bullying groups must communicate with one another in order to create the group intact. Very often, we see a high level of conformity in bullying groups as group members want to go along with the rest of the group even if they feel that the action is not right or unethical. We see extreme amounts of pressure in bullying groups that leads to hi conformity orientation.

Unfortunately, bullying groups are very common and start with at a very young age. We see bullying groups all through middle and high school, and even some evidence of bullying groups in elementary school. While the prevalence of bullying groups might decrease a bit upon entering college age, they do not necessarily go away. Moreover, as people enter the workplace, there is a large prevalence of bullying.

Workplace bullying

persistent patterns of aggressive behavior used with the intent to harm another person in the workplace

Workplace bullying is persistent patterns of aggressive behavior used with the intent to harm another person in the workplace. And if negative behavior occurs within the workplace one or two times, this is not considered bullying. It is considered a bullying when the behavior is consistent and persistent. Research shows that workplace bullying can occur for many different reasons. Competition among peer groups, Stress related to workload, conflict among employees, and other reasons contribute to the prevalence of workplace bullying.

In 2019, Monster.com conducted a study in which 90 percent of participants reported either having been involved or witnessing (which is being involved as a bystander) bullying.

When targets of bullying sought out advice from coworkers and others who knew about the workplace bullying events, certain pieces of advice such as "just stay calm" were not perceived as being very helpful (Tye-Williams & Krone, 2018). Still, communicating with others about workplace bullying is important.

Bullying groups – in any context - work together to create a situation that is hurtful for the person (or persons) being bullied. Although it might seem that keeping your emotions to yourself might be helpful to avoid for future bullying, in the long term, the lack of communication may only make things worse. Once we are able to effectively communicate with others and allow others to understand the experience of the bullies, helpful groups can be formed to combat this growing problem in our society.

COPING WITH BULLYING

No matter what context in which bullying occurs, and no matter if you are being bullied or are a bystander, there are actions you can take. Consider some of the following options to deal with bullying:

- Report the event(s) to an authority figure
- Surround yourself with supportive people
- Know your worth – no one deserves to be bullied
- Try not to react strongly; the more it is minimized, the less incentive for bullying behavior
- Avoid groups known to bully as much as possible
- Build up your own inner strength/confidence
- Work to understand bullies have their own issues causing the behavior

SUMMARY

In this chapter, we explored group communication in various contexts including healthcare, workplace, public advocacy, and social contexts such as friend and family groups. In our lives, we experience group communication in a variety of contexts. The manner in which groups communicate will depend, in part, on the context in which the communication occurs. For instance, group communication in health contexts may include jargon related to the health topic being discussed. When advocating for a particular issue, the communication is likely to include an element of persuasion. In the workplace, we can often find ourselves in both personal and professional relationships. Therefore, the group communication may represent a mix of communication styles. In our social groups, our communication will differ depending on if we are interacting with a group of friends versus family members gathered together for a holiday meal.

Most group contexts that we engage in will have a positive impact on our lives. From time to time, however, we may experience group contexts that are more aggressive. For instance, groups that engage in bullying are an unfortunate reality for some. If we find ourselves in a bullying situation, it is important to remember important communication skills that may help us in any context. This includes skills such as clarity, assertion, and effective listening.

When all is said and done, group communication can be effective in any context when group members are equipped with quality communication skills. If you find yourself in a group context which you are not familiar, remember the group communication skills learned in this text and apply them to the best of your ability. In the end, applying your skills will help you not only navigate the specific context, but enjoy it as well.

REFLECTION QUESTIONS

1. Why is it necessary to study group communication in context?
2. What is patient-centered communication and why is it important in health contexts?
3. Describe communication skills that are helpful when communicating in groups in health contexts.
4. How are social support groups helpful in health contexts?
5. Explain how one can satisfy needs via workplace groups.
6. Define and provide examples for two types of influence commonly used in workplace groups.
7. What is a public advocacy group? What communication skills are needed in this context?
8. Explain the role of persuasion in public advocacy groups.
9. Why are social groups important in our lives? What are some examples of social groups that are significant in your life?
10. How is bullying defined? Why is it important to study bullying groups?

LEARNING BY ACTION

Hands-on learning is invaluable. When students have the opportunity to learn about communication first-hand, they not only learn more but appreciate the lessons learned. Break the class into small groups of four-five students. Each group will choose one context to focus on and pick an organization from that context. For instance, groups may choose a health organization, retail company, political office, school or other context of their choosing. The students must then request to either 1) interview three organizational members about important communication skills needed specific to that context, or 2) request to shadow an organizational member for a day to observe communication norms. Students will then record all observations and create a list of "best practices" for communication in their assigned context. Groups may then share with the class and compare/contrast contexts.

VIDEO CLIP

Grey's Anatomy (2005 - present) is a well-liked television drama that highlights the social and professional lives of five surgery interns and their supervisors at Seattle Grace Hospital. Group communication can be found in nearly every episode. For a specific example, the episode titled "Back in the Saddle" (2019, Season 16, Episode 2) shows the group performing surgery on a man who caused a car accident involving one of their team members. The group is social (friendship) and also professional (workplace). Students can analyze the quality of the group communication and discuss how the group balances the personal and professional relationships.

CONTEMPORARY COMMUNICATION

When we communicate in groups, an efficient channel of communication includes the use of smartphones and tablets/iPad. When group members are working together to help a patient, accomplish a work project, or bind together to advocate for a specific cause, it is necessary for group members to quickly and consistently stay in communication. An application called Pronto Team Communication is a messaging application that allows group members to text, video-chat and even stream live communication when needed. This application can help groups members stay on task and work together to accomplish goals.

CASES IN COMMUNICATION

Jeanie, a sophomore in college, is a member of Alpha Delta Pi Sorority. Jeanie thoroughly enjoys the sorority and has developed close, life-long friendships through this groups. Unfortunately, another sorority, Gamma Zeta, has recently been accused of violating university hazing policies and is facing suspension. In managing the situation at Gamma Zeta, university leadership has announced that for an entire semester ALL sorority functions will be suspended. Jeanie and her sorority sisters are outraged by this decision as they have not violated any policies. As a group, they decide to publicly advocate against the decision by university leadership and organize a peaceful protest.

1. What communication skills must the group employ to effectively communicate their position?
2. When advocating for a cause such as this, is the communication more effective individually or in a group? Why? Defend your answer.
3. What advice would you give Jeanie and her sorority sisters as they map out their communication plan for the protest?

REFERENCES

Bortz, D. (2019). What can I do about workplace bullying? Monster. com. Retrieved from https://www.monster.com/career-advice/article/Workplace-Bullying-What-Can-You-Do

Chung, J. (2014). Social networking in online support groups for health: How online social networking benefits patients. *Journal of Health Communication*, *19*(6), 639–659. https://doi-org.proxy.library.ohio.edu/10.1080/10810730.2012.757396

Clark, P. G. (2014). Narrative in interprofessional education and practice: Implications for professional identity, provider-patient communication and teamwork. *Journal of Interprofessional Care, 28*, 34–39. doi:10.3109/13561820.2013.853652

Easton, S. S., & Aberman, A. (2008). Bullying as a group communication process: messages created and interpreted by bystanders. *Florida Communication Journal, 36*(2), 46–73.

Hall, E.D, Dilnora Azimova, M.M., Campbell, N., Ellithorpe, M., Plasencia, J., Chavez, M., Zeldes, G.A., Takahashi, B., Bleakley, A., & Hennessy, M. (2020) The mediating role of family and cultural food beliefs on the relationship between family communication patterns and diet and health issues across racial/ethnic groups. *Health Communication*, *13*, doi: 10.1080/10410236.2020.1733213

Haskins, W. A. (1996). Freedom of speech: Construct for creating a culture which empowers organizational members. *Journal of Business Communication*, *33*(1), 85–97. https://doi-org.proxy.library.ohio.edu/10.1177/002194369603300108

Henningsen, D. D., & Henningsen, M. L. M. (2015). A preliminary examination of perceptions of social influence in group decision making in the workplace. *International Journal of Business*

Communication, *52*(2), 188–204. https://doi-org.proxy.library. ohio.edu/10.1177/2329488414525448

Herbert, C. P. (2005). Changing the culture: Interprofessional education for collaborative Patient-centered practice in Canada. *Journal of Interprofessional Care, 19*, (1–4). doi:10.1080/ 13561820500081539

Jehn, K. A., & Shah, P. P. (1997). Interpersonal relationships and task performance: An examination of mediation processes in friendship and acquaintance groups. *Journal of Personality and Social Psychology, 72*(4), 775–790. https://doi.org/10.1037/0022-3514.72.4.775

Kaplan, M. F. (1989). Task, situational, and personal determinants of influence processes in group decision making. In E. J. Lawler (Ed.), *Advances in group processes* (Vol. 6, pp. 87–105). Greenwich, CT: JAI.

Kreps, G.L., & Thornton, B.C. (1992). *Health communication: Theory and practice* (2nd ed.). Prospect Heights, IL: Waveland Press.

Maslow, A. H. (1943). A theory of human motivation. *Psychology Review, 50,* 370-396.

Mayo Clinic. (2019, August 24). Friendships: Enrich your life and improve your health.https://www.mayoclinic.org/healthy-lifestyle/adult-health/in-depth/friendships/art-20044860

Mayo Clinic. (2018, June 26). Support groups: Make connections, get help. https://www.mayoclinic.org/healthy-lifestyle/stress-management/in-depth/support-groups/art-20044655

McLeod, J.M., & Chaffee. (1972). The construction of social reality. In J., Tedeshi (Ed.), *The social influence process* (pp. 50-59). Chicago, IL: Aldine-Atherton.

Read, B., Burke, P.J., & Crozier, G. (2020) 'It is like school sometimes': Friendship and sociality on university campuses and patterns of social inequality. *Discourse: Studies in the Cultural Politics of Education, 41*, 70-82, doi: 10.1080/01596306.2018.1457626

Thoele, D. G., Gunalp, C., Baran, D., Harris, J., Moss, D., Donovan, R., Yi Li, & Getz, M. A. (2020). Health care practitioners and families writing together: The three-minute mental makeover. *Journal of Applied Communications, 24*(1), 47–53. https://doi-org.proxy.library.ohio.edu/10.7812/TPP/19.056

Tye-Williams, S., & Krone, K. J. (2017). Identifying and re-imagining the paradox of workplace bullying advice. *Journal of Applied Communication Research, 45*(2), 218–235. https://doi-org.proxy.library.ohio.edu/10.1080/00909882.2017.1288291

Wanzer, M., Wojtaszczyk, A., & Kelly, J. (2009). Nurses' perceptions of physicians' communication: The relationship among communication practices, satisfaction, and collaboration. *Health Communication*, *24*(8), 683–691. https://doi-org.proxy.library.ohio.edu/10.1080/10410230903263990

Wong, E. M., Ormiston, M. E., & Tetlock, P. E. (2011). The effects of top management team integrative complexity and decentralized decision making on corporate social performance. *Academy of Management Journal, 54*, 1207-1228. doi:10.5465/amj.2008.0762

World Health Organization. (1948). Preamble to the Constitution of the World Health Organization. Official records of the World Health Organization (no. 2). Retrieved from www.who.int/about/definition/en

CHAPTER TEN

Mute Your Mic! Virtual Group Discussion

LEARNING OBJECTIVES

After studying chapter 10 you should be able to:

- Explain virtual group communication.
- Identify types of channels used in online group communication.
- Classify types of groups that meet online.
- Specify communication behaviors important when participating in online groups.
- Specify communication behaviors important when leading online groups.
- Assess the positives and negatives of virtual group communication.

When is the last time you participated in a Zoom meeting of some sort? How about an online meeting with co-workers, classmates, or even friends and family? For many, virtual group discussions are a regular part of our daily lives. If you did not know what Zoom was before the COVID-19 global pandemic, you likely learned about it during that time.

To begin thinking about the prevalence of online discussion groups, consider the following statistics:

- Over 30 million employees work from home (at least part-time) (Finance Online, 2020).
- Approximately 88 percent of corporate employees claim virtual teams are critical to workplace productivity (Finance Online, 2020).
- Generation Z is having a significant increase in the use of online platforms for group discussions (Finance Online, 2020).
- College student internships are increasingly moving to virtual platforms (yello.com, 2020).
- College students taking online classes can benefit from group projects and discussion (Inside Higher Education, 2018).

The list of statistics about the increase of online discussion groups can continue, but these are sufficient for now. In your own life, you may participate in many online group discussions for a variety of reasons. As the use of virtual formats for group work increases, it becomes

progressively more important for us to learn how to effectively communicate in groups online.

In chapter 10, we turn our attention specifically to virtual group discussions. We will explore what types of groups commonly communicate online guidelines for participating and leading virtual group discussions, as well as advantages and disadvantages of communicating in groups in virtual formats. To begin, let's examine the concept of virtual group communication.

© Yalcin Sonat/Shutterstock.com

VIRTUAL GROUP COMMUNICATION

To begin, lets refresh our memory of how we have defined group communication. At the start of this book, group communication was introduced as an interaction among a group of people who share a common purpose or goal. In turn, **virtual group communication** includes computer-mediated interaction among groups of people who share a common purpose or goal. Put differently, virtual group communication includes any group interaction that occurs using technology. Virtual group communication can take many forms. One very common channel used to communicate in groups is email, or electronic mail.

Virtual Group Communication

computer-mediated interaction among groups of people who share a common purpose or goal

Group Email

Email is a communication tool that most of us use daily. As you know, email can be accessed by any computer, iPad or tablet, and even on our smartphones. Thus, email is very accessible to most people. Although emails can be sent to only one other person, emails are frequently used for group interactions. It is often much easier to send an email to a group rather than contact each person individually.

Think of a group project you worked on in a college class. More often than not, you and your fellow group members were required to complete the project within a certain time frame. Therefore, the information that needed to be shared among group members was time sensitive. Email, as a form of virtual group communication, is a way to share that information very quickly and make sure that everyone is able to get it at the same time. Moreover, email is typically a free tool to use to communicate with groups. Free is always good!

In addition to being readily accessible, email is generally user-friendly. As a result, most people can quickly learn how to engage in group discussions via email. Imagine if you had to go out of town, yet you still had to work with group members on a class project. You can access your email from virtually anywhere as long as you have an Internet connection. While you may not be able to meet with your group face to face, you can participate in group discussions when this channel of online group discussion is used.

Finally, group communication via email can be archived. When something is archived, this means that the information is saved or preserved to be accessed in the future. The ability to archive and save information can be useful for many reasons. For instance, archiving is useful when sharing documents or information that might need to be retrieved at a later date and time period. This can also be useful for purposes of record keeping so that groups can keep a record of the online discussions that have taken place. As you can see, virtual group communication via email can be a very useful form of interaction. There are, however, also disadvantages when groups choose email as a means of group discussion.

One of the main disadvantages of virtual group email communication is the lack of nonverbal communication. When groups meet face-to-face, there is the opportunity to receive and react to nonverbal messages. As a reminder, nonverbal messages include any message sent from a sender to a receiver that is not language. Although advances in technology have allowed for some nonverbal communication to be included in emails (i.e., use of emoticons, bolding, increasing font to emphasize words or phrases), much of the nonverbal component of group discussion is missing when groups communicate via email. Therefore, what virtual group communication gains in terms of efficiency when using email, it gives up in terms of nonverbal messaging.

Another potential disadvantage to virtual group communication via email is the potential for information overload. Information overload occurs when information is received at a rate that surpasses one's ability to process the information effectively. In other words, we might experience information overload when we receive too much information in a short period of time. Depending upon how many people are included on the group email, there could be a significant amount of information shared very quickly with one another. In fact, it is possible that multiple group members could be sending an email simultaneously.

If you have ever received several email messages from the same group of people in a small period of time, you can see how the information can pile up quickly. Sometimes, when we experience information overload, we are unable to process all of the information, or miss certain key messages, which depreciates the effectiveness of the group communication. Keep in mind that what constitutes information overload for one person might be different for another. Accordingly, we

Archive

to save or preserve information to be accessed in the future

Information Overload

when information is received at a rate that surpasses one's ability to process the information effectively

need to be very careful when engaging in virtual email group communication so that we do not create an information overload situation for other group members.

Finally, communicating within groups via email can occasionally create uncertainty and confusion. When we are not able to discuss matters face-to-face, we can sometimes create misunderstandings within the group. If the communication is not synchronous (messages being sent and received at the same time), a receiver is left to interpret the message which may cause him or her to get confused and frustrated. We can send an email response and request clarification, but this could take time. Unlike face-to-face interactions, the asynchronous (messages not being sent and received at the same time) nature of email communication can be a drawback.

Do's and Don'ts on Group Emails

DO	DON'T
1. Respond to group emails in a timely manner. 2. Use professional language. 3. Be courteous in your emails to the group. 4. If you have an issue/conflict with only one group member, contact that person directly rather than in the group discussion. 5. Aim for clarity in all email messages. 6. If messages are not being communicated effectively in group email discussions, use a different channel of communication.	1. Do not use the "reply all" option if the information is not needed by the entire group. 2. Do not fail to include a "subject" in all group communication emails. 3. Do not get too overwhelmed with group emails. If you feel overwhelmed, take a break and clear your mind. 4. Delete emails with important information. Instead, create a folder to archive important group communication. 5. Do not forget to proofread messages before hitting "send".

Audio-only Group Conferencing

Groups can communicate using audio channels only. In an audio-only group conference, group members interact with one another, but there is no video component. Therefore, they can hear one another, but they cannot see one another.

One example includes telephone conference calling that has been used in organizations for many years. There are multiple services available for large groups and organizations who would like to use conference calling on a regular basis for group discussions. For those who would like to use a conference call to interact with groups, but do not want to subscribe to a specific service, conference calls can actually be made on regular landline telephones as well as smart phones.

Group conference calls have been used in a large variety of contexts. For example, families use conference calling so that multiple family members can engage in a conversation simultaneously. Also, audio-only conference calling has been a popular tool used in interviews so that a committee can interview a candidate for a position. Conference calls have also been used in other contexts such as health care settings, political settings, and even in classrooms. Audio conference group discussions are an efficient way for group members to collaborate quickly and easily.

Tips for Audio-Only Group Discussions

1. Assign a leader to facilitate the discussion.
2. Allow all group members to say "hello" so the group knows who is present.
3. When it is your turn to speak, make sure to identify yourself.
4. Try to ensure the group is not too large – this can cause confusion!
5. Remember to practice proper phone etiquette and turn-taking (i.e., don't interrupt).
6. Set an agenda for the group discussion (when appropriate) to keep the meeting on task.
7. Stick to the topic of group discussion.
8. Keep personal issues out of the discussion (unless appropriate).
9. Make sure you have a stable phone connection so that you do not miss parts of the discussion.
10. Be polite!

Video Conferencing

One of the most useful methods of virtual group communicate is through the use of videoconferencing. In fact, many people would argue that videoconferencing is the "new normal" for group discussions! Although video conferencing was popular before the COVID-19 pandemic, most would argue that it is used even more now.

Video conferencing can be defined as virtual group discussions that allow people from remote locations to interact face to face using both audio and video signals. In most video conferencing platforms, each user has the option to enable the audio and/or video signals. This means that a user may be both muted as well as have the video turned off, yet still participate in the virtual group discussion. Another option would be to have the video turned off, but the audio enabled so group members could hear what you are saying, but not see you. A third option would be to have the audio muted but the video enabled so that other group members can see you. This is a very popular option as many people might mute themselves until it is their turn to speak so as to keep the commotion in the online group discussion down a bit.

Video Conferencing
virtual group discussions that allow people from remote locations to interact face to face using both audio and video signals

© Andrey_Popov/Shutterstock.com

In addition to the various options for presentation in virtual group discussions, many platforms have capabilities such as screen sharing where one user can share what the view on their own computer screen with others in the group. There are also options such as a chat feature where group members can type in comments, questions, and other communication in a chat box. This is a very good way to make sure questions are raised to be answered later in the meeting.

An addition popular feature is the ability to record online virtual discussions. This is useful when some group members are not able to be present in the meeting but need to view the meeting at a later time period this is also great for archiving reasons.

Video conferencing as a means of virtual online group discussions is an efficient way for group members to communicate from remote locations yet still feel as if they are face-to-face. Unlike audio-only conferencing, much more opportunity to include nonverbal feedback is included with video conferencing. Considering the prevalence of video conferencing in this day and age, it is important to be familiar with video conferencing platforms and how to communicate on these platforms.

Popular Videoconferencing Platforms (July 2020)
- FaceTime
- Facebook Messenger
- Zoom
- Skype
- WhatsApp
- Google Duo
- Google Hangouts Meet
- Microsoft Teams

Information provided by Statista, 2020 – For most current information, go to https://www.pcmag.com/picks/the-best-video-conferencing-software

As with other forms of online group discussions, video conferencing has both advantages and disadvantages. One advantage of group video conferencing is flexibility. Many people have busy schedules and the time it takes to schedule a meeting, providing time to physically get to the meeting location, and setting up for a meeting, takes time. When meetings are scheduled using video conferencing, group members can easily access the meetings from virtually any location that has Internet access.

For example, just recently I had a doctor's appointment scheduled and my supervisor scheduled a meeting at the same time. I could not reschedule my doctor's appointment but as I sat in the waiting room for over 30 minutes waiting on the doctor to see me, I was able to log on to the video conference from my smartphone in the waiting room. This allowed me the flexibility to both be at my doctor's appointment yet participate in the virtual group meeting as well.

As you may have noted from that example, another benefit of many video conferencing sites available is that the online group discussions can be accessed using several different channels of communication. Many can be accessed on a computer, on a tablet or iPad, and even from smartphones.

As mentioned earlier in this section, another advantage of video conferencing is the capabilities provided in many platforms. For example, one's ability to be muted, have video on or off, record sessions, and have chats that can be saved for later use are all benefits of videoconferencing. Because of the capabilities provided by many video conferencing programs, corporations are consistently turning to this medium to host group discussions. The ease of video conferencing allows employees to participate in group discussions that otherwise may not be possible.

Although there are several benefits to utilizing video conferencing for virtual group discussions, there are also some drawbacks. One potential negative is the price tag occasionally associated with video conferencing software. Depending on the platform utilized, it can be expensive to subscribe to various video conferencing programs. Some platforms have versions available at no cost, but when the version needs upgraded to include more participants or greater capability, the price can get quite high. For instance, Zoom has a free version and several more advanced versions. Most larger organizations would need the greater package, inducing a cost for that organization.

Another potential disadvantage in group video conferencing is the reliance on technology. As we have all experienced at some point, technology is a great tool until it does not work correctly. Troubleshooting technology can be difficult for some people. Personally, I have been a part of many online group discussions using technology and due to technological issues, meetings have been disrupted or impossible to host. Unfortunately, any number of issues can arise when utilizing video conferencing. Therefore, it is always a good idea to have a backup plan for group communication.

The last drawback of video conferencing is a lack of physical presence among group members. Although there is certainly the opportunity for more nonverbal messages to be sent via video conferencing than audio-only conferencing, it is still not the same as meeting face to face. **Social presence** is the term used to indicate perceptions of the

Social Presence
perceptions of the existence of others in interactions

existence of others in interactions. In different contexts, it may be easier or more difficult to sense the presence of other group members. In face-to-face group discussions, it is certainly easier to experience the presence of others as opposed to virtual group discussions. This being said, some online group discussion platforms may provide the opportunity for one to experience social presence more than others.

A theory developed in the 1970's called **social presence theory** introduced the idea that different communication channels may have different abilities to convey social cues (Short, William & Christie, 1976). Originally, the two main communication channels studied were face-to-face communication an online communication. There was little differentiation between types of online communication. Nevertheless, as you would expect, face-to-face communication provided better opportunity to sense social presence than did virtual communication.

To this day, most communication scholars would argue that face to face group discussions are more involved and superior to virtual group discussions. That being said, considering the technology age in which we currently live, it is becoming more implausible to engage *solely* in face-to-face group discussions. As a result, it is important to understand that different virtual group discussion platforms may offer more or less of a chance to experience the social presence of other group members. These opportunities may, intern, impact the quality of group communication.

Keep in mind that some mediums lacking in social presence may suit the task perfectly fine. Other group goals that require more social presence in order to be achieved, may require channels of communication that allow for a richer interaction including both verbal and nonverbal cues. Hence, it is not necessarily good versus bad communication channels, but the job of the group to figure out what platform may best be used to accomplish goals.

Video conferencing can be used to accomplish a large variety of group goals. For instance, many workplaces are turning to video conferencing due to remote work situations. In addition, video conferencing can be used for health reasons, such as group exercise classes. In fact, research conducted by Statista in 2020 found that persons between the ages of 18 and 29 frequently use video conferencing for fitness classes since (and during) the coronavirus pandemic.

The increase of videoconferencing use for virtual group discussions is rising and will continue to do so in the future. While there are disadvantages to videoconferencing as a communication tool in some contexts, there are also numerous advantages. When working with group members, always remember to work together to identify the group goal and based on that objective decide on the best possible group discussion channel available.

Social Media Groups

Instagram. Facebook. Twitter. LinkedIn. Today, social media is a large part of our lives. Moreover, social media sites provide an accessible platform for group communication. Unlike other group contexts, however, social media also creates a space for group members to remain silent and unengaged many times. Therefore, while we may be a member of multiple social media groups, our personal group communication in those groups may be lacking.

© littleWhale/Shutterstock.com

It is important to note that there is a distinction between groups *formed on* social media sites and groups who communicate *through* social media sites. This distinction is important. When we join groups on social media, it is not uncommon to remain a "silent" group member. For instance, you may be a member of multiple groups on social media that are associated with organizations to which you belong, but you do not actively participate in those groups.

Other groups, however, that were created outside of social media, but also provide a space for interaction on social media sites, you may engage in frequently. Think of the groups to which you belong. Think about your interaction in the groups. Which are you most engaged in? In which are you more of a "bystander"?

For many groups, social media sites are not where the group is initiated but can provide an accessible place for group discussions. As an example, many instructors of our Communication Studies courses on my campus create group pages on Facebook for students to interact with one another as well as to increase communication with the instructor. Students often use these groups to ask questions and chat with one another more so than they do in face-to-face contexts, such as the classroom.

Think back to the various group contexts we learned about in chapter 9. One of the contexts reviewed included public advocacy groups. It is very common for public advocacy groups to engage in discussions virtually. Research has shown us that when public advocacy group members engage in virtual discussions with others who are advocating for the same cause, communication is plentiful. When the discourse *does not* align with a group member's attitudes, values, and beliefs, conversation is limited (Tsai, Tao, Chuan, & Hong, 2020).

What we can learn from this is that we are attracted to those that we perceive as being similar to us. Sometimes referred to as homophily, or our tendency to affiliate with others that we feel are similar, this can help increase engagement in online group discussions. Knowing that we tend to be attracted to others we perceive to be similar to us, the groups that we engage in most probably make a lot of sense. Those groups may include members like to us that make us feel empowered. As a result, when trying to encourage others to engage in virtual group discussion, highlighting similarities can be a great way to increase participation.

Virtual group discussions occurring on social media can include any type of group. For instance, group messaging on Facebook can occur among families, friendship groups, and coworkers to name a few. In addition, organizations may use social media platforms to discuss matters that are time sensitive. A good example of this was a Facebook discussion group created to address earthquake activity in Alaska in 2018 (Lambert, 2020). With regard to this crisis communication, or communication about a specific, non-routine, non-expected series of events created high levels of uncertainty (Ulmer, Sellnow, & Seeger, 2007) research, it was found that group discussions satisfy different needs for various groups. Specifically, public group members (who are not directly involved in the organization) and staff members used the group discussions to secure information about the crisis. Not only did group members hope to gain information, they also engaged in the online discussion to seek reassurance and create a shared identity of those going through the crisis.

As you can see, just as in face-to-face interactions, online group discussions can serve many different functions and center on a variety of topics. Instances of virtual group discussions that occur via social media are endless.

GROUPS THAT COMMUNICATE ONLINE

Now that we have reviewed different types of communication channels that may be used for virtual group discussions, as well as some advantages and disadvantages of each medium, we can explore some types

Homophily

the tendency to affiliate with others that we feel are similar

Crisis Communication

communication about a specific, non-routine, not expected series of events creating high levels of uncertainty (Ulmer, Sellnow, & Seeger, 2007)

of groups that may choose to engage in an online group discussion. Keep in mind that the types of groups included in this chapter do not represent an exhaustive list. Put differently, there is no way to review *every* single type of group that may choose to engage in virtual discussions. In this chapter, we will review some of the most common types of groups who communicate virtually.

Workplace Groups

To begin, it is well-known that companies across the United States are consistently turning to remote channels for group meetings and discussion. As of 2019, according to the U.S. Bureau of Labor Statistics, approximately 24 percent of Americans worked remotely, and this statistic is expected to rise. Many organizations have at least some employees working on teams remotely; thus, they have to engage in online group discussions.

Moreover, since COVID-19, the number of workplace groups working remotely had only increased. As a result of the rising occurrence of virtual workplace group meetings, some guidelines should be followed. First, effective virtual teams should use technology wisely to communicate and share information. Not all workplace meetings necessitate video conferencing necessarily. As mentioned earlier, consider the task to be accomplished and choose the medium appropriately.

If a task is small, a quick telephone conference or group discussion via email may be appropriate. When more involved workplace group discussions are necessary, group members should attempt to hold meetings similar to how they would be facilitated in person. This may include establishing leadership for the discussion, minding meeting etiquette, and be aware of time constraints. Just as you would do in a face-to-face group discussion, avoid distractions such as checking social media and texting. In other words, be polite.

Another guideline for virtual workplace group discussions to is engage in collaboration. In chapter 9, we learned that collaboration includes people working together to meet goals. This involves group members trying to capitalize on one another's abilities and talents as opposed to trying to achieve tasks independently. When workplace groups can collaborate and pool resources, they are more likely to not only accomplish the group goal(s), but to produce a quality outcome.

Finally, enter virtual group discussions with an open mind and a positive attitude. As with anything else in life, when we enter a situation with a sour attitude, the possibility arises for a self-fulfilling prophecy. A **self-fulfilling prophecy** occurs when a person or group of people predict that something will happen and, in turn, consciously or unconsciously behave in such a way that the prediction becomes reality.

Self-Fulfilling Prophecy
when a person or group of people predict that something will happen and, in turn, consciously or unconsciously behave in such a way that the prediction becomes reality

Imagine you are scheduled for a virtual group meeting for your job at 8:00 in the morning. Not only do you dislike early morning meetings, you are somewhat confused about the goal the group is trying to accomplish. On the morning of the meeting, you wake up in a bad mood and decide that you really do not want to participate in the group discussion. Therefore, you have a negative attitude when the discussion begins. Throughout the conversation you perceive every comment and idea negatively. This negativity comes through in your own interactions with the other group members. By the end of the meeting, nothing is accomplished because you and the other group members have spent time arguing instead of working collaboratively to achieve the task.

Not every time we enter into an interaction with a negative attitude does a self-fulfilling prophecy occur. In the same vein, this is not to say that when we begin the discussion in positive manner, there is not possibility for a negative interaction, but that our chances of being productive increase when we are optimistic. As your participation in workplace virtual group discussions continues to be required more and more, keep in mind that a positive attitude and a smile can go a long way!

Lastly, according to an article published in Forbes magazine in 2020, logistically there are some good things to keep in mind when engaging in virtual workplace group meetings and discussions. One tip is to establish regular morning team check-ins where workplace groups can simply touch base with each other every day or every week to make sure everyone is on the same page.

Another good tip is to take virtual coffee breaks in which you can spend time communicating with one another about topics other than work. We have all heard the cliché about "all work and no play…." even though our professional lives are significant, our social groups are also important. Online group discussions are not limited to work or academic groups, but also extend to those groups we participate in for social reasons.

Social Groups

When you hear "social groups" what type of groups do you automatically think about? Perhaps you think about your own circle of friends, a small group you are a part of through your church, or a group centered on a hobby or pastime that you enjoy.

One type of social group that communicates frequently online are groups of video gamers (or "gamers"). A study conducted on 22 gamers in Hong Kong found that individuals commonly identified groups of people who quickly became their online acquaintances (Lai & Fung,

2020). As their time online together grew, these relationships turned online friendships which then developed into offline friendships.

As we can see, some groups are formed online, and other social groups simply use online platforms as a means of communication. Social media sites have provided an accessible way for various social groups to communicate virtually. Using options such as Facebook live and Messenger are just a couple of ways that groups can communicate with one another very efficiently.

© Gorodenkoff/Shutterstock.com

When most of the United States was under some type of stay at home order in the spring of 2020, many social groups looked online to find channels of communication to communicate with other group members. Think about your own social groups. How do you interact with other group members?

Especially when life gets busy, virtual platforms are an excellent way to continue building and maintaining our social relationships with other people. Engaging in online social groups clearly has its benefits, but we must be careful at the same time. For example, when we enter into new groups online, we may not know the other group members personally. If that is the case, beware of whom you be friend and how much information you share with others.

Self-disclosure is sharing personal information with yourself to other people. Although self-disclosure is necessary when building relationships with others, disclosing personal information to the wrong person or groups of people can potentially be dangerous. When you meet a new group of friends online, it is always a good idea to take things slowly. Let the relationship develop naturally so that you can really get to know the other group members before you discover this is a group you do not want to be a part of. If at any point you feel uncomfortable participating in the online group discussions, you can simply stop interaction. Make sure to trust your instincts and if something feels "off," take action.

Self-Disclosure
sharing personal information with yourself to other people

Social groups are great for our mental, emotional, and physical health no matter what context in which they occur. Engaging in group discussions online with friends, family members, and other acquaintances can be good for all of us. Because so many social groups engage in interactions online, it is not surprising that social events are now also starting to occur virtually.

Virtual Group Events

During the COVID-19 global pandemic, many group events were cancelled due to concern over the spread of the coronavirus. Important events in people's life such as birthday parties, graduations, weddings, and the like had to be cancelled. As a result, groups began to get creative, finding ways to host events that are meaningful to so many people. Namely, many events went virtual.

At my own university, many disciplines hosted Zoom graduation receptions for students who would miss out on the physical graduation ceremony. Although the virtual event was not the same as the physical event, it did provide a way for students, faculty members, and families to celebrate this major milestone.

As time went on, we began to see more events go virtual. Entire professional conferences went online, weddings were viewed via Zoom, and even church services were held online. In 2020, we even saw classrooms around the country held virtually. Students engaged with other students and a teacher online. When no other options were available, this was an innovative method to allow students to continue learning. Groups quickly began to realize that holding the events virtually allowed many people to attend that ordinarily would not be able to attend due to proximity or other issues.

Primarily, there are two different ways in which virtual events can occur. The first is to provide a live stream of an actual event occurring so that other group members can view the event. An example would be two people getting married. The two persons getting married would be physically together and live stream the ceremony so friends and family members could view remotely.

A second method would be to host the virtual event so that all group members could participate in the actual event. This could include using video conferencing software that each person could log on to in order to interact with others at the virtual event. Although virtual events are certainly accessible for many people, they do entail quite a bit of work. Keep in mind if you choose to plan a virtual event that the work will not be less than the work put into a face to face event. There are many contingency plans that need to be put into place in order to make the virtual event successful.

Tips for Hosting Virtual Group Events

1. Design an event "theme" and make sure your plan is set.
2. Choose the virtual platform wisely – decide on need for audio and visual options.
3. Identify the number of attendees possible with each platform.
4. Make sure those invited have Internet access to "attend" the event.
5. Plan the event schedule as you would a face-to-face event.
6. Make sure to engage the attendees as much as possible.
7. Check, and recheck, the technology! Make sure all systems are set up correctly.
8. Have a backup plan! Technology can sometimes fail, so have a "Plan B".
9. Have fun!

Support Groups

Earlier in this text, we learned about the importance of social support and support groups. Support groups can interact face-to-face or online. Virtual support groups are increasingly popular to help people cope with issues related to health, personal problems, work related issues, and a wide variety of other problems.

Many online social support groups are created to help people cope with health-related issues. One of the positives of the support group interactions taking place virtually is that people can discuss their health issues and still retain a certain amount of privacy. They are able to protect their privacy a bit more when connecting with others online as opposed to in person (Coulson et al., 2007).

In addition to some protection of privacy, we know that support groups intended to help group members manage health issues can be beneficial in terms of reduction of depression and overall improvement of quality of life (Rains & Young, 2009). Moreover, we know that online social support groups help people combat negative health behaviors such as smoking cigarettes, and alcohol and drug abuse.

Another key component of online support group is the occurrence of reciprocal supportive communication. **Reciprocity** is the idea that the interaction is a mutual exchange of information; what one group member offers; other group members offer the same in return. In 2017, researchers Wang and Shen found that reciprocal supportive interactions in online support groups encourage other group members produce responses developing a group norm of sharing. On a related note, when group members self-disclosed using narration, or storytelling, group members were likely to respond sympathetically. As humans, we can relate to storytelling and often respond accordingly.

An entire book in-and-of-itself can be written on the benefits of online support groups. People seek out online support groups because they are looking to be affiliated with others that they perceive to have similar needs. As with any other type of virtual group discussion, however, when seeking out support online, we need to be careful of potential dangers. As always, be mindful of whom you are sharing personal information with, as well as whom you are taking advice from.

Reciprocity
the idea that the interaction is a mutual exchange of information; what one group member offers; other group members offer the same in return

PARTICIPATING IN VIRTUAL GROUP DISCUSSIONS

In this chapter, we have reviewed different types of online group discussions as well as specific group types that would lend themselves to using virtual discussions as a communication channel. What is your role when you are invited to participate in an online group discussion? What should you be doing in these online group discussions? In this section, let's review some guidelines about communication that will help make your participation in virtual group discussions beneficial to the group, as well as for yourself.

Be Engaged

Engagement

active participation in the group discussion through verbal and nonverbal means

First, as a participant, be engaged. Engagement includes active participation in the group discussion through verbal and nonverbal means. If you have ever participated in an online group discussion, you may have noted that it is very easy to get distracted. Surfing the web on your smartphone, returning text messages, or even doing tasks such as washing the dishes can take your attention away from the group discussion. When we are distracted from the group discussion, it is not uncommon to miss certain parts of the discussion or lack information presented once the discussion has ended. Therefore, for the benefit of the group overall as well as your own information, it is important to be actively engaged in group discussions online. How do we do this?

For starters, make sure that you eliminate as many distractions as possible. Set your phone to the side and try to focus exclusively on the group discussion for the allotted period of time. Next, make sure to provide feedback during the discussion both verbally and nonverbally. Verbally, you can ask questions, paraphrase information, and offer your own opinions and ideas as they become relevant to the group discussion. Nonverbally, you can provide feedback in various ways depending on the platform.

If the context is audio-only conferencing, providing backchanneling cues are a good way to deliver nonverbal messages to other group members indicating you are engaged in the conversation. If you are meeting via video conferencing, and your video is turned on, you can engage in other nonverbal messaging such as smiling and making eye contact to let others know that you are engaged. No matter what communication behaviors you choose, make sure you are letting other group members know that you were engaged in the group discussion period this communicates that you respect others and prioritize the goal of the group.

Listening

Listening is a communication behavior that has been addressed several times in this textbook. When we engage in listening, there are several benefits to the group as well as individually. Active listening communicates to other group members that you are engaged in the group work. This behavior allows the speaker to feel as if you are interested in what they have to say an involved. When we feel that our communication is confirmed in some way, we may see a positive impact on group cohesion.

Also, listening is important when groups must collaborate to achieve a goal. We should engage in listening to feed off of one another so that we can move forward and accomplished tasks. Individually, it is important to listen in group discussions. If you do not engage in listening, you are prone to miss important information or be left out of the decision-making process.

Listening is vital to group discussions for many reasons. Listening can impact the productivity of the group as well as relationship building within the group. When we are not face-to-face with other group members, it can become a bit more difficult to continuously engage in active listening. Distractions make it difficult to stay focused, but we need to prioritize listening and respect our group members.

Prepare for Group Discussions

As you would prepare for any face-to-face group meeting or discussion, you should always make sure you prepare for online group interactions. We never want to be *that* person in the meeting that has not done their part or has no idea what they can contribute to the group discussion.

Sometimes when we can hide behind a computer screen it seems easier to skirt accountability. This type of behavior, however, will not benefit the group in the long run. If every group member is unprepared at the start of a virtual group discussion, the discussion may ultimately be useless. When groups have a certain goal to achieve or task to accomplish, it is important for *all* group members to do their part and prepare accordingly.

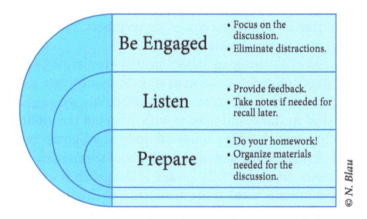

Be Engaged
- Focus on the discussion.
- Eliminate distractions.

Listen
- Provide feedback.
- Take notes if needed for recall later.

Prepare
- Do your homework!
- Organize materials needed for the discussion.

© N. Blau

LEADING VIRTUAL GROUP DISCUSSIONS

Participating in virtual group discussions is one thing, but sometimes we are called to lead the discussion. In chapter 7, we learned about the importance of group leadership and communication behaviors that help us lead groups to success. Many of those same communication behaviors can be applied in virtual group discussions.

Prepare, Prepare, Prepare!

Before the group discussion even begins, the leader must take steps to prepare for the group virtual group meeting. A good leader will always have an agenda, or schedule of items to be addressed during the group discussion, prepared prior to the start of the group discussion. If the leader can present the agenda to all group members prior to the start of the group discussion, that can help group members prepare for the meeting and plan their time accordingly. Right from the start, by sharing an agenda with group members, the tone of the group discussion will be met. This allows group members to prepare on how they will be able to participate in the group discussion and contribute to the overall group goal.

In addition, the leader must prepare the logistics for the group discussion. This includes determining the technology needed for the group discussion, testing the technology to ensure it will work properly, and inviting all group members. Just as a leader might set up a conference room or some other space for an in-person group discussion, the leader must take steps to set up a virtual group meeting, as well.

Engage Group Members

Next, as reviewed earlier in this chapter, engagement is very important in group discussions. It is important for participants to engage in group discussions, but this can sometimes be difficult. A good leader finds way to help group members actively engage in the group interactions. To begin, group leaders should point out similarities (homophily) among group members. As we have already learned, the more we perceive ourself as similar to our group members, the more likely we are to engage in communication.

One way to help group members identify similarities, especially in the early stages of group development, is to incorporate ice breakers into group discussions. An icebreaker is an activity where group members are asked to share information with others in the group, often in an entreating way. A leader could ask individual group members to share their favorite song, something silly about themselves, or a unique fact with other members of the group. If the group is quite large, the leader might initially break route members into small groups and have them share this type of information. The purpose of the icebreaker is to get the group members communicating with one another in a low-stakes manner. Most icebreakers are fine and upbeat, so group members readily engage in the activity.

When the leader cannot take time to engage the group in an icebreaker activity, they should minimally provide some time for group introductions. When we can check in and say "hello" to our fellow group members, this is a beginning step to get group members communicating with one another. Early on, in the group discussion, the goal is not necessarily to solve problems or buying decisions right away, but to break the ice and get the conversation flowing.

Encourage Openness

Once group members feel that they can communicate openly in virtual online discussions, the chances of increased creativity, brain storming, and problem solving significantly increase. Group leaders should create a **communication climate**, or tone of the group interaction, in which all group members feel that they can openly express their attitudes, beliefs, and opinions.

Communication Climate

tone of the group interaction

In order to do so, group leaders must create a space that is safe for all group members. Some group members have no problem verbally expressing their ideas directly with other group members. Others, however, may not feel so comfortable. Even when the communication climate is positive, some group members may not feel comfortable verbally communicating opinions.

One option is for group leaders to provide different types of spaces for virtual group openness. This could include opening a chat function in the virtual platform to allow group members to communicate questions and ideas in writing. Another possibility could be to allow group members to communicate ideas, questions, and opinions before or after the group discussion through another medium. Perhaps group members are encouraged to email their questions or speak with the leader privately before or after group discussions. The more opportunities the leader provides for group members to communicate their thoughts and feelings, the better.

Be Inclusive

Not only should group members allow for virtual spaces in which group members can openly communicate ideas and concerns, these spaces must be safe and inclusive for all group members. When a leader is **inclusive**, they support and encourage equal contribution from and provide equal resources to all group members. In other words, no group member's voice is muted for any reason.

If you have ever been part of a group, yet felt that you really didn't belong, you may have actually been part of an **outgroup**. An outgroup includes group members that are not really included in the majority group. The larger group, or the **ingroup**, tend to dominate the group discussions.

In virtual group discussions, it can be easy for the ingroup to mute the voices of the outgroup and not include them in group decision-making or problem-solving. It is the responsibility of *all* group members to ensure that outgroups do not form and feel isolated from an ingroup. Nevertheless, the ultimate responsibility falls on the shoulders of the group leader. The leader must take action steps in virtual group discussions to make sure everyone is included.

Some ways in which a leader can communicate inclusivity is to address every member of the group consistently and asked individually for ideas, thoughts, and opinions. Another option, if the group is large, is for the leader to break the group into smaller subgroups and spend equal amount of time to communicating with each group. Good leaders will go the distance to make sure all group members feel included, appreciated, and valued.

Watch Out for Symptoms of Groupthink

In chapter 1, we were introduced to the idea of groupthink where group members feel pressured to refrain from communicating dissent. It is vital that groups be mindful of any symptoms of groupthink creeping into group discussions. Groupthink can occur whether the group meets face-to-face or in a virtual context. When leading a virtual group discussion, assuming that the group meets regularly, group leaders need to be especially attentive to any symptoms of groupthink that creep into group interactions. For instance, leaders need to pay attention to any communication that indicates group members are beginning to feel invulnerable, collectively rationalize mistakes and actions of the group, stereotype outgroups, or in engage in self-censorship.

In addition, it is extremely important for leaders to watch communication in which direct pressure is placed on any group member who is dissenting from the majority opinion of the group. In virtual group discussions, leaders need to pay attention to the verbal interaction that is taking place as well as and the any written communication that may

---

Inclusive

when people support and encourage equal contribution from and provide equal resources to all group members

Outgroup

group members that are not really included in the majority group

Ingroup

a group of people who share a common goal similar to a clique

occur in chat rooms or group emails. If at any point, the group leader sees signs of groupthink creeping in, it is up to the leader to take immediate action. This might involve personal communication with specific group members or addressing the issues with the group as a whole.

Arguably, it may be easier in a virtual setting for group members to pressure members dissenting within the group. Sometimes, being behind a computer screen provides a sense of confidence to people that may not be there in face to face interactions. Because of this perceived confidence, occasionally group members communicate differently in the virtual setting than in person. For this reason, it is especially important that group leaders are continuously monitoring all communication to ensure that groupthink is avoided.

Hold All Group Members Accountable

Accountability is communicating responsibility for one's own action and behavior. Although group members should always be accountable for their own actions, it is important that the group leader hold each and every member accountable as well. When group members agree to complete a specific task, for example, the leader should ensure they get the task accomplished. Similarly, if there is a disagreement among group members during a discussion, it is the job of the leader to hold that person accountable. This can be a difficult job for a leader, especially in a virtual context.

In virtual group meetings, it is sometimes difficult to ascertain who should be accountable for which task or specific behaviors. If a group discussion online results in conflict, it may be difficult for the leader to figure out who initiated the conflict and who is right or wrong in the situation. Nonetheless, it is the responsibility of the leader to hold all group members accountable for their own actions and communication.

One way that group leaders can hold group members accountable is by establishing guidelines and norms for virtual group discussions. The guidelines for each group will depend on the purpose of the group, but guidelines for how group members should interact and what are what topics are appropriate may be included in the guidelines. In addition, guidelines help set the norm for the group so all members know exactly what they might be responsible for.

This, by no means, is an exhaustive list of the tasks and responsibilities of leaders in virtual groups. Any responsibility that a leader holds in a face-to-face group context also applies to a virtual context. The logistics on how to carry out each responsibility may differ, but the need for leadership remains the same.

If you have ever been involved in a group discussion online, you may have noticed that sometimes members get confused as to who should be leading the discussion. Virtual groups need leadership,

Accountability

communicating responsibility for one's own action and behavior perhaps even more than face to face groups. Utilizing the communication tool set provided in this text will help you develop your leadership skills both in person and in online groups.

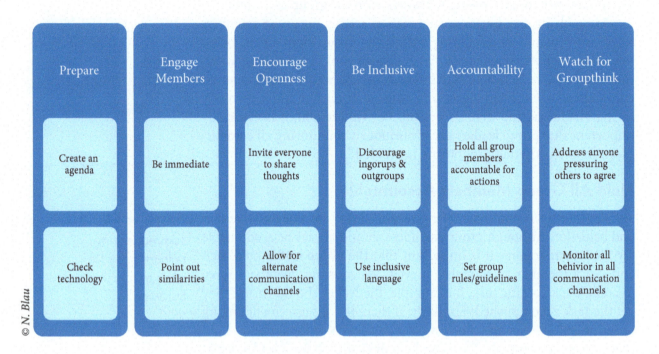

© N. Blau

Prepare	Engage Members	Encourage Openness	Be Inclusive	Accountability	Watch for Groupthink
Create an agenda	Be immediate	Invite everyone to share thoughts	Discourage ingorups & outgroups	Hold all group members accountable for actions	Address anyone pressuring others to agree
Check technology	Point out similarities	Allow for alternate communication channels	Use inclusive language	Set group rules/guidelines	Monitor all behivior in all communication channels

ADVANTAGES & DISADVANTAGES OF VIRTUAL DISCUSSIONS

Throughout this chapter, we have learned about several advantages and disadvantages to various types of online group discussions. Overall, what may be an advantage to for one type of group may be considered a disadvantage for another type of online group. Therefore, in this section, an overview of some advantages and disadvantages are addressed. As you review each, remember that what may be beneficial in some contexts, may be undesirable in others.

Advantages of Virtual Groups

Efficiency

As indicated multiple times in this chapter, one clear advantage of virtual group discussions is efficiency. When a group is facing a time constraint, taking the extra time to travel to a designated location, set up for a meeting, and arrange schedules can be a waste of precious time. When the group discussion is scheduled to take place virtually less time is spent preparing for the meeting as opposed to engaged in group discussion.

Flexibility

A second advantage of online group discussions is the amount of flexibility provided to group members. Not only does it save time for most group members (eliminating travel time and some preparation), group members can access the meeting/discussion from any location with Internet access which provides an abundant amount of flexibility.

In addition to ease of access, most virtual group discussions can be accessed by a variety of communication channels including a personal computer, smartphone, and/or iPad/tablet. You may have taken college classes via Zoom. If so, you have experienced the flexibility in this channel of communication. Instead of getting ready for class, driving to campus or walking to class, you can readily use that time to prepare for class or review for an exam.

Recording and Archiving Group Discussions

Another positive of virtual group discussions is the ability in many platforms too record group meetings. These meetings can then be archived for later use. Recording group meetings can be helpful for a few reasons. First, if any group members could not attend the discussion, they could catch up later by listening or watching the recording.

Moreover, if information is forgotten or unclear, group members can go back and view the recording at a later time. For some groups, record-keeping is necessary. Thus, by recording the group discussions and archiving that recording, this can satisfy requirements of record keeping.

Work-life Balance

For many, finding ways to balance the responsibilities in our personal lives and our professional lives, or finding **work-life balance**, can be stressful. Likewise, balancing academic responsibilities with personal life obligations can be difficult. When people are provided the opportunity to engage in group commitments remotely, this may help balance our work and personal obligations. For example, many people who work remotely are able to engage in group or team discussions online while also tending to children or other personal responsibilities simultaneously.

© Drazen Zigic/Shutterstock.com

Work-Life Balance

finding ways to balance the responsibilities in our personal lives and our professional lives

A result of the efficiency and flexibility created by virtual group meetings, we can better balance our professional or academic and personal lives. When we are able to better balance our work in family lives, this can alleviate a lot of stress in our lives. According to an article published on Indeed.com in 2018, many people who are able to work remotely attribute reductions in stress, improved morale, and less absences from work to the ability to engage in virtual group meetings.

Disadvantages of Virtual Groups

Lack of Nonverbal Cues

One of the clear disadvantages of virtual groups often cited by group members is the lack of nonverbal cues in many virtual communication channels. As reviewed earlier in this chapter, when introducing various types of virtual group meeting platforms, some forms of online discussions lend themselves to greater nonverbal communication then others. Even when using mediums that allow for synchronous video, there is still a degree of nonverbal communication missing in most interactions. In other words, no matter how good an online virtual discussion platform is, it can never fully for face-to-face interactions.

Virtual Bystanders

Another potential disadvantage in virtual group discussions is the potential for some group members to disengage and not participate in the interaction. Virtual bystanders are group members who log on (or call in) to virtual group discussions but participate little to none. A virtual bystander has the tendency to refrain from voicing their opinions, making comments, in engaging in the conversation. They simply sit back and watch and listen to other group members.

In some situations, a lack of communication can be beneficial. In most group discussions, however, if the group is focused on problem-solving or decision-making then the more opinions and ideas shared, typically the better. For this reason, virtual bystanders are often perceived as a drawback in virtual group discussions. Typically, it is more difficult disengage when the group meets in person. If you are a part of a virtual group discussion and you notice virtual bystanders, you may want to politely invite them to share their thoughts and ideas. Just a simple invitation to share with the group can be the nudge that makes a difference.

Less Visibility in an Organization

For some, another commonly mentioned disadvantage of virtual group discussions is not being as visible to leaders within an organization. In face-to-face discussions and meetings, very often, participation levels and contributions are easily noted by other group members. In a virtual setting, however, this is not always the case. Some people feel that they are lacking in visibility was in a company or organization when they don't have the "face time" to be seen and heard.

Virtual Bystanders

group members who log on (or call in) to virtual group discussions but participate little to none

If you are part of a virtual group or a team and you perceive this is happening to you, there are steps you can take to ensure that your visibility is where it needs to be. Make sure that you are fully engaged no matter what the platform. Do not become a virtual bystander. Make sure to share your ideas with the entire group. Also, make sure that you are communicating clearly and professionally. Even in virtual group discussions, leaders can spot effective communication. Utilize resources from your communication toolkit to make yourself stand out in the virtual group.

Distractions

One positive of virtual group discussions is flexibility and the ability to engage in group interactions from a wide range of remote locations. Depending on the location, though, distractions may be an obstacle for participation in virtual group discussions. As an example, when people attend virtual group meetings from home, there may be distractions in the setting that prevent complete engagement in the meeting. Interruptions from children running around, a leaky faucet dripping in the background, and even Amazon deliveries can be disruptive.

When we attend group discussions in face-to-face settings, most of those distractions are not present and we can more fully participate in the meeting. When you find yourself in a virtual group discussion in a location that presents disruptions, try your best to plan for those disruptions before the group meeting begins. If you can anticipate the disruptions and manage them before the meeting starts, you can then better turn your attention to the group conversation.

SUMMARY

In chapter 10, we have introduced the concept virtual group communication as well as types of groups that may choose to engage in online discussions. Moreover, we now know several different mediums available for virtual group discussions including both audio and video options. It is important to understand how virtual group communication can be both beneficial as well as potentially disruptive. If we want to effectively lead groups in virtual discussions, we need to practice communication skills learned throughout this entire textbook.

Key communication skills needed for work quality virtual group discussions include active listening, being engaged, having an open mind and attitude, as well as avoiding the symptoms of groupthink. As group interactions continue to take place in virtual formats, apply the tools learned in this textbook to capitalize on the opportunities presented in the virtual world of group discussion.

REFLECTION QUESTIONS

1. Why is virtual group communication useful for some types of groups?
2. Compare and contrast audio-only conferencing and video conferencing. What are the advantages and disadvantages of each?
3. What is crisis communication? How can social media be used to communicate during crises?
4. Provide some examples of types of groups that can easily engage in virtual group discussions.
5. What needs to be considered when planning group events virtually?
6. What communication behaviors are important to practice when participating in virtual group discussions? Which is most important? Why?
7. What communication behaviors are important to practice when leading virtual group discussions? Which is most important? Why?
8. What are some advantages to virtual group discussions?
9. What are some disadvantages to virtual group discussions?

LEARNING BY ACTION

As a class, have the students decide on a multi-day event that can be planned and carried out virtually. For instance, a Spring Fling or Fall Fest event on campus. After the class has collectively decided on an event, break the class into small groups of four-five students with each group being responsible for one activity in the main event. One group may plan a trivia contest while another group plans a social hour. Groups should be creative in planning the individual events. After the small groups have had time to plan the events, they will virtually host each event for the remainder of the class and/or others that could be invited to attend the event. When all events are completed, have each group evaluate the other groups and provide constructive feedback with regard to the execution of the online event.

VIDEO CLIP

Around the Horn (2002 - present) is a sports television show produced by ESPN in which panelists discuss and debate sports-related topics. The discussions are moderated by Tony Reali who is responsible for keeping the discussion on topic and has the ability to mute speakers as necessary. Since the COVID-19 pandemic, all panelists broadcast via videoconferencing from their own homes. Students may view any episode of the half-hour television show and asses the virtual group discussion. Specifically, students may assess the communication behaviors of the panelists and moderator and suggest areas for improvement.

CONTEMPORARY COMMUNICATION

Considering the reliance on virtual meeting spaces for groups, there are many platforms available for group communication. Some popular virtual meeting platforms included Slack, GoToMeeting, WebEx Meeting Center, and ezTalks Cloud Meeting. Depending on the online group needs (such as number of participants, time constraints, technology needs), one platform may work better than others. Take the time to read reviews on popular online meeting platforms before choosing one that will work for your group.

CASES IN COMMUNICATION

You are enrolled in an Intercultural Communication course. In the class, you will be learning about communication behaviors common in cultures different from your own. At the start of the semester, the instructor explains that there will be a group project and that the project may be different than projects in other classes. Particularly, you will be paired up with one other student in the class and your pair will be assigned to a group of five students total. The additional three students will be students in a communication course at a university in either Mexico or Germany. The instructor has partnered with instructors at universities in both Mexico and Germany and will be facilitating group projects wherein the groups are made up of students from various countries. You instantly feel anxious realizing this may be more difficult than simply working with group members in your own class.

1. What communication skills will be needed to work with students from other cultures?
2. What technology channels can you use to hold online group meetings with students in other countries? Which options are best? Worst? Defend your answer.
3. What challenges might you face when virtual group meetings are the only option for communication? How might you work to overcome those challenges?

REFERENCES

Anthony, J. (2020). *46 Virtual teams statistics you can't ignore: 2020 data analysis, benefits, & challenges*. Retrieved from https://financesonline.com/virtual-team-statistics/

Bendaly, N. (2020, March 20). Your team is now working remotely: 5 ways to strengthen communication and team cohesion in the COVID-19 world. Retrieved from https://www.forbes.com/sites/nicolebendaly/2020/03/20/your-team-is-now-working-remotely5-ways-to-strengthen-communication-and-team-cohesion-in-the-covid-19-world/#1615f1905b70

Coulson, N. S., Buchanan, H., & Aubeeluck, A. (2007). Social support in cyberspace: A content analysis of communication within a Huntington's disease online support group. *Patient Education and Counseling, 68,* 173–178. doi:10.1016/j.pec.2007.06.002

Indeed Editorial Team. (2018, November 14). *Remote work can bring benefits, but attitudes are divided*. Retrieved from https://www.indeed.com/lead/remote-work-survey

Lai, G., & Fung, K. Y. (2020). From online strangers to offline friends: a qualitative study of video game players in Hong Kong. *Media, Culture & Society, 42*(4), 483–501. https://doi-org.proxy.library.ohio.edu/10.1177/0163443719853505

Lambert, C. E. (2020). Earthquake country: A qualitative analysis of risk communication via Facebook. *Environmental Communication, 14*(6), 744–757. https://doi-org.proxy.library.ohio.edu/10.1080/17524032.2020.1719176

Lieberman, M. (2018, April 25). *Online students don't have to work solo. Inside Higher Ed.* Retrieved from https://www.insidehighered.com/digital-learning/article/2018/04/25/group-projects-online-classes-create-connections-and-challenge

Rains, S. A., and Young, V. (2009). A meta-analysis of research on formal computer-mediated support groups: Examining group characteristics and health outcomes. *Human Communication Research, 35,* 309–336. doi:10.1111/j.1468-2958.2009.01353.x

Short, J., Williams, E., & Christie, B. (1976). *The social psychology of telecommunications*. London: John Wiley & Sons, Ltd.

Statista. (2020, June 18). Use of video conferencing for fitness classes during the coronavirus (COVID-19) pandemic in the United States as of April 2020, by age. Retrieved from https://www.statista.com/statistics/1110989/covid-video-conferencing-fitness-age/

Tsai, W.-H. S., Tao, W., Chuan, C.-H., & Hong, C. (2020). Echo chambers and social mediators in public advocacy issue networks. *Public Relations Review, 46*. https://doi-org.proxy.library.ohio.edu/10.1016/j.pubrev.2020.101882

Ulmer, R.R., Sellnow, T.L., & Seeger, M.W. (2007). *Effective crisis communication: Moving from crisis to opportunity.* Thousand Oaks, CA: Sage Publications.

U.S. Bureau of Labor Statistics. (2020, June 25). Employed persons working at home, workplace, and time spent working at each location by full- and part-time status and sex, jobholding status, and educational attainment, 2019 annual averages. Retrieved from https://www.bls.gov/news.release/atus.t06.htm

Wang, W., & Shen, F. (2017). Reciprocal communication in online health support groups: Effects of message format and social support on individual responses to health issues. *Media Psychology, 20*, 240–266. https://doi-org.proxy.library.ohio.edu/10.1080/15213269.2016.1142381

Yello. (2020). *Virtual internship statistics and trends: A 2020 COVID-19 Impact study.* Retrieved from https://yello.co/blog/virtual-internship-statistics/

APPENDIX

The Group Presentation Toolkit

As we know, at some point in our lives we will be asked to participate in a group presentation. For many, this is a task we have already faced. Although information on things to consider and communication in groups has been the primary focus of this textbook, this additional section is centered on providing hands-on advice and tangible tools that may be used in group presentations. In this section, tools will be reviewed that you can use as appropriate in your own personal, academic, and/or professional group presentations.

Specific strategies will be addressed for each of the following:

- Preparing for group presentations
- Delivering group presentations
- Tools for virtual group presentations
- Assessing group presentations

Before we dive into hands-on strategies in each of these areas, it is important to always keep in mind that the basic components of the well-known Shannon-Weaver Communication Model1.[1]

S = Sender (person whom communicates a message to a receiver)
R = Receiver (person whom receives and assigns meaning to a message)
Message = verbal or nonverbal
Channel = the medium by which the message is sent from sender to receiver
Feedback = the message sent from receiver to sender
Noise = anything that interferes with a message being sent/received; can be physical or psychological
Context = the situation (time, place) in which the interaction takes place

---

[1] Shannon, C., & Weaver, W. (1949). *The Mathematical Theory of Communication*. Urbana: University of Illinois

*All components of the communication model are *interdependent*, meaning they influence one another. When one element changes, it may influence change in other elements.

*All components must be considered in each and every stage of the group presentation process from preparation to assessment. Keep in mind each element as we review useful tools to help you create and deliver high quality group presentations.

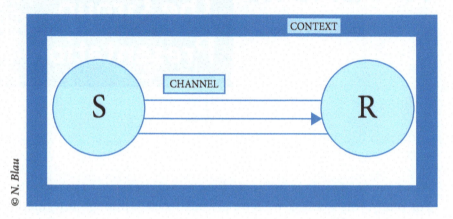

© N. Blau

Preparing for Group Presentations Part One: Setting the Stage

1. Get to know your group members!
   - If you do not already know your group members, begin the forming phase and get acquainted with your group members.
   - Exchange contact information and identify preferred channels of communication.
2. Decide on the presentation goal/purpose.
   - All group members must fully understand the purpose and goal of the presentation in order to prepare accordingly.
   - Make sure presentation goals are specific.
     - **DON'T**: Make goals vague (i.e., "to earn a good grade" or "do well")
     - **DO**: Identify tangible outcomes to work toward (i.e., specific length, topics to cover)
   - Ensure the presentation goal is attainable in the time allotted.
   - Is the goal to entertain? Inform? Persuade?
3. Determine and analyze the target audience.
   - Who is your audience?
   - Work to identify as many characteristics of the audience as possible (i.e., age range, sex/gender, and other demographics that my impact how you present the message).
   - Try to determine how much the audience knows about your topic prior to your presentation so that you can engage listeners.

4. Consider the context in which the group will present.
   - Think about the date, time, and location for the presentation.
   - The time of day can impact audience engagement.
   - Consider the actual location in which the presentation will take place – can the group maximize space and other elements physically to enhance the presentation?
     - Check on the seating arrangement, noise level, lighting

© N. Blau

Preparing for Group Presentations Part Two: Working Toward the Goal

1. Delegate tasks for group members
   - Decide on logical ways to divide the workload.
   - Based on skills and interest, divide the tasks among group members.
   - Make sure all group members have a voice – encourage all to share ideas.
2. Hold all group members accountable
   - As a group, discuss the importance of teamwork early in the process.
   - Put a system of "checks-and-balances" in place to ensure all group members are accountable for their actions.
   - Prepare back up plans in the event a group member cannot complete the assigned task.
3. Choose a group member to moderate the presentation
   - This person will ensure transitions between topics and speakers goes smoothly.
   - This person will facilitate a Q&A session (if included in the presentation).
4. Work together to put the presentation together
   - After all tasks have been completed, work together to compile the presentation.
   - As a group, make sure the presentation includes all necessary components including an introduction, body, and conclusion.
   - Tailor the message to the audience as much as possible.
   - Decide on the details of the delivery including speaker order, topic order, and presentation tools (i.e., PowerPoint, Prezi, etc.).

- All group members should participate in the editing process.
- **DON'T:** Allow only one or two group members to compile the presentation and expect others to understand the flow of the presentation.

5. Practice, practice, practice
   - Carve out time for a dry run with all group members present.
   - Practice the presentation *in the location* if possible.
   - Make sure to practice time limits for each speaker, and the overall presentation.
   - Practice transitions between speakers.
   - Practice using any visual aids that will be used for the actual presentation.

© N. Blau

It's "Go Time": Delivering the Group Presentation

1. Get into a positive mindset
   - Do not underestimate the power of positive thinking! Envision success.
   - Work together to manage nervousness (if any is experienced).
     - Take deep breaths; practice various breathing techniques to calm nerves.
   - Group members should encourage another.
   - Dress for success!
     - Wear clothing that is appropriate given the presentation topic.
     - Make sure all group members agree on how to dress before the presentation day.
2. Nonverbal messages matter
   - In addition to personal appearance, pay attention to nonverbal cues from audience members.

- **DON'T:** Sway when speaking, use too many vocal fillers (i.e., "um", "uh"), speak at an extremely high rate so that audience members cannot understand the message.
- **DO:** Make eye contact with the audience, incorporate appropriate gestures when possible, use an appropriate and positive tone.
- Smile!

3. Stick to the script
   - All group members should deliver the presentation as practiced.
   - **DON'T:** Add in more information not prepared and approved by the group.
   - **DON'T:** Change the order of the presentation throwing other presenter off his/her plan.
   - **DO:** Make minor adjustments to nonverbal and verbal messages as necessary to keep the audience engaged.

4. Handouts and extra information
   - When possible, avoid passing out pamphlets and handouts during the presentation (this may be distracting for audience members).
   - Provide additional information to audience members post-presentation if requested.

DO	DO DON'T
Go into the presentation positively	Change the presentation mid-delivery
Dress confidently	Let your nerves get the best of you
Be aware of nonverbal cues being communicated	Pass out handouts or other materials that may distract your audience during the presentation

The Virtual Group Presentation Toolkit

When presenting virtually, the same tools used to prepare for and deliver the presentation can be used. There are, however, a few *additional* guidelines that should be kept in mind:

- Practice the presentation using the virtual platform that will be used in the presentation.
- Make sure to check all technology well in advance of the presentation to ensure it works properly (including your Internet connection).
- Explore all options available in the virtual platform that may potentially be used to enhance the presentation.
- Remember you may have to work harder to keep your audience engaged and attentive during the presentation.
  - Ask audience members questions throughout the presentation.

- Allow for comments and questions to be entered in a chat box during the presentation.
- Allow audience members to voice thoughts and opinions where appropriate.
- Make the presentation lively by using short stories, humor, and relatable examples.
- Avoid outside distractions!
  - Do not answer phone calls or texts during the presentation.
  - Make sure you are in a location where others will not provide distraction.
  - Close all other applications and browsers during the presentation.
  - Use the restroom before the presentation begins.

© N. Blau

How Did it Go?: Assessing Group Presentations

Another tool we often forget about is learning to evaluate group presentations. Assessment is not something that only happens once a presentation has been delivered. A group can – and should – engage in assessment before, during, and after presentations.

*NOTE: Assessments can take many forms. Therefore, the following are samples of possible ways to evaluate group preparation and presentations. Certain group compositions and/or presentation topics may necessitate differing forms of assessment.

Assessing Group Preparedness

DIRECTIONS: Check off each item as completed. Once all items are completed, the group should be well-prepared for the presentation.

_____ Introductions/meet group members

_____ Exchange contact information/establish how group communication will take place

_____ Identify the presentation goal/purpose

_____ Analyze the target audience

_____ Discuss how the presentation may be tailored to the audience

_____ Analyze the presentation situation (context)

_____ Delegate tasks to all group members

_____ Choose a group presentation moderator

_____ Create presentation introduction, conclusion, and transitions

_____ Choose presentational aids

_____ Practice

_____ Check technology

_____ Plan to arrive early for presentation

Assessment During Group Presentations

During group presentations, there are many ways we can assess the situation and determine if minor adjustments are needed. This may be done by the group member speaking and/or others in the group. Keep in mind, even if you are not the current speaker, you are still presenting as part of the group and need to be aware of messages you are communicating to the audience!

In order to (silently) assess the group *during* the presentation, group members may ask themselves the following questions:

1. Do audience members seem to be engaged and interested in the presentation?
2. Can the audience members hear the presentation or does sound need to be adjusted?
3. Does it appear that audience members understand the message being delivered? Do they look confused?
4. How is the timing of the presentation? Is everything on time as planned? Will the group be able to deliver the entire presentation in the allotted time?
5. Is every group member sending appropriate and positive nonverbal messages (even when not speaking)?
6. Are presentational aids being used effectively in the presentation?

As these questions are asked and answered (mentally), group members may adapt as necessary. For instance, if the audience does not seem engaged, it may be time to ask a question, insert a brief (related) story, or change some nonverbal behaviors such as tone of voice or facial expressions. If it appears as if audience members are unable to hear, the speaker may need to adjust their volume or the volume on a microphone. Monitoring audience feedback – both verbal and nonverbal – is crucial to delivering an effective group presentation. As a group member, if you see something that can be easily fixed, take the initiative and make the change. In the end, it can mean the difference in the success of the presentation!

Post-Presentation Feedback

After a group has completed a presentation, it is always a good idea to solicit feedback from audience members. Groups can obtain feedback in many ways. Some common strategies are as follows:

- Verbally ask audience members for comments on the presentation.
- Ask audience members to complete a feedback form outlining positives and negatives of the group presentation.
- Monitor nonverbal feedback from audience members. Do they seem excited about the topic? Are they smiling? Are they rushing to leave as soon as the presentation is completed?
- Groups can follow up with audience members electronically after some time has passed. For instance, soliciting comments via email or sending a link to an online evaluation form.

Sample Assessment Form for Group Presentations

DIRECTIONS: Use the key (on the right) to assess the group presentation.	SD = Strongly Disagree D = Disagree N = Neutral A = Agree SA = Strongly Agree N/A = Not Applicable					
	SD	D	N	A	SA	NA
Introduction						
Captured attention of audience						
Clearly stated purpose of presentation						
Speakers seem to be credible to speak on this topic						
Body of presentation						
The information is organized in a clear manner (easy to follow)						
Speakers transitioned well between topics						
Presentational aids were used effectively						
Technology was used effectively						
The presentation was interesting/engaging						
Group members stayed within time limits						
Supporting materials were used effectively						
Presentation content related well to the audience						
Conclusion						
There was a clear conclusion for the presentation (summarized presentation information)						
The presentation concluded in a memorable way						
IV. Delivery						
The speakers spoke clearly						
The speakers used vocal variety and appropriate tone and volume						
The speakers used nonverbal behaviors appropriately (facial expressions, eye contact, posture, personal appearance)						

Presentation Strengths:

Areas for Improvement:

GLOSSARY

Accommodation: putting another's needs ahead of your own

Accountability: communicating responsibility for one's own action and behavior

Active listening: when a person concentrates on the message being received, works to process the information, and then provides noticeable feedback to the speaker (verbal or nonverbal)

Active listening: when a person concentrates on the message being received, works to process the information, and then provides noticeable feedback to the speaker verbally and/or nonverbally

Adjourning phase: the "wrap-up" phase where groups are no longer focused on task achievement but wrapping up any loose ends and concluding the group

Affiliation: connection with others

Affiliation need: a human need to be connected to others

Agenda: schedule of items to be addressed during the group discussion

Altuism: asserting that if one complies with a request it would be helpful to others

Analysis paralysis: when groups spend too much time analyzing the problem to the point where a decision never gets made

Appreciation: showing that we are grateful for another's work and efforts in the team

Archive: to save or preserve information to be accessed in the future

Assertiveness: "the ability to communicate the full range of your thoughts and emotions

Asynchronous: messages not being sent and received at the same time

Audio-only group conference: group members interact with one another, but there is no video component

Authoritarian leadership style: leadership style in which the leader typically seizes control within the group and does not often relinquish such control

Aversive stimulation: continuous punishments that only end when a compliance occurs

Avoidance: characterized by not engaging in the physical, psychological, or communicative functions of conflict

Brainstorming: group members communicate as many ideas as they possibly can; the more the better

Bullying: persistent patterns of physical, emotional, or verbal behaviors used with the intent to harm another person (Olweus, 1993)

Bystander: someone who observes the bullying interaction

Closed-minded: when group members are not willing to listen to and respect others

Closure stage: the phase where the group communicates any decisions made to whomever necessary and confirm that is the decision made as a group

Coercive power: power granted to a person when they have the ability to punish others when a request is not fulfilled

Collaboration: when group members work together through conflict to ensure the needs and/or wants of all members are met

Collaboration: when people work together to meet goals

Collectivist culture: a culture that emphasizes community over independence

Commitment: one's dedication to a goal, person, or group of people

Communication: sharing meaning with others through verbal and nonverbal codes

Communication climate: tone of the group interaction

Competent communication: effectively sending and receiving verbal and nonverbal messages; a person's ability to speak in a way that others can understand and receive messages with accurate understanding.

Competing: when group members disagree with other viewpoints and do not necessarily attempt to see things from a different point of view

Complementary skills: abilities that match up well with the talents of others

Compliance-gaining: when a sender verbally or nonverbally sends a message to a received requesting he/she conform to a specific request or behavior

Compromising: when we work with others to get part of what we want, and they also get part of what they want

Confirmation: communication that acknowledges the other person's message and feelings

Conflict: "an expressed struggle between at least two interdependent parties who perceive incompatible goals, scarce resources, and interference from the other party in achieving their goals" (Wilmot & Hocker, 2011, p. 11)

Conflict management: using communication skills effectively to manage conflict legitimately and efficiently

Conflict resolution strategies: ways that we can solve conflict within groups

Conflict stage (Fisher): the phase in which group members share perspectives and offer solutions; this may or may not lead to interpersonal conflict

Conflict stage (Tubbs): the phase in which the problem to be solved or decision to be made identified by group members

Conformity orientation: the extent to which a family group encourages family members to adopt similar ways of behaving, feeling, and thinking

Consensual family groups: high in conversation orientation and also high in conformity orientation

Consensus: when group members unanimously agree on the decision

Consensus stage: the phase that the group settles on one of the solutions posted in the previous stage of the model

Context: the situation in which the communication takes place

Contingency theory of leadership: the belief that the best leadership style in a group situation is dependent on specific variables

Convergence: changing your communication to better match others

Conversation orientation: the level of openness and regularity that a family group discusses topics

Credibility: the perception that a person is competent, trustworthy, and shows goodwill toward others

Credibility: when others perceive a person or group of people as being trustworthy, competent, and genuine

Crisis communication: communication about a specific, non-routine, not expected series of events creating high levels of uncertainty (Ulmer, Sellnow, & Seeger, 2007)

Cultural orientation: one's perspective on phenomena based on your cultural beliefs and practices

Cultural sensitivity: the recognition of cultural differences without judgment

Culture: the values, beliefs, attitudes, opinions, behaviors and practices of a group of people

Cynicism: a negative attitude whereas one communicates doubts in the team's ability to achieve goals and be effective

Debt: requesting compliance as "re-payment" for past favors; paying back debt

Delegating style: the leader simply divvies up tasks and "hands out" jobs to group members

Democratic leadership style: shared governance and power among group members Designated leader: leaders are appointed to or from the group

Destructive message: a message that demolishes team cohesion and prevent teams from achieving goals

Disconfirmation: when we verbally ignore another person's message

Disruptive roles: roles enacted by group members who are more focused on themselves than the group and work to disturb the group

Divergence: changing your communication to set yourself apart and stress the differences between yourself and others

Diversity: the state of being distinctive, or unlike others

Dysfunctional conflict: conflict that has a damaging effect on the group members, or even the group as a whole

Emergence stage: the phase where a decision is made by the group

Emotional intelligence: one's ability to consciously control emotions and the communication of those emotions

Emotional stability: one's ability to remain emotionally in balance when necessary

Emotional support: performing some behavior to make another feel valued and cherished

Empathy: seeing things from another's perspective

Employee burnout: when an employee becomes disengaged with their work often showing signs of exhaustion and apathy

Empowerment: when we relinquish power so that others may make their own decisions and choose their own behaviors

Engagement: active participation in the group discussion through verbal and nonverbal means

Ethics: the study of beliefs of what is right or wrong, good or bad, moral or immoral

Ethnicity: a group of people who share common cultural characteristics

Ethnocentrism: the belief that our own culture is superior to other cultures

Expert power: power granted because of one's level of expertise, or skill set, in a certain area

Explicit norms: guidelines for the group that are clearly stated so there is little to no uncertainty

Expressed struggle: the conflict must be communicated in some way

Family of origin: the family in which we were raised

Feminine culture: a culture that stresses more conventional gender role characteristics as accommodation and nurturing behaviors

Formal roles: positions assigned by a group leader or voted on by group members; official roles in the group

Forming phase: when group members are placed together in a group by either assignment or choice

Functional conflict: conflict that ultimately results in a positive outcome and sometimes even strengthens the relationship among group members

Gender: masculine or feminine roles enacted by people

Group: three or more people brought together by a common goal who depend on one another to achieve their goal

Group: three or more people brought together by a common goal who depend on one another to achieve their goal

Group communication: "an interaction among a small group of people who share a common purpose or goal, who feel a sense of belonging to the group, and who exert influence on one another" (Beebe & Masterson, 1997, p. 6).

Group communication climates: the tone or the feeling within the group

Group conflict: as expressed struggles between two or more group members where in at least one group member perceives incompatible goals, scarce group resources and interference from other group members when working to attain goals

Group identity: anything that will unify or unite a group together

Group polarization: individual group members are influenced by the remainder of the group to view things from a specific perspective

Group socialization: the process group members use to influence one another and communicate in order to create agreed-upon norms for the group

Groupthink: extreme pressure felt by group members to agree with the behavior(s) of the group; a less than optimal decision is made by the group in order to come to an agreement

Health: "a state of complete physical, mental and social well-being and not merely the absence of disease or infirmity" (WHO, 1948)

Health communication: "the way we seek, process, and share health information" (Kreps & Thornton, 1992, p. 2)

High-context culture: a culture that places great emphasis on the context to interpret messages

High-power distance orientation: when a minority of people have most of the power within a group

High uncertainty avoidant culture: cultures that avoid uncertainty as much as possible

Homophily: the tendency to affiliate with others that we feel are similar

Icebreaker: an activity where group members are asked to share information with others in the group, often in an entreating way

Identity management: when a compliance request is resisted by manipulating the identity of the person initiating the request

Immediacy: the perception of physical or psychological closeness between persons

Implicit norms: guidelines that are understood by group members, though not necessarily expressed outright

Inclusive: when people support and encourage equal contribution from and provide equal resources to all group members

Independent: when people do not rely one on another, they do not meet this definition of team

Individualistic culture: a culture in which the focus is on personal needs as opposed to that of the broader group

Indulgent cultures: cultures that focus on doing whatever will provide instant gratification; the goal is enjoyment with little regard to social rules and norms

Informal roles: positions that transpire from group interactions and are not formally assigned

Informational influence: attempts to influence or persuade others by providing information in the form of facts and evidence and providing logical arguments

Informational support: providing information to someone that assists them in some way

Information overload: when information is received at a rate that surpasses one's ability to process the information effectively

Ingroup: a group of people who share a common goal similar to a clique

Instrumental support: aid that is given in the form of tangible items such as providing resources or assisting with tasks

Inter-group conflict: when one group engages in conflict with other (external groups)

Interdependence: a change in one component of the process will create change in the other components

Interdependence: when group members depend on one another for tangible or intangible things

Interdependence: when one's behavior influences that of another person

Interference: when there are impediments from other group members in achieving one's goals

Interprofessional communication: group communication that occurs when healthcare providers include the voices of multiple professionals

Intra-group conflict: when groups experience conflict amongst their own group members, or internal to the group

Intrapersonal conflict: conflict experienced within yourself

Jargon: a specialized language used by a group of people

Justification: when an individual resists compliance by providing reasons whey he/she cannot or will not comply

Laissez-faire family group: low in conversation orientation and also low in conformity orientation

Laissez-faire leadership style: the leader provides very little structure for the group

Leadership: the communication process used by persons in an attempt to influence followers to meet group goals

Legitimate power: power granted based on a person's position

Liking: behaving in a way to increase others' liking of you so that they may subsequently comply to your request

Logo: a symbol used to represent or help identify team characteristics

Logos: appeals to people's logic

Lose-lose resolution strategy: when no group members are happy with the decision or group outcome

Low-context culture: cultures that do not relay on the context in order to understand communication

Low-power distance orientation: when power in a group is more evenly distributed making the distance between those who have power (and those who) do not much smaller

Low uncertainty avoidance cultures: cultures that do not shy away from uncertainty

Maintenance roles: roles that are focused on creating and sustaining relationships within the group

Majority rule: group members vote on the solutions and whichever has support from the largest group is the final decision

Manager: someone who is assigned authority within a group to administer group functions and maintain the current state of the group

Masculine culture: a culture that focuses on achievements and being successful

Me-orientation: when group members are more concerned about their self (or immediate friends/family) as opposed to the greater group

Minority rule: allowing a small number of people (or even one leader) to make a decision

Moral appeal: asserting that one will be perceived as sinful or not moral if they do not comply to a request

Motivation: one's drive to accomplish a goal or behave in a certain way

Motto: a word, phrase, or even a sentence that adequately depicts the character of an individual, a team, group, or product

Negative altercasting: asserting that only a "bad person" or a person with negative qualities would not comply with the request

Negative esteem: communicating that others will think badly of you if you do not comply to the request

Negative expertise: implicit punishments for noncompliance (i.e., you will feel horrible about yourself if you do not comply)

Negative identity management: when one resists power by making the requestor feel negatively, or bad, about him/herself

Negative self-feeling: communicating that one will feel worse/badly if they do not comply with the request

Negotiation: offering a compromise and attempting to comply with part of the request, but not all of it

"Nobody upstairs" power play: when the person essentially ignores a request repeatedly: by acting as if they don't know common social rules, they simply ignore requests for compliance

Nominal group technique (NGT): a form of structured brainstorming where group members write down individual ideas to be shared with the group after each person has had time to think independently

Non-negotiation: one's outright refusal to comply with a request

Nonverbal communication: sending a message to a receiver using non-speech symbols (such as gestures, body movements, and non-speech vocalics)

Nonverbal immediacy: the perception of psychological and/or physical closeness via the use of nonverbal behaviors

Normative influence: when group members attempt to alter attitudes and behaviors of others based on people's desire to "belong" or be accepted by the group

Norming phase: power struggles and other issues begin to get resolved and group members begin to understand what is normal for the group

Norms: rules and guidelines for the group

Open-minded: group members whom are willing to listen and respond to the ideas and opinions of others

Orientation stage: the phase where group members get to know another and share information about themselves

Outgroup: group members that are not really included in the majority group

Paralanguage: how we say something, as opposed to what we say

Participating style: leaders relinquish some control and allow group members to actively play a role in decision-making and problem-solving

Passion: a strong emotion or feeling one has for others or a phenomenon

Pathos: appeals to people's emotions

Patient-centered communication: the type of interaction that occurs among health-care providers and the patient or loved ones of the patient in an effort to help the patient and share concerns

Perceived incompatible goals: at least one group member that his/her goals contradict the goals of other group members and/or the overall group goal

Perceived scarce resources: when one believes that there is not enough means to meet all needs/desires

Perception: how we sense and attribute meaning to a phenomenon

Performing phase: communication is better defined within the group and group members better understand how to communicate differing ideas and opinions while staying focused on the group goal; group roles are solidified

Persuasion: the process of getting others to comply with a request or change an attitude or opinion

Pluralistic family groups: high in conversation orientation and low in conformity orientation

Poise: the way we hold our body

Positive altercasting: asserting that a "good person" would comply with the request

Positive esteem: communicating that others will think highly of you if you comply to the request

Positive expertise: promises of implicit rewards for compliance (i.e., you will feel good about yourself if you comply)

Positive identity management: when one resists power by making the requestor feel positive, or good, about him/herself

Positive self-feeling: assurance that one will feel better about themselves if they comply with the request

Power: the ability to influence another's attitudes, beliefs, values, and communication

Power plays: patterns of communication used repeatedly by an individual to manipulate them in some manner

Power struggles: competition for the ability to assert dominance over others,

Pregiving: providing a reward before someone complies to a request

Problem analysis: the step where group members must take care to strategically figure out the scope and cause of the issue

Problem identification: step in which group members must clearly identify the problem

Promise: the promise to provide a reward for compliance

Protective family groups: typically low in conversation orientation but high in conformity orientation

Public advocacy: when a group gathers together to engage in some activity intended to raise awareness for some cause or change public policy

Questions of fact: questions that inquire whether something is true or false

Questions of policy: questions that ask about the need for guidelines or rules that may be needed to enact change

Questions of value: questions that probe the worth of a phenomenon

Race: a group of people who share common biological traits

Readily detectable traits: traits/attributes that are easily seen and identifiable

Reciprocity: the idea that the interaction is a mutual exchange of information; what one group member offers; other group members offer the same in return

Referent power: power that is granted when others look up to you and, in some way, want to be like you

Reflective thinking: a process rooted in the scientific method that indicates a set of logical steps must be followed when a decision is to be made

Reinforcement stage: the phase in which a decision has been made and individual group members attempt to understand the decision through their own perspective

Rejection: when we openly acknowledge another person's message but quickly reject or disagree with it

Relationship conflicts: conflict that occur within groups when interpersonal relationships experience strains

Requisite functions: functions necessary for a group to perform in order to make a quality decision.

Resource: an asset, or something valued by a person such a time, materials, or money

Respect: when we deeply admire someone for certain qualities, they possess such as expertise, values, or commitment

Restraint-based cultures: cultures that do not worry about instant gratification and are more focused on following norms set forth

Reward power: when power is given to a person based on their capacity to provide reward for a certain behavior or attitude change

Risky shift phenomenon: when groups are more likely to engage in risky behaviors than members would have done individually

Role ambiguity: a lack of understanding about how to fulfill one's role

Role clarity: when group members to know exactly what they are responsible for and how their contribution will help achieve the group goal

Role conflict: when our roles contradict each other

Self-disclosure: sharing personal information with yourself to other people

Self-fulfilling prophecy: when a person or group of people predict that something will happen and, in turn, consciously or unconsciously behave in such a way that the prediction becomes reality

Selling style: a leader tries to "sell" his or her ideas to the group and negotiate with group members in an attempt to get them to follow their lead

Servant leadership: when a leader shares power with group members and provides service in an effort to create positive change

Situational theory of leadership: appropriate leadership is determined by the situation; different situations call for diverse leadership styles

Social categorization perspective of diverse group decision-making: on an individual level, group members who differ ethnically are often less cohesive, which can lead to lower individual performance; at the group level, the social categorization perspective states that ethnically diverse groups often experience increased conflict and decreased group cohesion

Social dimension: the relationships formed among group members as a result of their interaction; the output of this dimension is cohesiveness.

Social influence: when group members agree with others (often the majority opinion) even if they do not agree

Social presence: perceptions of the existence of others in interactions

Social support: providing assistance to another person

Social support groups: groups that provide emotional, mental, and/or physical support for others experiencing a similar situation

Solution criteria: the step in which group members develop criteria that will ultimately be used to evaluate possible solutions

Solution evaluation and selection: the step where group uses the criteria set forth in step three to assess each proposed solution

Solution implementation: the final step in the Standard Agenda in which the solution is employed (and later evaluated)

Stage model: a process model that explains behaviors as it moves through various phases in a particular order

Standard Agenda: a multi-step model of decision-making centered on analysis and reflection in order to identify the best solution possible which includes six steps: problem identification, problem analysis, solution criteria, alternative generation, solution evaluation and selection, and implementation

Static: unchanging

Storming phase: communication is increased, and group members are getting to know one another and trying to figure out group roles; conflict often occurs in this phase

Synchronous: messages being sent and received at the same time

System: "a set of elements standing in interrelation among themselves with the environment" (von Bertalanffy, 1975, p. 159)

Task conflict: when group members perceive incompatibilities with regard to the achievement of group tasks

Task dimension: the functions and work achieved by the group; productivity is the output of this dimension

Task roles: roles that help the group function in ways to achieve a specific task or goal, solve a problem, or make a decision

Team: a cohesive group of two or more people who are interdependent, committed to a common goal with similar passion and a shared identity

Telling style: the group leader "tells" or instructs followers on what to do as well as how to do it

Theory: ideas logically linked together that can be used to explain, predict, and understand human phenomena

Threat: establishing punishment for noncompliance

Trait: a distinct quality or characteristic a person has that is relatively stable over time

Trait theory of leadership: the idea that leaders are born with certain traits that make them an effective leader

Transactional communication: when communicators simultaneously exchange messages both verbally and/or nonverbally

Transformational leadership: leaders who bring about change

Transparency: the act of clearly communicating so that group members can easily understand the entire message

Typology: classification

Uncertainty: a state of not knowing or inability to predict phenomena

Underlying attributes: traits/attributes that are not indefinable just by looking at someone

Value conflicts: when two or more group members find themselves disagreeing on fundamental attitudes and beliefs

Verbal communication: using words to send a message between sender and receiver

Verbal immediacy: using words to create perceptions of physical and/or psychological closeness

Video conferencing: virtual group discussions that allow people from remote locations to interact face to face using both audio and video signals

Virtual bystanders: group members who log on (or call in) to virtual group discussions but participate little to none

Virtual group communication: computer-mediated interaction among groups of people who share a common purpose or goal

Visual dominance behavior: the theory that states when communicating power, or dominance, in an interpersonal interaction, we alter our normal eye contact behaviors; when listening we engage in less eye contact to communicate positions of power

We-orientation: the tendency to be inclusive of others and focus on the group (we) instead of the self (me)

We-orientation: when group members are more concerned with the needs of the group as opposed to their own needs

Wholeness: viewing a system as a larger, whole entity instead of as a summation of individual parts

Win-lose resolution strategy: where some group members are satisfied, while others are dissatisfied

Win-win resolution strategy: when the goal is to satisfy the needs/wants of all group members with confidence and skill" (Adler, 1977, p. 6)

Work-life balance: finding ways to balance the responsibilities in our personal lives and our professional lives

Workplace bullying: persistent patterns of aggressive behavior used with the intent to harm another person in the workplace

"Yougottobekidding" power play: responding to communication in a way that puts down the other persona and makes them feel stupid or embarrassed for presenting an idea or opinion

"You owe me" power play: when one person does something (a task, favor) for another and subsequently request something in return

INDEX